T0206952

Lecture Notes of the Institute for Computer Sciences, Social Informatics and Telecommunications Engineering 425

More information about this series at https://link.springer.com/bookseries/8197

Joao L. Afonso · Vitor Monteiro ·
José Gabriel Pinto (Eds.)

Sustainable Energy for Smart Cities

Third EAI International Conference, SESC 2021
Virtual Event, November 24–26, 2021
Proceedings

Springer

Editors
Joao L. Afonso ⓘ
Department of Industrial Electronics
University of Minho
Guimaraes, Portugal

Vitor Monteiro ⓘ
Department of Industrial Electronics
University of Minho
Guimaraes, Portugal

José Gabriel Pinto ⓘ
University of Minho
Guimaraes, Portugal

ISSN 1867-8211   ISSN 1867-822X (electronic)
Lecture Notes of the Institute for Computer Sciences, Social Informatics
and Telecommunications Engineering
ISBN 978-3-030-97026-0   ISBN 978-3-030-97027-7 (eBook)
https://doi.org/10.1007/978-3-030-97027-7

This Springer imprint is published by the registered company Springer Nature Switzerland AG
The registered company address is: Gewerbestrasse 11, 6330 Cham, Switzerland

Preface

We are pleased to present the proceedings of the third edition of the International Conference on Sustainable Energy for Smart Cities (SESC), sponsored by the European Alliance for Innovation (EAI) in close cooperation with the University of Minho, Portugal. Following the previous editions, this edition of SESC was also organized within the Smart City 360° event and, due to the COVID-19 pandemic situation, it was a fully-fledged online conference, whilst still ensuring quality of experience. The main aim of the SESC 2021 conference was to offer a multidisciplinary scientific online meeting covering the emerging and complex technical aspects of smart cities. Within the scope of smart cities, topics associated with sustainable energy were also discussed at the SESC 2021 conference as it is essential to ensure a balance between economic growth and environmental sustainability, as well as to contribute to reducing the effects of climate change.

The SESC 2021 technical program included 13 full papers, which were distributed into four sessions. A double-blinded peer review process was respected for each submitted paper, ensuring a minimum of three reviews per paper. Regarding the committees, cooperation with the EAI team was vital for the success of the SESC 2021 conference. Furthermore, we would like to present our appreciation to all the members of the Technical Program Committee, who were fundamental to the high-quality technical program, as well as to ensuring the quality of the peer review process. Last but not least, we would like to thank all the external reviewers from numerous countries around the world, who were specifically invited based on the areas of expertise included in the SESC 2021 conference.

The SESC 2021 conference was a distinguished scientific meeting for all researchers, developers and practitioners, offering the opportunity to discuss all scientific and technological directions targeting smart cities. Aligned with the success of the SESC 2021 conference, which is reflected in the distinct subjects covered in the papers presented in this volume, we anticipate a successful and stimulating future series of SESC conferences.

January 2021

Joao L. Afonso
Vitor Monteiro
J. G. Pinto

Organization

Steering Committee

Imrich Chlamtac	University of Trento, Italy
Joao L. Afonso	University of Minho, Portugal
Vitor Monteiro	University of Minho, Portugal
Gabriel Pinto	University of Minho, Portugal

Organizing Committee

General Chairs

Joao L. Afonso	University of Minho, Portugal
Vitor Monteiro	University of Minho, Portugal
Gabriel Pinto	University of Minho, Portugal

Technical Program Committee Chair

Carlos Couto	University of Minho, Portugal

Sponsorship and Exhibit Chair

Paula Ferreira	University of Minho, Portugal

Local Chair

Madalena Araújo	University of Minho, Portugal

Workshops Chair

Delfim Pedrosa	University of Minho, Portugal

Publicity and Social Media Chair

Luis Barros	University of Minho, Portugal

Publications Chair

Tiago Sousa	University of Minho, Portugal

Web Chair

Jose Afonso   University of Minho, Portugal

Panels Chair

Luis Machado   University of Minho, Portugal

Technical Program Committee

Edson H. Watanabe	Federal University of Rio de Janeiro, Brazil
Alberto-Jesus Perea-Moreno	University of Cordoba, Spain
Joao A. Peças Lopes	University of Porto, Portugal
Hfaiedh Mechergui	University of Tunis, Tunisia
Richard Stephan	Federal University of Rio de Janeiro, Brazil
Walter Issamu Suemitsu	Federal University of Rio de Janeiro, Brazil
Chunhua Liu	City University of Hong Kong, China
Mauricio Aredes	Federal University of Rio de Janeiro, Brazil
Guilherme Rolim	Federal University of Rio de Janeiro, Brazil
Carlos Hengeler Antunes	University of Coimbra, Portugal
Adriano Carvalho	University of Porto, Portugal
Jelena Loncarski	Polytechnic University of Bari, Italy
Marcelo Cavalcanti	Federal University of Pernambuco, Brazil
Joao P. S. Catalão	University of Porto, Portugal
Jose A. Afonso	University of Minho, Portugal
Antonio Lima	State University of Rio de Janeiro, Brazil
Antonio Pina Martins	University of Porto, Portugal
Rosaldo Rossetti	University of Porto, Portugal
Luis Monteiro	State University of Rio de Janeiro, Brazil
Joao P. P. Carmo	University of São Paulo, Brazil
A. Caetano Monteiro	University of Minho, Portugal
Luis Martins	University of Minho, Portugal
Marcello Mezaroba	Santa Catarina State University, Brazil
J. Aparicio Fernandes	University of Minho, Portugal
Paulo Pereirinha	University of Coimbra, Portugal
Orlando Soares	Instituto Politécnico de Bragança, Portugal
Jose L. Lima	Instituto Politécnico de Bragança, Portugal
Carlos Felgueiras	Polytechnic Institute of Porto, Portugal
Amira Haddouk	University of Tunis, Tunisia
Manel Hlaili	University of Tunis, Tunisia
Joao C. Ferreira	ISCTE – University Institute of Lisbon, Portugal
Stefani Freitas	Federal University of Tocantins, Brazil
Julio S. Martins	University of Minho, Portugal
Luiz Artur Pecorelli Peres	State University of Rio de Janeiro, Brazil

Kleber Oliveira	Federal University of Paraíba, Brazil
Joao L. Monteiro	University of Minho, Portugal
Mohamed Tanta	Vestas, Portugal
M. J. Sepúlveda	University of Minho, Portugal

Contents

Power Electronics

Fault Analysis of a Non-isolated Three-Level DC-DC Converter Integrated in a Bipolar DC Power Grid

Catia F. Oliveira, Joao L. Afonso, and Vitor Monteiro[⊠]

ALGORITMI Research Centre, University of Minho, Guimarães, Portugal
{c.oliveira,jla,vmonteiro}@dei.uminho.pt

Abstract. DC power grids present significant advantages over AC power grids, namely higher stability and controllability, and the absence of harmonic currents and reactive power. Moreover, DC grids facilitate the interface with renewable energy sources (RES) and energy storage systems (ESS). DC grids can be either unipolar or bipolar, where the latter consists of three wires and provides higher flexibility, reliability and transmission capacity. However, failures in bipolar DC grids (especially in the power semiconductors) can occur. The consequences of these failures can result in increased costs, depending on the damage, e.g., if it occurs a wire of the DC grid or in the connected power converter. Thus, in this paper is presented a fault analysis of a non-isolated three-level DC-DC converter used to interface solar photovoltaic (PV) panels into a bipolar DC power grid. The fault analysis is conceived through computational simulations, where can be observed the performance of the presented DC-DC converter under fault conditions in each wire of the bipolar DC grid. The simulation results demonstrate the DC-DC converter operating in two different situations: steady-state and transient-state. The control strategy applied in normal and fault conditions, as well as the different operation modes, are explained in detail.

Keywords: Bipolar DC power grid · Three-level DC-DC converter · Solar PV panels · Fault analysis

1 Introduction

The increasing emission of greenhouse gases caused by industrialization and transport sector requires the development of viable solutions to mitigate environment degradation [1]. In view of this, the integration of renewable energy sources (RES), namely solar photovoltaic (PV) panels and wind turbines contributes to a clearer environment [2, 3]. Moreover, the power management from RES can be efficiently achieved in a DC grid, due to its high controllability and absence of harmonic currents and reactive power [4, 5]. For this reason, a PV-based grid can be implemented, for instance, in fast charging stations, whose energy extracted from solar PV panels is used to not overload the power grid and to charge the electric vehicle batteries [6–8]. However, the interface of RES

© ICST Institute for Computer Sciences, Social Informatics and Telecommunications Engineering 2022
Published by Springer Nature Switzerland AG 2022. All Rights Reserved
J. L. Afonso et al. (Eds.): SESC 2021, LNICST 425, pp. 3–15, 2022.
https://doi.org/10.1007/978-3-030-97027-7_1

demands efficient power converters to attend the innumerous failures that can occur either in the power converters or in the DC grid [9, 10]. Due to this fact, it is a constant challenge for researchers to develop solutions to respond to unavoidable failures [11]. In the presence of failures, the power semiconductors that constitute the power converters, and its drivers are quite vulnerable [12–14]. To circumvent those problems caused by the presence of failures in the power converters or in the DC grid, the development of fault-tolerant converters is required [15]. This type of topologies can require additional hardware in order to guarantee the normal operation under fault conditions, avoiding the damage of adjacent hardware [16–18]. Due to the necessity of additional hardware, the development of fault-tolerant converters can lead to increased costs, namely sensors to the application of fault diagnostic strategies or the introduction of power semiconductors [19, 20]. Despite that, the damage caused by non-fault-tolerant converters can be more expensive and harmful [21].

In this paper, a non-isolated three-level DC-DC converter integrated in a bipolar DC grid is presented. The DC-DC converter is used to interface RES, namely solar PV panels [22] as demonstrated in Fig. 1. The main application of this DC-DC converter is to continuously extract, considering the weather scenarios, the maximum energy from PV panels at each moment. However, the aim of this paper is analyzing the behavior of the three-level DC-DC converter in the presence of failures in the positive, neutral, and negative wires of the bipolar DC grid. Thus, it is proved the fault-tolerance of the DC-DC converter, without adding any electronic components.

The presented paper is organized as follows: In Sect. 2 are described in detail the operation modes of the non-isolated three-level DC-DC converter in normal conditions and in the presence of a failure in the DC wire. Furthermore, it is described the adopted control strategy to extract energy from the solar PV panels (boost-mode). In Sect. 3 are discussed the simulations results for steady-state and transient-state operations of the three-level DC-DC converter under normal and fault conditions. Finally, Sect. 4 presents the main conclusions.

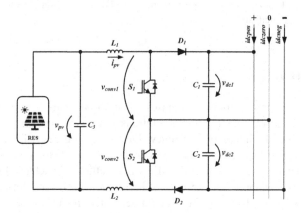

Fig. 1. Electric schematic of the three-level DC-DC converter interfacing solar PV panels connected to a bipolar DC power grid.

2 Operating Principles of the Three-Level DC-DC Converter

This section presents a detailed description of the different operation modes of the three-level DC-DC converter under normal and fault conditions. In normal conditions, there is not any fault in the bipolar DC grid, whereas in fault conditions are presented three possible failures: (a) a failure in the positive wire of the bipolar DC grid; (b) a failure in the neutral wire of the bipolar DC grid; (c) a failure in the negative wire of the bipolar DC grid.

2.1 Operation Modes in Normal Conditions

The presented three-level DC-DC converter integrated in a bipolar DC-DC converter aims to extract the energy from the solar PV panels. The topology demonstrated in Fig. 1 consists of two power semiconductors totally controlled (IGBTs in this case), two diodes, two inductors and a split DC-link. The output voltages, v_{conv1} and v_{conv2}, depend on the states of the semiconductors S_1 and S_2 and the DC-link voltage. In case of the semiconductors S_1 and S_2 are disabled, the current flows through the diodes D_1 and D_2. The value of v_{conv1} is $+v_{dc1}$ and v_{conv2} is $+v_{dc2}$. If the semiconductors S_1 and S_2 are enabled, v_{conv1} and v_{conv2} are zero. When the diode D_1 is directly polarized and the semiconductor S_2 is enabled, v_{conv1} is $+v_{dc1}$ and v_{conv2} is zero. Finally, if S_1 is enabled and D_2 is directly polarized, v_{conv2} assumes the value of $+v_{dc2}$ and v_{conv1} is zero. The values $+v_{dc1}$ and $+v_{dc2}$ corresponds to $+v_{dc}/2$ since the capacitors C_1 and C_2 of the DC-link are equal.

2.2 Operation Modes in Fault Conditions

As mentioned previously, the three-level DC-DC converter is connected to a bipolar DC grid composed by three wires (positive, neutral and negative wires), where can occur failures in those wires of the DC grid. In this section is described the different operation modes of the DC-DC converter under fault conditions. Figure 2 demonstrates the operating modes of the DC-DC converter under a failure in the positive wire. As it can be observed, the DC-DC converter presents two different operation modes. In case of the current value from PV panels, i_{pv}, presents a lower value than the reference current, i_{pv} flows through the semiconductor S_1 and the diode D_2 (Fig. 2(a)), otherwise i_{pv} flows through the semiconductors S_1 and S_2 (Fig. 2(b)). For both cases, the diode D_1 is not conducting due to the presence of a failure in the positive wire, as well as the voltage in capacitor C_1 is zero. Despite the failure in the positive wire in the DC grid, the DC-DC converter operates in boost-mode, as it is intended.

Figure 3 shows the operations modes of the three-level DC-DC converter under a failure in the neutral wire. When i_{pv} is lower than the reference current, the current flows through the diodes D_1 and D_2 and the capacitors C_1 and C_2 (Fig. 3(a)). Thus, the inductors store the energy until reaching the intended current. Otherwise, i_{pv} flows through the semiconductors S_1 and S_2 (Fig. 3(b)). Depending on the value of i_{pv} according to its reference, the voltage v_{conv1} assumes the value $+v_{dc}$ which corresponds to the sum of the voltage v_{dc1} with the voltage v_{dc2} or the value zero.

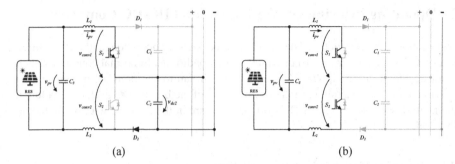

Fig. 2. Operating principles of the three-level DC-DC converter under a failure in the positive wire of the bipolar DC power grid: (a) $v_{conv1} = 0$ and $v_{conv2} = +v_{dc2}$; (b) $v_{conv1} = 0$ and $v_{conv2} = 0$.

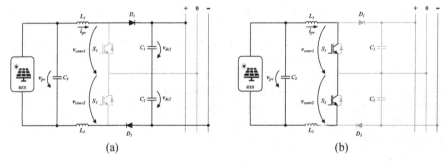

Fig. 3. Operating principles of the three-level DC-DC converter under a failure in the neutral wire of the bipolar DC power grid: (a) $v_{conv1} = +v_{dc}$ and $v_{conv2} = 0$; (b) $v_{conv1} = 0$ and $v_{conv2} = 0$.

Figure 4 presents the operating principles of the three-level DC-DC converter in the presence of a failure in the negative wire of the DC grid. In this case, the output voltage v_{conv1} assumes the value $+v_{dc1}$ or zero and v_{conv2} is zero. Depending on the current value in the inductors relatively to the reference current, there are two possible operation modes. Figure 4(a) shows the operation mode when i_{pv} is lower than the established reference current, where the current from the PV panels flows through D_1 and S_2. When i_{pv} is higher than the reference current, the current flows through the semiconductors S_1 and S_2, as demonstrated in Fig. 4(b).

For both situations (normal and fault conditions) the control strategy applied to the three-level DC-DC converter is presented through expression (1). The voltages to be synthetized by the three-level DC-DC converter correspond to v_{cv_dc1} and v_{cv_dc2}. On the other hand, the voltage in the solar PV panels is presented by v_{pv} and $i_{Lx}[k]$ is the current in inductor L_1 or L_2 at instant $[k]$. The established reference current that the DC-DC converter must synthetize corresponds to the parameter $i_{Lx}[k + 1]$ at instant $[k + 1]$.

$$v_{cv\_dcx} = v_{pv} - (L_1 + L_2)f(i_{Lx}[k + 1] - i_{Lx}[k]), \quad x = \{1,2\} \qquad (1)$$

where f is the sampling frequency.

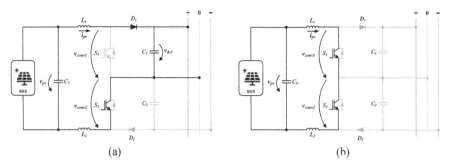

Fig. 4. Operating principles of the three-level DC-DC converter under a failure in the negative wire of the bipolar DC power grid: (a) $v_{conv1} = +v_{dc1}$ and $v_{conv2} = 0$; (b) $v_{conv1} = 0$ and $v_{conv2} = 0$.

The comparison between v_{cv_dc1} and v_{cv_dc2} with two triangular carriers phase shifted 180°, results in the control signals of semiconductors S_1 and S_2.

3 Simulations of the Three-Level DC-DC Converter

In this section are described the simulation results of the three-level DC-DC converter carried out with the software PSIM. The presented simulation results include the steady-state and transient-state operations in two different scenarios: normal conditions and fault conditions. It is used a voltage source of 100 V to emulate the solar PV panels, since the aim of this paper is the fault analysis of the DC-DC converter, and the maximum power tracking control of PV panels is not in the scope of this paper. Moreover, it is considered a voltage value of 200 V in each DC-link capacitor. The DC-link capacitors, C_1 and C_2, assume a capacitance value of 8.2 mF and the inductors L_1 and L_2 have an inductance value of 1.2 mH.

3.1 Steady-State Operation: Normal and Fault Conditions

Figure 5 shows the steady-state operation of the three-level DC-DC converter in normal conditions, i.e., in the absence of any failure in the DC grid. In this case, it is established a reference current of 10 A. As it can be observed, the ripple frequency of i_{pv} is 40 kHz, which corresponds to the double of the switching frequency (20 kHz). As the DC-DC converter is operating in normal conditions, the voltages synthesized by the DC-DC converter, v_{conv1} and v_{conv2}, can assume the voltage values of zero and $+v_{dc}/2$ (200 V). Thus, when the semiconductors S_1 and S_2 are enabled, v_{conv1} and v_{conv2} is zero. If S_1 is enabled and S_2 is disabled, v_{conv2} is 200 V and v_{conv1} is 0 V, otherwise v_{conv2} is 0 V and v_{conv1} is 200 V. In this case, the duty-cycle of S_1 and S_2 is 75%, whose command signals are the result of the comparison with two triangular carriers of 20 kHz 180° phase shifted, resulting in the voltages v_{conv1} and v_{conv2}.

Figure 6 presents the steady-state operation of the three-level DC-DC converter in normal and fault conditions in the positive wire for a reference current of 8 A. Initially, the three-level DC-DC converter is operating normally until time instant 0.004 s, when a failure occurs in the positive wire of the bipolar DC grid. In the presence of the failure, it can be observed that the ripple frequency of i_{pv} is half the frequency (20 kHz) verified in normal conditions (40 kHz). Since there is a failure in the positive wire of the bipolar DC grid, there is no energy in capacitor C_1, so the current never flows through the diode D_1 and the energy from the PV panels is not injected into the positive wire of the bipolar DC grid. Thus, v_{conv1} is 0 V and v_{conv2} can assume the values 0 V and 200 V. Due to this, the semiconductor S_1 is always enabled, and the duty-cycle of S_2 is reduced from 75% to 50% to maintain the current value according to its reference. As voltage v_{conv1} is zero, the ripple of i_{pv} is higher than the current ripple verified for normal conditions. The two possible operation modes for this case are presented in Fig. 2.

Figure 7 shows the steady-state operation of the three-level DC-DC converter in normal and fault conditions in the neutral wire of the bipolar DC grid, for a reference current of 6 A. The three-level DC-DC converter is operating in normal conditions until time instant 0.008 s. However, in the presence of a failure in the neutral wire of the bipolar DC grid, the ripple frequency of i_{pv} changes from 40 kHz to 20 kHz, as observed in the previous case. Moreover, v_{conv1} assumes the values 0 V and 400 V, whose last value corresponds to the total voltage value of the DC-link, whereas v_{conv2} is 0 V. On the other hand, as v_{conv2} assumes the value 0 V the ripple of i_{pv} is higher than the current ripple verified in normal conditions. In the presence of a failure in the neutral wire, both semiconductors S_1 and S_2 switch and the current flows through D_1 and D_2, resulting in the operation modes presented in Fig. 3.

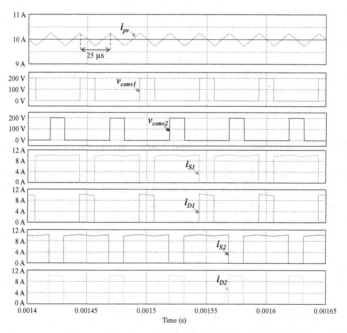

Fig. 5. Steady-state operation of the three-level DC-DC converter in normal conditions for a reference current of 10 A.

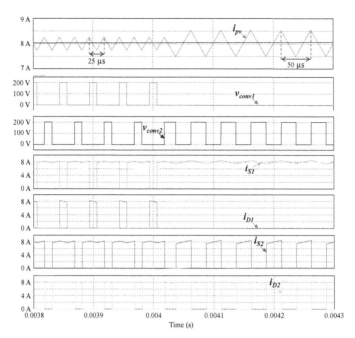

Fig. 6. Steady-state operation of the three-level DC-DC converter in normal and fault condi-tions in the positive wire for a reference current of 8 A.

Figure 8 presents the steady-state operation of the three-level DC-DC converter in normal and fault conditions in the negative wire of the bipolar DC grid, for a reference current of 4 A. As the previous case, the ripple frequency of i_{pv} in the presence of a failure in the bipolar DC grid, changes from 40 kHz to 20 kHz. Due to the presence of a failure in the negative wire of the bipolar DC grid, there is no energy in C_2 and the energy from the PV panels is not injected into the negative wire of the bipolar DC grid, so the current in D_2, i_{D2}, is 0 A. For this reason, v_{conv2} is 0 V and v_{conv1} can assume the values 0 V and 200 V. As voltage v_{conv2} is 0 V, the ripple of i_{pv} is higher than the current ripple verified for normal conditions. Furthermore, the semiconductor S_2 is always enabled, and the duty-cycle of S_1 is reduced from 75% to 50% in order to maintain the current value according to its reference. The two possible operation modes for this case are presented in Fig. 4.

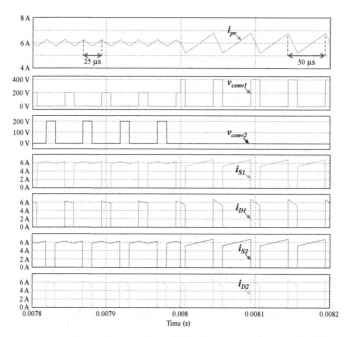

Fig. 7. Steady-state operation of the three-level DC-DC converter in normal and fault conditions in the neutral wire for a reference current of 6 A.

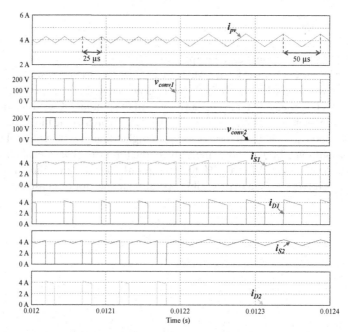

Fig. 8. Steady-state operation of the three-level DC-DC converter in normal and fault conditions in the negative wire for a reference current of 4 A.

3.2 Transient-State Operation: Normal and Fault Conditions

Figure 9 illustrates the transient-state operation of the three-level DC-DC converter in normal conditions. Initially, the reference current is 10 A and it is reduced to 8 A at time instant 0.002 s. In this case, the transition time takes 25 μs. Moreover, the ripple frequency of i_{pv} is 40 kHz, i.e., the double of the switching frequency. As the three-level DC-DC converter is operating in normal conditions, the output voltages, v_{conv1} and v_{conv2}, assume the values 0 V and 200 V. When S_1 and S_2 are enabled, v_{conv1} and v_{conv2} are zero. If S_1 is enabled and S_2 is disabled, v_{conv2} is 200 V and v_{conv1} is 0 V, otherwise v_{conv2} is 0 V and v_{conv1} is 200 V. The duty-cycle of S_1 and S_2 is 75%.

Figure 10 shows the transient-state operation of the three-level DC-DC converter in the presence of a failure in the positive wire of the bipolar DC grid. At time instant 0.0055 s the reference current is reduced to 6 A, whose transition time is 50 μs. The transition time verified is higher than in normal conditions (25 μs). Moreover, the ripple of i_{pv} is the same verified in fault conditions, i.e., the ripple is higher than in normal conditions. This is since the output voltage v_{conv1} is 0 V, where S_1 is always enabled and there is no energy injected into the positive wire of the bipolar DC grid. So, i_{D1} is 0 A and the current flows through S_1 and S_2 or S_1 and D_2.

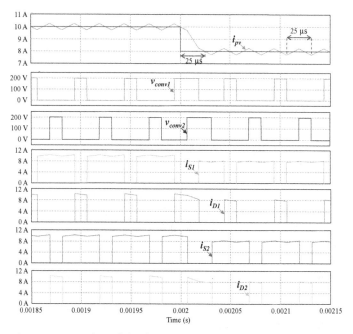

Fig. 9. Transient-state operation of the three-level DC-DC converter in normal conditions for reference currents of 10 A and 8 A.

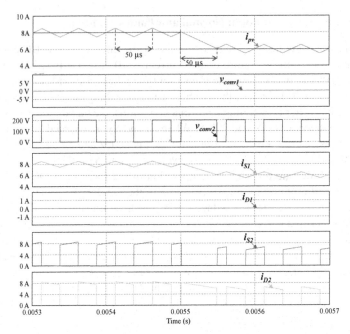

Fig. 10. Transient-state operation of the three-level DC-DC converter in the presence of a failure in the positive wire of the DC power grid for reference currents of 8 A and 6 A.

Figure 11 presents the transient-state operation of the three-level DC-DC converter in the presence of a failure in the neutral wire of the bipolar DC grid. Initially, the established reference current is 6 A and at time instant 0.0095 s the reference current is reduced to 4 A, whose transition time took 25 μs. As mentioned above, in the presence of a failure in the neutral wire of the bipolar DC grid, v_{conv1} assumes the values 0 V and 400 V and v_{conv2} is 0 V. As v_{conv2} is null, the ripple of i_{pv} is higher than the current ripple verified in normal conditions.

Figure 12 illustrates the transient-state operation of the three-level DC-DC converter in the presence of a failure in the negative wire of the bipolar DC grid. At time instant 0.0135 s the reference current changes from 4 A to 2 A, whose transition time is 50 μs. In the presence of a failure in the negative wire of the bipolar DC grid, v_{conv1} assumes the values 0 V and 200 V and v_{conv2} the value 0 V. In this case, the energy is injected from the PV panels into the bipolar DC grid, through the semiconductors S_2 and S_1 or S_2 and D_1.

Despite the presence of failures in the positive, neutral or negative wire of the bipolar DC grid, i_{pv} follows correctly the reference current.

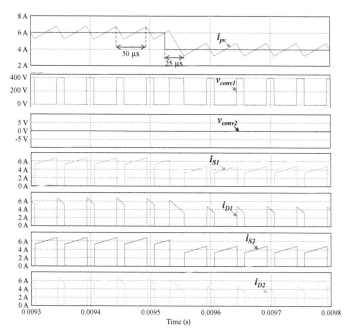

Fig. 11. Transient-state operation of the three-level DC-DC converter in the presence of a failure in the neutral wire of the DC grid for reference currents of 6 A and 4 A.

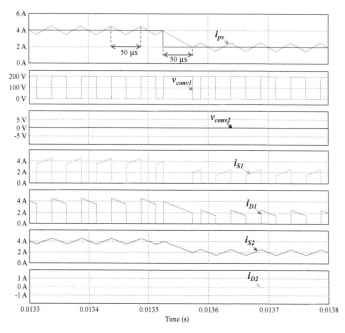

Fig. 12. Transient-state operation of the three-level DC-DC converter in the presence of a failure in the negative wire of the DC power grid for reference currents of 4 A and 2 A.

4 Conclusions

In this paper, a three-level DC-DC converter is analyzed in normal and fault conditions connected to a bipolar DC power grid. The three-level DC-DC converter aims to interface solar photovoltaic (PV) panels into a bipolar DC power grid. The presented DC-DC converter is analyzed in normal conditions considering steady-state and transient-state operations. The results are compared with the DC-DC converter operating in the presence of a failure, individually, in the positive, neutral and negative wires of the DC grid. Moreover, the validation was performed for different values of the reference currents. It is demonstrated that, despite the presence of failures in the bipolar DC grid, the current from the PV panels, i_{pv}, correctly follows the established reference current. However, the ripple of i_{pv} is higher in presence of failures than in normal operating conditions, but analyzing the presented simulation results, this aspect is not critical. As shown, the three-level DC-DC converter presents good results in normal and in the fault conditions reported in this paper, without compromising the power extraction from the solar PV panels.

Acknowledgment. This work has been supported by FCT – Fundação para a Ciência e Tecnologia within the R&D Units Project Scope: UIDB/00319/2020. This work has been supported by the FCT Project newERA4GRIDs PTDC/EEI-EEE/30283/2017.

References

1. Li, J., Zhang, X., Ali, S., Khan, Z.: Eco-innovation and energy productivity: New determinants of renewable energy consumption. J. Environ. Manage. **271**, 111028 (2020)
2. Akintande, O.J., Olubusoye, O.E., Adenikinju, A.F., Olanrewaju, B.T.: Modeling the determinants of renewable energy consumption: evidence from the five most populous nations in Africa. Energy **206**, 117992 (2020)
3. Ahmed, M., Kuriry, S., Shafiullah, M., Abido, M.: DC Microgrid energy management with hybrid energy storage systems. In: 2019 23rd International Conference on Mechatronics Technology (ICMT), pp. 1–6 (2019)
4. Matayoshi, H., Kinjo, M., Rangarajan, S.S., Ramanathan, G.G., Hemeida, A.M., Senjyu, T.: Islanding operation scheme for DC microgrid utilizing pseudo Droop control of photovoltaic system. Energy Sustain. Dev. **55**, 95–104 (2020)
5. Cui, S., Hu, J., De Doncker, R.: Fault-tolerant operation of a TLC-MMC hybrid DC-DC converter for interconnection of MVDC and HVdc grids. IEEE Trans. Power Electron. **35**(1), 83–93 (2019)
6. Wang, D., Locment, F., Sechilariu, M.: Modelling, simulation, and management strategy of an electric vehicle charging station based on a DC microgrid. Appl. Sci. **10**(6), 2053 (2020)
7. Sechilariu, M., Molines, N., Richard, G., Martell-Flores, H., Locment, F., Baert, J.: Electromobility framework study: infrastructure and urban planning for EV charging station empowered by PV-based microgrid. IET Electr. Syst. Transp. **9**(4), 176–185 (2019)
8. Monteiro, V., Pinto, J.G., Afonso, J.L.: Experimental validation of a three-port integrated topology to interface electric vehicles and renewables with the electrical grid. IEEE Trans. Industr. Inf. **14**(6), 2364–2374 (2018)
9. Monteiro, V., Tashakor, N., Sousa, T.J., Kacetl, T., Götz, S., Afonso, J.L.: Review of five-level front-end converters for renewable-energy applications. Front. Energy Res. **8**, 172 (2020)

10. Abdelghani, A.B.-B., Sakly, J., Abdelghani, H.B., Slamabelkhodja, I.: Reliable, efficient and fault tolerant power converter for grid-connected PV system. In: 2018 International Conference on Electrical Sciences and Technologies in Maghreb (CISTEM), pp. 1–6 (2018)
11. Csaba, S., Razvan, S.: Transient phenomena and failures analysis in redundant power converters. In: 2019 8th International Conference on Modern Power Systems (MPS), pp. 1–6, (2019)
12. Bento, F., Cardoso, A.J.M.: A comprehensive survey on fault diagnosis and fault tolerance of DC-DC converters. Chin. J. Electr. Eng. **4**(3), 1–12 (2018)
13. Wen, H., Li, J., Shi, H., Yihua, H., Yang, Y.: Fault diagnosis and tolerant control of dual-active-bridge converter with triple-phase shift control for bidirectional EV charging systems. IEEE Trans. Transp. Electr. **7**(1), 287–303 (2021)
14. Hu, K., Liu, Z., Yang, Y., Iannuzzo, F., Blaabjerg, F.: Ensuring a reliable operation of two-level IGBT-based power converters: a review of monitoring and fault-tolerant approaches. IEEE Access **8**, 89988–90022 (2020)
15. Pires, V.F., Cordeiro, A., Foito, D., Pires, A.J., Martins, J., Chen, H.: A multilevel fault-tolerant power converter for a switched reluctance machine drive. IEEE Access **8**, 21917–21931 (2020)
16. Bi, K., An, Q., Duan, J., Sun, L., Gai, K.: Fast diagnostic method of open circuit fault for modular multilevel DC/DC converter applied in energy storage system. IEEE Trans. Power Electron. **32**(5), 3292–3296 (2017)
17. Givi, H., Farjah, E., Ghanbari, T.: Switch and diode fault diagnosis in nonisolated DC–DC converters using diode voltage signature. IEEE Trans. Industr. Electron. **65**(2), 1606–1615 (2018)
18. Farjah, E., Givi, H., Ghanbari, T.: Application of an efficient Rogowski coil sensor for switch fault diagnosis and capacitor ESR monitoring in nonisolated single-switch DC–DC converters. IEEE Trans. Power Electron. **32**(2), 1442–1456 (2017)
19. Kumar, G.K., Elangovan, D.: Review on fault-diagnosis and fault-tolerance for DC-DC converters. IET Power Electron. **13**(1), 1–13 (2020)
20. Zhuo, S., Xu, L., Gaillard, A., Huangfu, Y., Paire, D., Gao, F.: Robust open-circuit fault diagnosis of multi-phase floating interleaved DC-DC boost converter based on sliding mode observer. IEEE Trans. Transp. Electr. **5**(3), 638–649 (2019)
21. Bento, F., Cardoso, A.J.M.: Open-circuit fault diagnosis in interleaved DC-DC boost converters and reconfiguration strategy. In: 2017 IEEE 11th International Symposium on Diagnostics for Electrical Machines, Power Electronics and Drives (SDEMPED), pp. 394–400 (2017)
22. Rodrigues, A., Oliveira, C., Sousa, T.J.C., Machado, L., Afonso, J.L., Monteiro, V.: Unified three-port topology integrating a renewable and an energy storage system with the grid-interface operating as active power filter. In: 2020 IEEE 14th International Conference on Compatibility, Power Electronics and Power Engineering (CPE-POWERENG), vol. 1, pp. 502–507 (2020)

A Comprehensive Comparison of Voltage and Current Control Techniques for Three-Phase VSI Converters

Daniel F. S. Fernandes[1(✉)], Rui F. O. Costa[1], Luis A. M. Barros[1,2], Delfim Pedrosa[1,2], João L. Afonso[1,2], and J. G. Pinto[1,2]

[1] Department of Industrial Electronics, University of Minho, Guimarães, Portugal
a81700@alunos.uminho.pt
[2] Centro ALGORITMI, University of Minho, Guimarães, Portugal

Abstract. Converting electrical energy from direct current to alternate current, or vice versa, is one of the most frequently performed tasks in today's electrical systems. The Voltage Source Inverter (VSI) is the most widely used topology to accomplish this task. This paper compares the performance of three control algorithms for voltage source inverter (VSI) with PI, PR and MP control algorithms were applied for voltage control and current control. For voltage control the VSI synthesizes the sinusoidal voltage system for an islanded application. In current control the VSI injects energy into the power grid by synthesizing sinusoidal currents. A general comparison is made of the performance of the three control algorithms under the presented conditions, helping to choose the control algorithm to use in a given application.

Keywords: Voltage source inverter · Current control · Voltage control

1 Introduction

Nowadays, electrical energy is indispensable for the execution of many tasks. With their increasing relevance, power electronics converters have become the focus of research to improve their performance and applicability. Power electronics converters can be grouped into four categories: DC-DC, DC-AC, AC-DC and AC-AC [1]. Within each category there are several topologies aimed at the most varied applications related to the production, transport and distribution of electrical energy (transformers, power generation systems, power grid interfaces for alternative energy resources such as solar photovoltaic panels, wind turbines and energy storage systems) [2, 3], industry (motor drive systems) [4], household activities (air conditioners, computers, electric vehicle chargers) [5] among others.

Regarding the DC-AC power converters, these can be classified according to their power supply, being divided into two large groups: voltage source inverter (VSI) and current source inverter (CSI) [6].

J. L. Afonso et al. (Eds.): SESC 2021, LNICST 425, pp. 16–31, 2022.
https://doi.org/10.1007/978-3-030-97027-7_2

The VSI are the most used. Through the control algorithm it is possible to adjust the output amplitude and frequency. The VSI are used in various applications such as AC motor adjustable speed drives or interfacing energy production systems from renewable sources with the power grid [7].

Although it is widely used, there is a gap in the literature in explaining and comparing control algorithms for VSI. The schematic in Fig. 1 (a) shows the voltage-controlled VSI used in this study where the converter generates the sinusoidal voltage system responsible for feeding a set of loads islanded from the power grid. The Fig. 1 (b) shows the block diagram of the current-controlled VSI assembly used in this work, where it is responsible for injecting energy into the power grid.

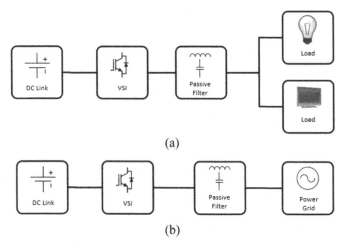

Fig. 1. Block diagram of the VSI applications using: (a) voltage-control; (b) current-control.

In this paper, three control algorithms for VSI are described and implemented: Proportional Integral (PI), Proportional Resonant (PR) and Model Predictive (MP). The objective of the paper is to compare the performance of these three algorithms in current-control and voltage-control modes.

This document is organized into five sections, as follows: Sect. 1 provides an introduction to the subject; Sect. 2 describes the VSI topology and its applications; in Sect. 3 the three control algorithms used, the PI, PR and MP, are described; in Sect. 4 the simulation results for the VSI controlled by voltage and current are presented; and, finally, in Sect. 5, the main conclusions and some ideas for future work are presented.

2   VSI Converter Topologies

The diagram of a VSI with three legs and four wires is represented in Fig. 2. This VSI requires a DC-Link division to generate a midpoint. The main advantage of this topology is the fact that this converter can control the voltage of each phase in relation to the neutral point. With its connection to the system neutral, a return path for the neutral current is created, which is an asset in unbalanced systems or for compensating power quality (PQ) problems. For its correct operation, it is necessary to ensure that the voltages V_{DC1} and V_{DC2} have similar values.

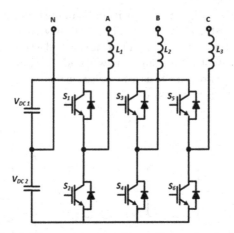

Fig. 2. VSI with 3 legs and 4 wires with a split capacitor in the DC-Link.

Since this type of converter is bidirectional (it can transfer energy from the DC side to the AC side or from the AC side to the DC side), its use is quite wide. In [8] is a study of the application of a 3-leg 4-wire VSI with split capacitor in the charging of an electric vehicle was presented.

In [9] the author used a 3 leg and 3 wire VSI as a shunt active filter in order to compensate the current harmonics in a three-phase power grid system. The author was able to significantly reduce the Total Harmonic Distortion (THD%) of the currents on the power grid side.

This converter is widely used in renewable energy applications. In [10] is used to inject the energy produced by an array of PV modules into the power grid. In [11] the author used a VSI topology for a wind power system based on a six-phase permanent magnet synchronous generator with fixed switching frequency.

Another application of the VSI is in motor control. In [12] a VSI based on Silicon Carbide Metal Oxide Semiconductor Field Effect Transistor (SiC MOSFET) was developed in order to feed a squirrel cage induction motor controlled using a constant *V/f* (it is an induction motor control method which ensures the output voltage proportional with the frequency) control achieving good results under different motor operating conditions.

3 Voltage and Current Control Techniques

In this topic the different control algorithms implemented for the comparative study are presented and analyzed. For each one of them, a block diagram of its constitution or the mathematical equation for its implementation is presented.

3.1 Proportional Integral (PI) Control

The PI voltage control technique is based on the calculation of the error, v_{error}, between the reference voltage, v_{ref}, and the converter output voltage, v_{out}. The error resulting from this operation is multiplied by a proportional gain, K_P, and an integral gain, K_I. The resulting variable, $v_{control}$, is used to synthesize the command signals of the semiconductors to be controlled. In Fig. 3 the block diagram of the PI voltage control algorithm is represented. For the current control, the diagram is similar, replacing the voltage signals with their respective current signals.

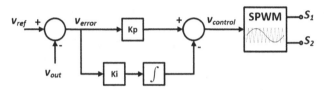

Fig. 3. Block diagram of the PI voltage-control algorithm.

In [13] a modified PI control was applied to a brushless DC motor (BLDC) with the objective of contributing to the application of this type of motor in electric vehicles.

3.2 Proportional Resonant (PR) Control

In Fig. 4 the diagram of the PR controller is represented. This control algorithm uses the error, v_{error}, between the reference signal, v_{ref}, and the synthesized signal, v_{out}, as inputs. The resulting value v_{error} is multiplied by a resonant gain, K_S, that will be the input from a second order generalized integrator (SOGI) [14]. Its output is added to the error multiplied by a proportional gain, K_P, resulting in the signal that will be the input to the sinusoidal pulse width modulation (SPWM) technique, $v_{control}$. The ω_0 constant represents the fundamental frequency of the signal to be synthesized. For 50 Hz applications, this value is approximately 314 rad/s ($2\pi f$). For the current control, the diagram is similar, replacing the voltage signals with their respective current signals.

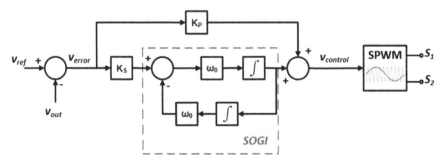

Fig. 4. Block diagram of the PR control algorithm.

In the literature there are some applications of this algorithm. For example, in [15] this algorithm was applied to a shunt active power filter used in unbalanced systems. The results prove its good operation for compensation of harmonics and neutral currents. In [16] PR control was applied to an inverter in order to inject the energy produced by a photovoltaic module into the power grid.

3.3 Model Predictive (MP) Control

The MP control technique is based on the electrical model of the system to predict the future behavior of the variables to be controlled, taking advantage of the finite number of possible switching states for a static energy converter (such as the VSI) [17]. In the literature there are several predictive controls [18–20].

This control algorithm has the advantage of having no gains in its closed loop, depending only on the constituent elements of the system and the quality of the electrical model used. This allows the control system to have a good response to the unpredictability of the loads that can be connected to the system [17].

In this work the control algorithm described below was used. The explanation is oriented towards a single-phase VSI since, for the case of a three-phase converter, it is only necessary to replicate the control for the remaining phases of the system. In Fig. 5 is the electrical representation of a grid connected single-phase VSI.

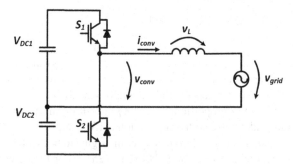

Fig. 5. Electrical diagram of a single-phase inverter connected to the power grid.

Considering the model presented in Fig. 5 and applying Kirchhoff's voltage laws, it is possible to deduce the Eq. (1). The converter output voltage (v_{conv}) results from the sum of the voltage at the inductor terminals (v_L) and the power grid voltage (v_{grid}). This model assumes that the inductor internal resistance is very small and can be neglected.

$$v_{conv} = v_{grid} + v_L \tag{1}$$

Using an equation characteristic of the voltage in an inductor, v_L, it is possible to obtain the Eq. (2).

$$v_{conv} = v_{grid} + L\frac{di_{conv}(t)}{dt} \tag{2}$$

This control is applied in closed-loop. The error current (i_{error}) is calculated from the subtraction of the converter output current (i_{conv}) and the reference current (i_{ref}), as represented in (3).

$$i_{error} = i_{ref} - i_{conv} \tag{3}$$

By updating the Eq. (2) of the electrical model of the system with the Eq. (3) of the reference current, it is possible to obtain the Eq. (4)

$$v_{conv} = v_{grid} - L\frac{di_{error}(t)}{dt} + L\frac{di_{ref}(t)}{dt} \tag{4}$$

To cancel the current error (i_{error}), the controller must allow the converter to generate a voltage that, when applied to the inductor, causes a current with equal amplitude but in phase opposition to the calculated in the Eq. (3). So, it is possible to obtain the Eq. (5).

$$v_{Conv} = v_{grid} + L\frac{di_{error}(t)}{dt} + L\frac{di_{ref}(t)}{dt} \tag{5}$$

Microcontrollers cannot work in the continuous domain. They have a minimum time between samples which makes them discrete domain devices. Converting Eq. (5) to the discrete domain, it was obtained Eq. (6), where T_a is the acquisition period.

$$v_{conv}[k] = v_{grid}[k] + \frac{L}{T_a}\left(2i_{ref}[k] - i_{ref}[k-1] - i_{conv}[k]\right) \tag{6}$$

The same principle and equations can be applicate to the voltage-controlled MP by replacing the reference and produced currents by the reference and produced voltages.

4   Simulation Results

This chapter presents the simulations carried out in this work. These are divided into two subchapters: voltage-controlled VSI and current-controlled VSI. In the simulations performed for this paper, equal parameters were used to make a fair comparison between algorithms. Table 1 shows the general parameters used in these simulations.

Table 1. General parameters of the simulations.

Parameter	Value	Unit
Inductors L_1, L_2, L_3	5	mH
Switching frequency	20	kHz
Sampling frequency	40	kHz
Upper peak of the triangular carrier	3750	-
Lower peak of the triangular carrier	0	-

4.1 Voltage Controlled VSI

In the presented simulation, the VSI is controlled by voltage. A group of loads has been added, as shown in Fig. 6. A configuration in star of 3 resistive loads of 50 Ω each was used. Regarding the nonlinear load, it was used a three-phase full-bridge diode rectifier with a RC load. The capacitor used was 500 μF and the resistor has the value of 200 Ω. An LC filter was placed at the output of the converter, where the inductor is 5 mH, the capacitor is 30 μF and the resistor is 2.2 Ω.

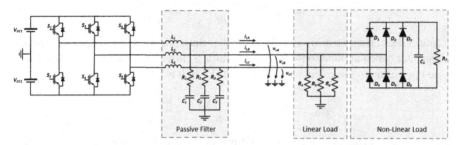

Fig. 6. Electrical diagram of the circuit used for the voltage-controlled VSI study.

During this study are used different voltage control algorithms applied to the VSI. The objective is to see the different behaviors of the different controls with linear loads and nonlinear loads connected to the system. The control algorithms used in this simulation are the PI, PR and MP. The simulation conditions are the same for the three voltage control algorithm under study. In this simulation, the linear load is connected at 0.2 s and at 0.25 s the nonlinear load is added until the end of the simulation time. For the nonlinear load is used a pre-charge circuit to charge the capacitor in such a way as not to cause disturbances in the system at its connection.

PI Voltage Control Algorithm
The first control algorithm implemented was PI. The simulation starts with the linear load connected to the electrical system and after 0.25 s a nonlinear load is added. From that time the system is powering the linear load and the nonlinear load. With this simulation, it is intended to verify the differences in the behavior of the voltage control algorithm with the two different loads and seeing the behavior of the control when the load addiction occurs. In Fig. 7 are presented the results of this simulation with the linear and nonlinear loads. These results are obtained using a K_p of 130 and a K_i of 5.

Analyzing the obtained results, it is possible to conclude that the PI control algorithm works correctly not only with a linear load but also with a nonlinear load. The voltage THD increased a little bit with a nonlinear load comparing with the results obtained with the linear load. In Table 2 is presented the THD% voltage results during this simulation.

PR Voltage Control Algorithm
The second control algorithm implemented was PR. The simulation starts with the linear load connected to the system and after 0.25 s the load addiction occurs, becoming the

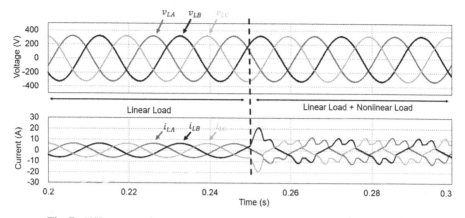

Fig. 7. VSI output voltages and load currents with PI voltage control algorithm.

Table 2. PI voltage control algorithm THD% comparison using different loads.

Load	Voltage	THD%
Linear	v_{LA}	1.18%
	v_{LB}	1.14%
	v_{LC}	1.14%
Linear + Nonlinear	v_{LA}	1.27%
	v_{LB}	1.23%
	v_{LC}	1.23%

linear load and the nonlinear load connected to the system. In Fig. 8 are presented the results of this simulation with the linear and nonlinear loads. These results are obtained using a K_p of 200 and a K_s of 1000.

Analyzing the obtained results, it is possible to conclude that the PR voltage control algorithm works correctly with a linear load as well as with a nonlinear load on the system. The THD% voltage results are presented in Table 3.

The THD% voltage increased when the nonlinear load is connected to the system comparing with the results with a linear load. Although, the THD% results are very satisfactory for both loads. Comparing this control to the results obtained for the PI control, they are very similar, but the THD% results are a little higher for the PI control.

MP Voltage Control Algorithm

The last voltage control algorithm implemented was the MP. As for the PI and for PR voltage control algorithms, the simulation for testing MP voltage control algorithms use a linear load and a nonlinear load. The loads have the same values as used for the other control under study. Also, at 0.25 s it is added the nonlinear load to the linear load previously used. In Fig. 9 are presented the results of this simulation with the linear and nonlinear loads using the MP voltage control algorithm for VSI.

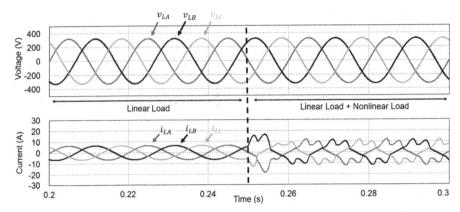

Fig. 8. VSI output voltages and load currents with PR voltage control algorithm.

Table 3. PR voltage control THD% comparison using different loads.

Load	Voltage	THD%
Linear	v_{LA}	1.16%
	v_{LB}	1.06%
	v_{LC}	1.09%
Linear + Nonlinear	v_{LA}	1.25%
	v_{LB}	1.16%
	v_{LC}	1.18%

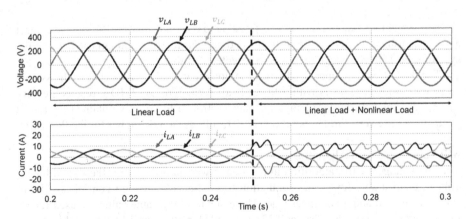

Fig. 9. VSI output voltages and load currents with MP voltage control algorithm.

Analyzing the results it was possible to validate the MP voltage control algorithm for the VSI to produce three-phase sinusoidal voltages. In terms of THD% results, in Table 4, is possible to conclude the increasing values with linear load to nonlinear load. Comparing these THD% voltage results with the values obtained for the other two controls, the MP voltage control algorithm presents the higher values. Although, the THD% results are very satisfactory.

Table 4. MP voltage control THD% comparison using different loads.

Load	Voltage	THD%
Linear	v_{LA}	1.21%
	v_{LB}	1.18%
	v_{LC}	1.18%
Linear + Nonlinear	v_{LA}	1.35%
	v_{LB}	1.31%
	v_{LC}	1.30%

4.2 Current Controlled VSI

For the simulation of current control algorithms, the electrical schematic is presented in Fig. 10. The component values are the same as those used in the previous section. In this, the VSI is responsible for injecting energy into a three-phase 400 V/50 Hz power grid from its DC-Link (in this case using DC energy sources).

The simulation conditions are the same for all the three algorithms under study. A perturbation was caused (the reference current increases to double) to verify the response of each of the current control algorithms. Variation of current in a system is quite common as for example as the resulting from the solar radiation or wind speed change in a renewable energy application.

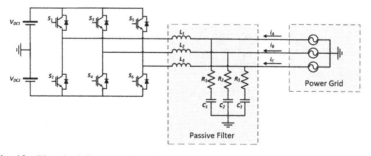

Fig. 10. Electrical diagram of the circuit that integrates the current-controlled VSI.

PI Current Control Algorithm

In Fig. 11 are represented the results obtained with the application of the PI algorithm to current control. As can be seen, the PI current control algorithm causes a current spike when the references change. This spike is approximately 17 A (considering peak values) and it is evidenced in phase B because it is the phase in which the current takes the highest value at the time of the references change. These results are obtained using a K_p of 100 and a K_i of 15.

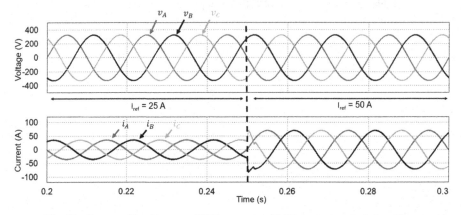

Fig. 11. Power grid voltages and VSI currents with PI current control algorithm.

Analyzing the results, it is possible to validate the PI current control algorithm for the VSI to inject energy into the power grid. In terms of THD% results, in Table 5, is possible to conclude the decreasing values with the increase of the current reference because the impact of switching noise is less with higher amplitude.

Table 5. PI current control THD% comparison using different reference amplitudes.

Reference	Current	THD%
25 A	i_A	2.31%
	i_B	2.32%
	i_C	2.30%
50 A	i_A	1.22%
	i_B	1.23%
	i_C	1.21%

PR Current Control Algorithm

The simulation results for the PR current control algorithm are shown in Fig. 12. Like the previous algorithm, it occurs a current spike in the references change. In this case, this phenomenon has an amplitude of 9 A. These results are obtained using a K_p of 120 and a K_s of 800.

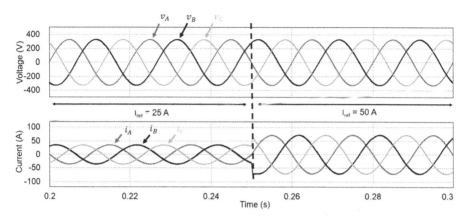

Fig. 12. Power grid voltages and VSI currents with PR current control algorithm.

This control produced similar results to the PI current control algorithm. The THD% results are similar, with the same behavior as in the previous control, as it can be seen in Table 6.

Table 6. PR current control THD% comparison using different reference amplitudes.

Reference	Current	THD%
25 A	i_A	2.29%
	i_B	2.32%
	i_C	2.27%
50 A	i_A	1.18%
	i_B	1.20%
	i_C	1.17%

MP Current Control Algorithm

The Fig. 13 shows the simulation results obtained by applying the MP current control algorithm. This algorithm does not cause current spikes during the references change transient, resulting in a smoother behavior.

In terms of results, the MP control algorithm has the most advantages over previous current control algorithms. It has a lower THD, being able to synthesize currents with less than 1% THD% with a 50 A reference, as shown in Table 7.

The PI and PR voltage control algorithms present a problem. If the gains are static, variations in the reference can cause current peaks. The predictive algorithm does not

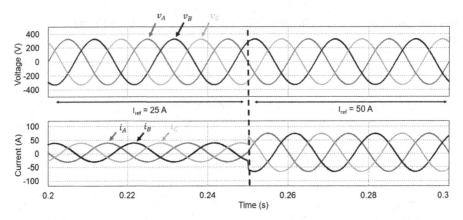

Fig. 13. Power grid voltages and VSI currents with MP current control algorithm.

have this disadvantage. However, the application of this algorithm is more complicated than the others since, in a real system, the components that constitute a converter are not ideals, making obtaining an accurate electrical model of the system a difficult process.

Table 7. MP current control THD% comparison using different reference amplitudes.

Reference	Current	THD%
25 A	i_A	1.81%
	i_B	1.86%
	i_C	1.79%
50 A	i_A	0.91%
	i_B	0.96%
	i_C	0.91%

4.3 Comparative Analyses

Table 8 shows the comparison between the three control algorithms in voltage control. In terms of harmonic distortion, the algorithms are quite similar, with the PR showing slightly better results. Regarding the difficulty of implementation, the PI and PR algorithms are similar, with the MP being slightly more complex due to obtaining the system model.

Table 9 shows the comparison of the results of the application of the three algorithms in current control. The implementation difficulty is like the in the voltage control. In terms of THD% the MP control gives slightly better results. Furthermore, this algorithm does not cause current spikes, unlike PI and PR. The PI is the one with the largest current spike of 17 A.

Table 8. Comparison between the results of control algorithms in voltage control.

Control algorithm	THD% (Average)	Implementation complexity
PI	1.25%	Moderate
PR	1.15%	Moderate
MP	1.25%	Moderate/High

Table 9. Comparison between the results of control algorithms in current control.

Control algorithm	THD% (Average)	Implementation complexity	Current transient (Overcurrent)
PI	1.75%	Moderate	17 A
PR	1.75%	Moderate	9 A
MP	1.35%	Moderate/High	0 A

5 Conclusions

This paper compared the performance of three control algorithms for voltage source inverter (VSI). The Proportional Integral (PI), Proportional Resonant (PR) and the Model Predictive (MP) control algorithms were applied for voltage control and current control. As demonstrated in the simulations, all algorithms show good results in terms of Total Harmonic Distortion (THD%), and as expected, the THD% decreases with increasing current amplitude.

In the voltage controlled, the PR control algorithm gives slightly better results in terms of THD%. The implementation difficulty is similar for PI and PR control, the MP being slightly more difficult to implement.

In the current control, the PI and PR algorithms show very similar results, and since they have static gains, they cause an overcurrent transient in the current references change because the error is too high at this instant. The MP algorithm shows better results with respect to the transient. It also has a lower THD% in the current control. Nevertheless, it should be noted that this algorithm only works well with a good model of the electrical system, which, depending on the case, can be difficult to obtain. As future work it is planned to validate experimentally the three control algorithms to have a better perception of their behavior in real application in comparison with the simulation results.

Acknowledgements. This work has been supported by FCT – Fundação para a Ciência e Tecnologia with-in the Project Scope: UIDB/00319/2020. This work has been supported by the FCT Project QUALITY4POWER PTDC/EEI-EEE/28813/2017, and by the FCT Project DAIPESEV PTDC/EEI-EEE/30382/2017. Mr. Luis A. M. Barros is supported by the doctoral scholarship PD/BD/143006/2018 granted by the Portuguese FCT foundation.

References

1. Zhang, G., Li, Z., Zhang, B., Halang, W.A.: Power electronics converters: past, present and future. Renew. Sustain. Energy Rev. **81**, 2028–2044 (2018). https://doi.org/10.1016/j.rser. 2017.05.290
2. Barros, L.A., Tanta, M., Sousa, T.J., Afonso, J.L., Pinto, J.: New multifunctional isolated microinverter with integrated energy storage system for PV applications. Energies **13**(15), 4016 (2020). https://doi.org/10.3390/en13154016
3. Duarte, R.E.G., Moreira, L., Barros, L.A.M., Monteiro, V.D.F., Afonso, J.L., Pinto, J.: Power Converters for a Small Islanded Microgrid based on a Micro Wind Turbine and an Battery Energy Storage System. ISBN: 978–972–99596–4–6. (2018)
4. Uma, D., Vijayarekha, K.: Modeling and simulation of VSI fed induction motor drive in Matlab/Simulink. Int. J. Electr. Comput. Eng. **7**(2), 584 (2017). https://doi.org/10.11591/ ijece.v7i2.pp584-595
5. Pinto, J., Monteiro, V., Gonçalves, H., Afonso, J.L.: Onboard reconfigurable battery charger for electric vehicles with traction-to-auxiliary mode. IEEE Trans. Veh. Technol. **63**(3), 1104–1116 (2013). https://doi.org/10.1109/TVT.2013.2283531
6. Azmi, S., Ahmed, K., Finney, S., Williams, B.: Comparative Analysis Between Voltage and Current Source Inverters in Grid-Connected Application (2011). https://doi.org/10.1049/cp. 2011.0138
7. Sarkar, A.: Modeling and Control of a Three Phase Voltage Source Inverter with an LCL Filter. Arizona State University (2015)
8. Mandrioli, R., Hammami, M., Viatkin, A., Barbone, R., Pontara, D., Ricco, M.: Phase and neutral current ripple analysis in three-phase four-wire split-capacitor grid converter for EV chargers. Electronics **10**(9), 1016 (2021). https://doi.org/10.3390/electronics10091016
9. Castillo, T.D., Castro, J.R.: Renewable energy source PV connected to the grid through shunt active power filter based in PQ Theory. In: 2018 IEEE Third Ecuador Technical Chapters Meeting (ETCM), pp. 1–5 (2018). https://doi.org/10.1109/ETCM.2018.8580274
10. Mohammed, A.Y., Mohammed, F.I., Ibrahim, M.Y.: Grid connected Photovoltaic system. In: 2017 International Conference on Communication, Control, Computing and Electronics Engineering (ICCCCEE), pp. 1–5 (2017). https://doi.org/10.1109/ICCCCEE.2017.7867659
11. Milev, K., Yaramasu, V., Dekka, A., Kouro, S.: Predictive control of multichannel boost converter and VSI-Based six-phase PMSG wind energy systems with fixed switching frequency. In: 2020 11th Power Electronics, Drive Systems, and Technologies Conference (PEDSTC), pp. 1–6 (2020). https://doi.org/10.1109/PEDSTC49159.2020.9088419
12. Mishra, P., Munk-Neilsen, S., Maheshwari, R.: Testing of SiC voltage source inverter fed induction motor drive and its control with output sinusoidal LC filter. In: 2020 IEEE International Conference on Power Electronics, Drives and Energy Systems (PEDES), pp. 1–5 (2020). https://doi.org/10.1109/PEDES49360.2020.9379605
13. Haque, M.R., Khan, S.: The modified proportional integral controller for the BLDC motor and electric vehicle. In: 2021 IEEE International IOT, Electronics and Mechatronics Conference (IEMTRONICS), pp. 1–5 (2021). https://doi.org/10.1109/IEMTRONICS52119.2021. 9422548
14. Ortiz, A., Aredes, M., Rolim, L.G., Bueno, E., Rodriguez, P.: A new current control for the STATCOM based on secondary order generalized integrators. In: 2008 IEEE Power Electronics Specialists Conference, pp. 1378–1383. (2008)
15. Santiprapan, P., Areerak, K., Areerak, K.: Proportional plus Resonant Control for Active Power Filter in Unbalanced System. International Electrical Engineering Congress (iEECON) **2017**, 1–4 (2017). https://doi.org/10.1109/IEECON.2017.8075733

16. Abdel-Rahim, O., Furiato, H., Switched inductor quadratic boosting ratio inverter with proportional resonant controller for Grid-Tie PV applications. In: IECON 2014–40th Annual Conference of the IEEE Industrial Electronics Society, pp. 5606–5611 (2014). https://doi.org/10.1109/IECON.2014.7049358
17. Pirooz, A., Noroozian, R.: Predictive voltage control of three-phase voltage source inverters to supply nonlinear and unbalanced loads. In: The 6th Power Electronics, Drive Systems & Technologies Conference (PEDSTC2015), pp. 389–394 (2015)
18. Shi, H., Zong, J., Ren, L.: Modified model predictive control of voltage source inverter. In: 2019 IEEE 4th Advanced Information Technology, Electronic and Automation Control Conference (IAEAC), vol. 1, pp. 754–759 (2019). https://doi.org/10.1109/IAEAC47372.2019.8997737
19. Vitor Monteiro, J.L.A., Meléndez, A.A.N.: Novel single-phase five-level VIENNA-type rectifier with model predictive current control. In: IECON 2017–43rd Annual Conference of the IEEE Industrial Electronics Society, pp. 6413–6418 (2017)
20. Boukezata, B., Chaoui, A., Gaubert, J.-P., Hachemi, M.: Implementation of predictive current control for shunt active power filter. In: 2017 6th International Conference on Systems and Control (ICSC), pp. 133–138 (2017)

Development of a Modular Multilevel Cascade Converter Based on Full-Bridge Submodules with a Common DC Bus

João Rego[1(✉)], Fábio Lúcio Pereira[1], Luis A. M. Barros[1,2], António P. Martins[3], and J. G. Pinto[1,2]

[1] Department of Industrial Electronics, University of Minho, Guimarães, Portugal
a81341@uminho.pt
[2] Centro ALGORITMI, University of Minho, Guimarães, Portugal
[3] SYSTEC Research Center, University of Porto, Porto, Portugal

Abstract. The Modular Multilevel Cascade Converters (MMCC) present themselves as one of the solutions for high power and high voltage applications. Modularity and low voltage stress in each semiconductor are some of the features of this solution. This paper presents a study with experimental results concerning an MMCC composed by three full-bridge submodules with a common DC-bus and with low frequency cascaded transformers. Sharing the DC bus for each submodule al-lows for a simpler control algorithm as well as a simpler interface point with renewable energy sources or energy storage systems. Along the paper, it is presented the step-by-step methodology to obtain the main parameters of the elements that constitute the MMCC, namely the transformers equivalents model. Thus, it was possible to develop a more realistic simulation model, whose results obtained are very similar to the experimental results.

Keywords: Modular multilevel cascade converter (MMCC) · Cascade transformers · Simulation model

1 Introduction

The increasing technological evolution combined with the increase in electrical energy demand encourages the investigation of more efficient and effective power conversion solutions. In this sense, power electronic converters have been gaining popularity due to their versatility and features. The evolution of power semiconductors has led to the appearance of more robust and compact topologies for power electronic converters. Two and three-level DC-AC power electronic converters are the most widely used topologies. These power converters are used in several applications, such as interfacing renewable energy sources with the power grid, driving electric motors, charging electric vehicles, and other applications [1, 2]. Regarding the control, they are usually controlled by Pulse Width Modulation (PWM) technique. As such, the output harmonic content is dispersed, which causes high losses in the system, namely in the output passive filters

J. L. Afonso et al. (Eds.): SESC 2021, LNICST 425, pp. 32–50, 2022.
https://doi.org/10.1007/978-3-030-97027-7_3

[1]. Furthermore, the semiconductors have a higher volt-age stress [1, 3]. For that reason, conventional converters are not feasible for high power and high voltage applications.

The Multilevel Converter (MLC), namely the Modular Multilevel Converter (MMC) and the Modular Multilevel Cascaded Converter (MMCC) concepts, presents themselves as innovative solutions to mitigate the mentioned problems. The MMCC allows the connection of different submodules, being the number of added submodules adjusted in order to withstand the desired voltage. The more submodules added, the more voltage levels the MMCC can synthesize [1]. Consequently, it is possible to obtain a waveform closer to the sinusoidal one, which minimizes the harmonic spectrum, being more concentrated on the fundamental component and the switching frequency [1, 4]. Therefore, it is possible to reduce the *dv/dt* variations at the output, allowing the integration of smaller passive filters and more robust semiconductors [1]. For these reasons, system losses are lower, and the efficiency is higher, which is important for high power applications [1, 5–8]. In [1] and in [9] it is possible to conclude the impact of the number of levels that the MMCC can synthesize on the out-put signals, both in the time domain and in the frequency domain. With a smaller number of voltage levels, the harmonic spectrum is wide and with considerable amplitude values. On the other hand, with a higher number of voltage levels, the harmonic spectrum is more concentrated in the fundamental frequency and switching frequency, having reduced amplitudes along the rest of the harmonic spectrum. This feature facilitates the design of passive filters. In [9], the influence of the modulation index on the number of levels that an MMCC composed of cascaded full-bridge can synthesize was studied. The total harmonic distortion (THD) has a higher value for low voltage levels.

Due to lower voltages in each submodule, the voltage stress is reduced. Furthermore, with the integration of MMCC based solutions, it is possible to increase the output frequency without changing the switching frequency, taking advantage of the complementarity of the different constituent submodules [1]. Also, given the modular concept, it is relatively easy to adapt or replace any damaged module. With the creation of redundant states and auxiliary submodules, it is possible to obtain a more fault tolerant system. In this way, continuous operation of the system is guaranteed [10, 11]. Finally, the modularity and scalability of the MMCC allow meeting any voltage level requirements [1, 5–8].

The MMCC became the most attractive MLC topology for high voltage DC transmission systems (HVDC) [4, 5, 12, 13], medium voltage drives [4, 13], active filters [4], integration with renewable energy sources [4, 9, 13, 14] and energy storage systems (ESS) [13, 14], and electrical railway systems [14, 15].

The MMCC is mentioned several times in the literature. In [16] several topologies and control strategies for MMCC with a power grid connection with a large-scale solar photovoltaic (PV) system interface are analyzed. In turn, in [17] it is presented a connection between a battery ESS and an MMCC through a non-isolated DC-DC converter. In [13] the MMCC is reviewed in respect to the submodule and overall topologies, mathematical modeling, control methods and modulation techniques. The power losses with the incorporation of advanced wide-bandgap power devices, such as Silicon Carbide (SiC) and Gallium Nitride (GaN) is also presented. Additionally, in [18] it is presented a study about the PWM techniques to a MMCC and their impact on the MLC harmonic pollution, efficiency and ripple synthetized across its capacitors. In [1] it is presented a comparative analysis based on computer simulations of the different PWM techniques to an MMCC with 4 full bridges. In this analysis, it is demonstrated that the phase-shift carriers (PSC) and the phase-shift disposition (PSD) allow the synthetization of an output waveform with a low THD ratio. When applying the PSC PWM technique in a hybrid MMCC based on the half-bridge and full-bridge submodules, undesirable harmonics on the output voltage and uneven loss distributions between the submodules arise. To deal with these issues an im-proved PSC PWM technique is presented in [19]. Also, in [20] it is demonstrated that the use of a hybrid modulation technique could be the most indicate when the MMCC has a lower number of submodules due to the extra switching losses with the increase of the submodules.

Despite its numerous advantages, the MMCC presents some challenges from the hardware and control system point of view, such as: (i) the complex structure be-cause of the need to manage a large number of switching signals; (ii) the need to measure several voltages and currents through sensors, which contributes to an enormous exchange of data at each sampling; (iii) the difficulty in keeping the DC-bus capacitor voltages balanced as well as the potential increase in energy losses due to circulating currents [4, 20]; it is not the case in the present application.

An existing solution in the literature of an MMCC consists of the parallel association of different full-bridge power electronic converters in parallel, thus allowing the same DC bus to be shared. A transformer is connected to the output of each full-bridge, the secondary winding being connected to the adjacent transformer. The transformation ratio can be different between transformers, thus increasing the input voltage as well as increasing the number of levels that can be synthesized. In the literature, there are some projects related to this topology. However, there is a research gap that allows the correct design of transformers, as well as a methodology that helps to create a more realistic simulation model based on the parameters measured in a real transformer.

In [21–27] different approaches are presented, with different numbers of voltage levels, control techniques and power levels. However, no further information regarding transformers and their sizing is provided. Additionally, the methodology for determining the simulation model parameters is not explicit. In turn, in [28] a switching technique for power balancing between submodules is proposed. In [29] they show a solution composed of 4 cascade transformers, where some transformer parameters are presented. However, the methodology used to determine the parameters of the transformers is not presented, nor is information regarding the sizing of the transformers disclosed. However, the parameters of the transformers used in simulation do not support the values used experimentally. In [30] an analysis of the existing state-of-the-art methodologies for the design of cascaded transformers is presented. In the end, a sizing methodology is proposed, which is compared with the conventional methodology. Experimental results were presented for transformers sized for 100 VA. In general, it is possible to identify a research gap that could support the development of this solution for high voltage applications as well as for higher powers. The methodology for determining the transformer parameters so that the implementation of more realistic simulation models is possible is a critical step for the correct implementation and validation of the system.

The purpose of this paper is to demonstrate the development of an MMCC composed of 3 full-bridge submodules with a common DC-bus and with cascaded power transformers. Therefore, this paper is organized as follows: Sect. 1, presents an introduction to the topic of research and explains the concept of MMCC; Sect. 2 shows the topology of MMCC used in this study; Sect. 3 describes the control algorithms implemented; Sect. 4 presents the step-by-step methodology for the MMCC analyses based on cascaded transformers, which served as the basis for the implementation of the simulation. The obtained simulation results are also presented in this section; Sect. 5 shows the experimental results of the MMCC; finally, in Sect. 6, the main conclusions of this study as well as some suggestions for future work are presented.

2 Full Bridge with Cascaded Transformers Topology

In Fig. 1 is illustrates the MMCC composed of full-bridge converters with cascaded power transformers. The MMCC consists of the parallel association of three full-bridge submodules sharing the same DC-bus. The output of each submodule connects to the primary side of a power transformer, while the secondary side is connected in series with the adjacent transformers [16]. In this study, these power transformers have a transformer ratio of 1:1 and are used to create the multilevel feature, since there is only one DC-bus.

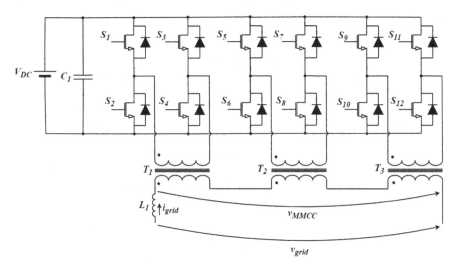

Fig. 1. MMCC composed of full-bridge with cascaded transformers and common DC-bus.

Considering that exists N submodules on the MMCC, by adding the voltages of each secondary winding of adjacent transformers, the number of obtained voltage levels is given by the Eq. (1).

$$N_L = 2N + 1 \tag{1}$$

For this topology, it is necessary $4N$ power semiconductors, N transformers, and only one voltage source. It should be noted that, due to the versatility of changing the transformers transformation ratios, it is possible to obtain different output voltage levels even with few submodules [1]. A maximum of 3^N output voltage levels can be obtained, with N being the number of submodules connected in parallel. For example, in a topology with three submodules, it would be possible to obtain 27 voltage levels at the output by applying transformers with 1:1, 1:3 and 1:9 ratios [16]. However, it is necessary to implement a space vector modulation (SVM) control algorithm, as presented in [4, 7, 16, 31]. Additionally, each submodule would contribute with different powers, losing the concept of modularity.

Sharing a single DC-bus between the different submodules facilitates the control algorithms as well as the integration of other power converters. These power converters could be interfaced with an ESS or renewable energy source. From an implementation point of view, the use of only one DC-bus and the existence of a common reference for fully controlled power semiconductors make the implementation easier [1, 10]. Furthermore, this topology makes it possible to synthesize an output sinusoidal current at lower switching frequencies [16]. In fact, with the increase in the number of submodules, it is possible to reduce the switching frequency of semiconductors and the output presents less harmonic distortion [11]. This increase further reduces the value of dv/dt, mitigating the problems associated with electromagnetic interference [32].

Due to the use of a power transformer for each submodule added, the system implementation costs may be higher [9, 16]. However, it is possible to use medium-frequency transformers. These allow the integration of power semiconductors with high switching frequencies which enable the use of smaller passive filters. Additionally, the volume, weight, and implementation costs would be lower compared to low-frequency transformers [10]. Although high-frequency increases switching losses and the skin effect, it is possible to reduce losses in the passive elements [10]. Another drawback of the use of transformers in this topology is that they are not suitable for variable frequency applications [9]. Another aspect to consider is the voltage drop in each semiconductor. Considering N the number of submodules of the MMCC and V_{CE} the voltage drop in each power semiconductor, the total voltage drop in the power converter can be express by Eq. (2). The multiplication by 2 is explained by the fact that in a full-bridge submodule 2 semiconductors are simultaneously in conduction. As an example, considering the typical $V_{CE\_SAT} = 3.3$ V on the SKM 100GB125DN Insulated Gate Bipolar Transistor (IGBT) module of the Semikron and 3 submodules, a total voltage drop of 19.8 V is obtained.

$$\sum V_T = 2NV_{CE} \tag{2}$$

3   Control Algorithms

The control algorithms of MMCC that interface with the power grid need to be synchronized with the fundamental component for an accurate and efficient operation. This synchronization algorithm must detect the signal phase as quickly as possible and the synchronization process must be continuously updated, to increase efficiency [33]. The synchronization technique used in this study was the Enhance Phase Locked Loop (EPLL), described in [33]. The EPLL can detect the phase and amplitude of the fundamental component of a given input signal. The output signal is sinusoidal and in phase with the fundamental component of the input signal, even if it contains harmonics. Multiplying the unitary sinusoidal signal, pll, by the amplitude value, A, is possible to obtain a signal, v_{pll}, with the same phase and amplitude of the input signal fundamental component. The biggest advantage of the EPLL is the fast response to disturbances and the high rejection of the harmonic content [33]. In Fig. 2 is shown the diagram of the implemented EPLL algorithm. In the digital implementation of the EPLL the integrals were replaced by summations.

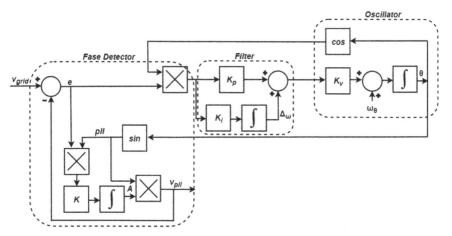

Fig. 2. Diagram of the implemented EPLL algorithm.

In this study, the main purpose of the MMCC is to inject energy into the power grid. Therefore, the MMCC will have the function of synthesizing a sinusoidal current in phase opposition with the power grid voltage, thus with unitary power factor. The reference current, i^*, is obtained by multiplying the desired amplitude value by the unitary sinusoidal signal, pll, resulted from the EPLL algorithm. The amplitude of the current reference depends on the power reference, and its value is given by the division between twice the power reference, P^*, and the peak value of the voltage grid, $\widehat{V}_{pk}$, constructed using the EPLL algorithm. That said, the calculation of the reference current is depicted in Eq. (3) which is similar to the presented in [34] and in [35].

$$i^* = \frac{2P^*}{\widehat{V}_{pk}} * pll \tag{3}$$

After calculating the i^* it is necessary to control the output current of the MMCC, i_{grid}, through power electronics semiconductors, specifically, through IGBT devices used in this study. For this purpose, a Proportional Integral (PI) current control algorithm and a PWM modulation technique was used, as shown in the block diagram presented in Fig. 3. Initially, the difference between i^* and i_{grid} results in an error value, $error$. This error value is then used in the PI current control algorithm to produce a command voltage, $v_{control}$. This command voltage establishes the modulating wave in the PWM technique.

Before the modulation process takes place and, to avoid undesirable operations, the command voltage is delimited between two pre-defined values. Regarding the PWM technique, in [1] it is demonstrated that the PSC allows the synthesis of an output waveform with a low THD ratio and is easy to implement in a Digital Signal Controller (DSC) platform, namely in the Texas Instruments C2000 platform utilized in the MMCC prototype. Therefore, the PSC was adopted to be implemented in the control system of the MMCC prototype. Finally, the modulation technique triggers the respective IGBT devices (S_1, ..., S_n, where n is the total number of IGBT devices).

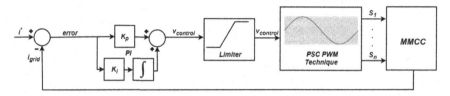

Fig. 3. Block diagram of current control used in the MMCC.

4 Simulation Results

In this section, the simulation results of the MMCC topology implemented are presented and analyzed. These simulations were performed in PSIM software. To obtain realistic results it is important to get an accurate model of the transformer, which is a key component in the studied topology. The transformer used in the tests has a nominal voltage of 230 V, a nominal power of 500 VA and a transformation ratio of 1:1. Considering the equivalent model of a transformer presented in Fig. 4 is important to consider:

- R_P the electrical resistance of the primary winding;
- R_S the electrical resistance of the secondary winding;
- L_P the leakage inductance of the primary winding;
- L_S the leakage inductance of the secondary winding;
- L_M the magnetizing inductance.

To obtain a more realistic transformer model to use in the simulation, an LCR bridge equipment, with the references 3532-50LCR HiTESTER from the manufacture Hioki, was used to measure the transformer inductances. At this stage, was necessary to measure with the windings in series (terminal b connected to terminal c and measured from a to d) and anti-series (terminal b connected to terminal d and measured from a to c). When measure with the winding in series, a value of 4.9 H was obtained. On the other hand, when measured with the winding in anti-series, a value of 3.6 mH was obtained.

The measurement of these two inductances allows the calculation of the self-inductance of the primary winding (L_1), the self-inductance of the secondary winding (L_2), and the mutual inductance between the primary and secondary windings (M), through Eq. (4) and Eq. (5). Since the primary and secondary windings have the

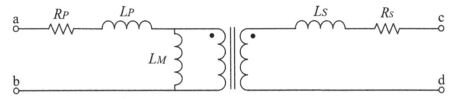

Fig. 4. Equivalent model of the transformer used in this study.

same number of turns, L_1 is approximately equal to L_2 and thus, in the equations, the self-inductance of the windings was represented by L, as represented in Eq. (6) [36].

$$L_{series} = 2L + 2M = 4.9\,H \tag{4}$$

$$L_{anti-series} = 2L - 2M = 3.6\,mH \tag{5}$$

$$L = L_1 = L_2 \tag{6}$$

To obtain the values of the inductances L and M, it is necessary to solve a system of equations with Eqs. (4) and (5). Therefore, by substituting the L of Eq. (5) into Eq. (4), is possible to obtain the Eq. (7). Thus, the value of M can be calculated. Having the value of M, the value of L can be easily obtained by substituting the value of M in Eq. (8).

$$M = \frac{L_{series} - L_{anti-series}}{4} = 1.224\,H \tag{7}$$

$$L = \frac{L_{series} + 2M}{2} = 1.226\,H \tag{8}$$

The self-inductance of the windings, L_1 and L_2, represents the electromotive force induced in each winding due to the magnetic field produced by the current in the winding itself. The mutual inductance between the windings, M, represents the electromotive force induced in the primary winding due to the magnetic field produced by the current in the secondary winding [36]. Once have been calculated the self-inductance of the windings and the mutual inductance between the windings, it is possible to calculate the coupling coefficient between the windings, k, through Eq. (9). The k is a value between 0 and 1. When this coefficient has the value of 0 it means that there is no magnetic coupling between the primary and the secondary winding. When the coefficient is 1, the coupling is ideal, that is, all the magnetic flux produced by the primary winding links the secondary winding, and vice versa. Thus, the magnetic flux is equal throughout the magnetic circuit [36]. To highlight that the obtained value of k was close to 1, as desired.

$$k = \frac{M}{\sqrt{L_1 L_2}} = 0.999 \tag{9}$$

Finally, after calculating the coupling coefficient between the windings, it is possible to calculate the leakage inductances, L_P and L_S, as well as the magnetization inductance,

L_M, present in the equivalent transformer model, through Eq. (10), Eq. (11), and Eq. (12) [36].

$$L_P = (1 - k)L_1 = 1.8\,mH \tag{10}$$

$$L_S = (1 - k)L_2 = 1.8\,mH \tag{11}$$

$$L_M = kL_1 = 1.22\,H \tag{12}$$

To obtain the values of the winding resistances, R_P and R_S, a precision multimeter equipment was used, with the reference 34450 A from the manufacture Keysight Technologies. For the resistance R_P, the transformer terminals a and b were measured, leaving terminals c and d in an open circuit. For resistance R_S the transformer terminals c and d were measured, leaving terminals a and b in an open circuit. The obtained value of resistance R_P was 3.1 Ω and the value of resistance R_S was 3.7 Ω, all measured at a frequency of 1 kHz.

After performing these measurements and calculations, it is now possible to place these parameters in the simulation model to be able to obtain results closer to reality. Table 1 presents the values of the main components used in the computational simulation of the studied topology. The values of the components used were obtained in such a way as to be the closest to the ones used in the laboratory prototype. Moreover, the power grid voltage presents the harmonic content presented in the Table 2.

The implementation and respective simulation of the EPLL algorithm for power grid voltage synchronization were carried out, and the obtained simulation results are shown in Fig. 5. As it can be seen, the EPLL algorithm quickly synchronizes with the frequency and phase of the power grid voltage fundamental component and determines the amplitude in a maximum of 4 power grid cycles. In this way, the dynamic response of the algorithm is verified, which can detect and monitor voltage variations in the power grid. Additionally, despite the power grid voltage has harmonic content, the EPLL waveform presents a residual THD value. Once concluded, the correct functioning of the EPLL algorithm allows the synchronization of the converter with the power grid, which provides a dynamic response to the system.

In Fig. 6 is shown the output voltage waveform of the MMCC. In Fig. 6(a) using an ideal transformer and in Fig. 6(b) using an equivalent model of real transformer. As can be seen in Fig. 6(a), the use of three submodules in series allows, as predicted, the existence of seven voltage levels at the output. In a real application, transformer windings contain inductances and resistances, which cause losses, as seen in Fig. 4. The influence of this parameters can make it difficult to visualize the output voltage levels because of the slower dv/dt response. Even so, the presence of inductances in the transformer windings allows obtaining a voltage waveform close to a sinusoidal (Fig. 6(b)). Nevertheless, it should be noted that with the ideal simulation model, it would be possible to obtain an MMCC output voltage with a maximum value of 180 V, three times the DC-bus voltage. On the other hand, with a real simulation model, the voltage drops in the IGBT devices and in the magnetic elements is considerable to the point that only a maximum value of 90 V can be obtained. Note that the MMCC based on cascade transformers should start operating at 90° or −90°. This is due to the fact that the variation of the magnetic flux

Table 1. Specification of the simulation parameters.

Description	Variables	Value	Units
Coupling coil	L_1	4	mH
Power grid voltage	v_{grid}	60	V_{RMS}
DC-bus voltage	V_{DC}	60	V
Power grid line inductance	L_z	100	μH
Power grid line resistance	R_z	2	mΩ
Resistance of the primary winding of the transformer	R_P	3.1	Ω
Resistance of the secondary winding of the transformer	R_S	3.7	Ω
Inductance of the primary winding of the transformer	L_P	1.8	mH
Inductance of the secondary winding of the transformer	L_S	1.8	mH
The magnetizing inductance	L_M	1.22	H
Transformers turns-ratio	N	1:1	–
IGBT saturation voltage	V_{CE}	3.3	V
IGBT collector-emitter resistance	r_{CE}	8.1	mΩ
IGBT diode threshold voltage	V_F	2	V
IGBT diode resistance	r_F	12	mΩ
IGBT switching frequency	f_w	1	kHz
Sampling frequency	f_s	50	kHz

Table 2. Main harmonic components in the power grid voltage [37].

Harmonic order	Amplitude (V_{RMS})	Phase (°)
1	60	0
3	0.26	95
5	0.15	135
7	2.18	44
9	0.42	−147
11	0.97	−134
13	0.05	29
15	0.07	−20
THD	4.1%	

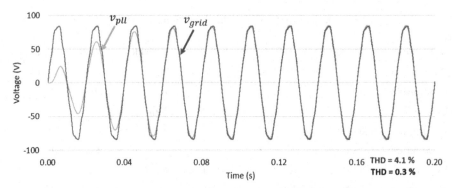

Fig. 5. Simulation result of the EPLL synchronism: power grid voltage, v_{grid}, and pll signal, v_{pll}.

does not present an average value of zero at each switching period. In this topology, the variation of the magnetic flux presents an almost sinusoidal wave along the period of the fundamental component of the output signal. If the start is different from 90° or −90°, the variation of the magnetic flux will present an average value, being able to saturate the ferromagnetic core.

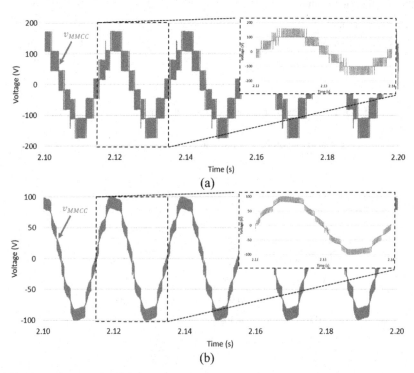

Fig. 6. Simulations results of the MMCC injecting energy into the power grid: (a) output voltage waveform, v_{MMCC}, with ideal transformers model; (b) output voltage waveform, v_{MMCC}, with real transformers model.

After completing the system initialization processes, the MMCC control is fully functional within 0.5 s, as is a highlight in Fig. 7. The MMCC will have the ability to inject energy into the power grid, depending on the P^* value. Therefore, with the introduction of P^* value, the active power injected into the power grid, P_{grid}, must follow the reference, P^*, as shown in Fig. 7.

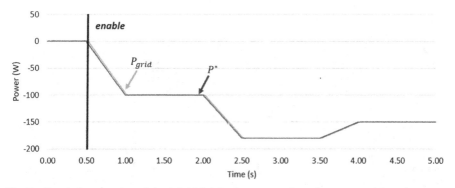

Fig. 7. Simulations results of the MMCC injecting energy into the power grid: active power injected into the power grid, P_{grid}, and the power reference, P^*.

Analyzing Fig. 8, it is possible to see that the synthesized current, i_{grid}, follows the reference current, i^*. It can be concluded the correct operation of the current control algorithm implemented, resulting in grid current, i_{grid}, with low harmonic distortion (THD% = 2.5%). Nevertheless, to highlight that the PI current control algorithm allows the MMCC to synthesize a sinusoidal current, 180° lag in relation to the power grid voltage, injecting energy into the power grid.

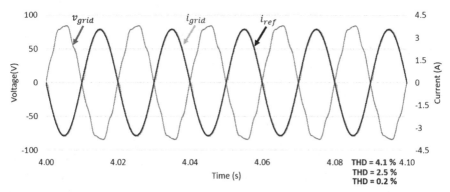

Fig. 8. Simulations results of the MMCC injecting energy into the power grid: power grid voltage, v_{grid}, reference current, i_{ref}, and grid current, i_{grid}.

5   Experimental Results

Once the computer simulations have been validated, all the hardware was assembled, highlighting the control system and the power system. Figure 9 shows a general overview of the laboratory workbench, where the hardware was assembled and tested. In this section are presented some experimental results of the MMCC composed of full-bridge with cascaded power transformers implemented.

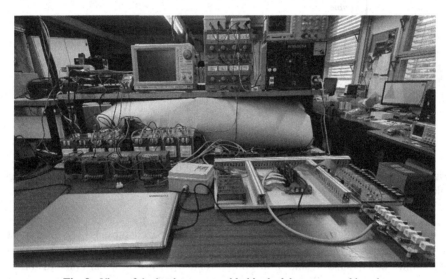

Fig. 9. View of the hardware assembled in the laboratory workbench.

Table 3 shows the specification of the operation conditions of the laboratory prototype implemented for the experimental tests. The DSC platform used was the Control Card-F28379D from Texas Instruments.

The PWM peripheral was configured in the DSC with 3 μs of dead time to avoid a short circuit of the DC-bus voltage source caused by the simultaneous conduction of semiconductors in the same arm of the full-bridge submodule. Other parameters were also configured, such as the time period and phase offset of the carrier wave in each arm of the full-bridge submodules, to obtain the desired PSC PWM technique. That is, six carrier waveforms were implemented with a frequency equal to 1 kHz and out of phase with each other by 60°.

To produce a sinusoidal current in phase opposition relativity to the power grid voltage, it is necessary to produce a signal synchronized with the fundamental component of the power grid voltage, as already mentioned. Thus, the synchronism of the EPLL signal algorithm with the power grid voltage is shown in Fig. 10, based on the algorithm used in the computational simulations. Note that the v_{grid} and v_{pll} are visualized using a Digital-Analog Converter (DAC) with the reference TLV5610 by the manufacturer Texas Instruments with 0.016 V/V scale.

In an ideal scenario, the output voltage of the MMCC would be 3 times the voltage on the DC-bus (3 * 60 V). However, considering the voltage drops in the IGBT devices,

Table 3. Specification of the MMCC main components and operation conditions.

Description	Variables	Value	Units
Coupling coil	L_1	4	mH
DC-bus capacitor	C_1	1	mF
DC-bus voltage	V_{DC}	60	V
Power grid voltage	v_{grid}	60	V_{RMS}
Transformers turns-ratio	N	1:1	–
IGBT switching frequency	f_w	1	kHz
Sampling frequency	f_s	50	kHz
Current sensor	CYHCS-B6-100A		
Voltage sensor	CYHVS5-25A		
IGBT	SKM 100GB125DN[a]		

[a] Although used in the experimental results this device is oversized for this application

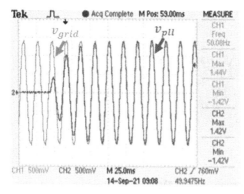

Fig. 10. Experimental results of the EPLL synchronism: power grid voltage, v_{grid}, and output signal, v_{pll}.

and in the low frequency transformers, the output voltage presents a similar waveform to the obtained on the real model simulations. Analyzing Fig. 11 it can be concluded that the MMCC can synthesize all the expected voltage levels, with a maximum voltage variation up to 106 V and minimum of −118 V.

To inject energy into the power grid, the current synthesized by the MMCC must be in phase opposition relativity to the power grid voltage. Moreover, the output voltage of the MMCC must be higher than the peak value of the power grid voltage. The experimental results obtained for the injection of energy into the power grid with the variation of the power reference from 80 W to 110 W are shown in Fig. 12.

A power reference of 80 W and 100 W was given to the MMCC. Considering the power grid voltage, the control system determined a reference current of 1.85 A_{peak} and 2.3 A_{peak}, respectively. The results presented in Fig. 13 prove the correct functioning of the MMCC, where i_{grid} follows i_{ref}. Note that the i_{ref}. and i_{grid} are visualized using a DAC with a 1 V/A scale.

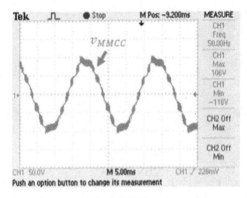

Fig. 11. Experimental results of the MMCC: output voltage waveform, v_{MMCC}.

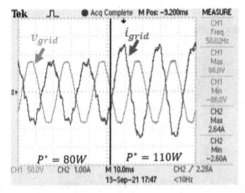

Fig. 12. Experimental results of the MMCC while injecting energy into the power grid: power grid voltage, v_{grid}, and grid current, i_{grid}.

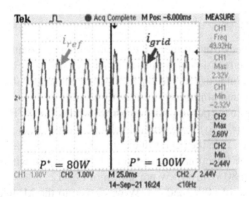

Fig. 13. Experimental results of the MMCC while injecting energy into the power grid: reference current, i_{ref}, and grid current, i_{grid}.

6   Conclusions

This paper presents the development of a Modular Multilevel Cascade Converter (MMCC) composed of full-bridge submodules with a common DC-bus and with low frequency cascaded transformers. The MMCC was first validated based on computer simulations, with the entire methodology being presented step by step as well as the control algorithms. Regarding the simulation model, the parameters of the real were used, namely in the transformers equivalents model. As such, it was necessary to carry out experimental tests and measurements in order to obtain the important parameters for the implemented model. The entire procedure is presented in detail in order to be easily replicable by other researchers. The simulation model was validated based on the experimental results, obtaining experimental results similar to those of simulation.

Regarding the operation of the MMCC, it was possible to prove the correct functioning of the system, validating the control algorithms implemented either in simulation or in the laboratory prototype. In the experimental tests the synthesized output current follows the reference, presenting low ripple and THD, being very similar to the results achieved in simulation.

As the main technical conclusions of the work, it can be concluded that the low-frequency transformers generate audible noise due to vibrations during the operation of the MMCC. In order to maximize the system efficiency, the inclusion of LCL filters at the input of each transformer, in order to apply a sinusoidal waveform to each low-frequency transformer would be studied. This solution could increase transformer efficiency despite increasing losses in passive filters, since they would have to be replicated depending on the number of submodules added. This solution, instead of adding square waves, presenting a stair output waveform, would add sine waves, which could reduce the output harmonic spectrum. However, this approach eliminates one of the advantages of the MMCC, which is the frequency multiplication applied to the output filter. The frequency multiplication could aid to reduce the weight, volume, and cost of the final solution. Another solution would be the study, design and development of medium-frequency transformers for the specific application. The use of amorphous ferromagnetic materials would present an added value since they allow a higher magnetic flux density, allowing operation with higher switching frequencies, as well as it would be possible to obtain a more compact solution.

It is possible to highlight that there is a research gap in the MMCC topology based on cascade transformers. Despite its potential, presenting a common DC-bus, which facilitates not only control algorithms but also the integration of other interfaces, such as renewables energies or energy storage systems, also presents some implementation challenges. Since the solution of cascade transformers with full-bridges allows the bidirectional flow of energy, this characteristic would be more widely explored if there were an interface with bidirectional energy system, such as in the case of an energy storage system. The interface with renewable energy sources, despite its unidirectional energy flow, would appear as an additional interface.

Acknowledgements. This work has been supported by FCT – Fundação para a Ciência e Tecnologia with-in the Project Scope: UIDB/00319/2020. This work has been supported by the FCT Project QUALITY4POWER PTDC/EEI-EEE/28813/2017, and by the FCT Project DAIPESEV

PTDC/EEI-EEE/30382/2017. Mr. Luis A. M. Barros is supported by the doctoral scholarship PD/BD/143006/2018 granted by the Portuguese FCT foundation.

References

1. Barros, L.A.M., Tanta, M., Martins, A.P., Afonso, J.L., Pinto, J.G.: Submodule topologies and PWM techniques applied in modular multilevel converters: review and analysis. In: Afonso, J.L., Monteiro, V., Pinto, J.G. (eds.) SESC 2020. LNICSSITE, vol. 375, pp. 111–131. Springer, Cham (2021). https://doi.org/10.1007/978-3-030-73585-2_8. ISBN 978-3-030-73584-5
2. Steimel, A.: Electric traction-motive power and energy supply: basics and practical experience. Oldenbourg Industrieverlag (2008). ISBN 978-3-8356-3132-8
3. Sharifabadi, K., Harnefors, L., Nee, H.-P., Norrga, S., Teodorescu, R.: Design, Control, and Application of Modular Multilevel Converters for HVDC Transmission Systems. Wiley (2016). ISBN 9781118851548
4. Perez, M.A., Bernet, S., Rodriguez, J., Kouro, S., Lizana, R.: Circuit topologies, modeling, control schemes, and applications of modular multilevel converters. IEEE Trans. Power Electron. **30**(1), 4–17 (2014). https://doi.org/10.1109/TPEL.2014.2310127,ISSN:0885-8993
5. Debnath, S., Qin, J., Bahrani, B., Saeedifard, M., Barbosa, P.: Operation, control, and applications of the modular multilevel converter: a review. IEEE Trans. Power Electron. **30**(1), 37–53 (2014). https://doi.org/10.1109/TPEL.2014.2309937,ISSN:0885-8993
6. Liao, J., Corzine, K., Ferdowsi, M.: A new control method for single-DC-source cascaded H-bridge multilevel converters using phase-shift modulation. In: 2008 Twenty-Third Annual IEEE Applied Power Electronics Conference and Exposition, pp. 886–890 (2008). https://doi.org/10.1109/APEC.2008.4522825. ISBN 978-1-4244-1873-2
7. Brenna, M., Foiadelli, F., Zaninelli, D.: Electrical Railway Transportation Systems. Wiley (2018). ISBN 978-1-119-38680-3
8. Zhao, C., Li, Y., Li, Z., Wang, P., Ma, X., Luo, Y.: Optimized design of full-bridge modular multilevel converter with low energy storage requirements for HVDC transmission system. IEEE Trans. Power Electron. **33**(1), 97–109 (2017). https://doi.org/10.1109/TPEL.2017.266 0532. ISSN:1941-0107
9. Yellasiri, S., Panda, A.: Performance of cascade multilevel H-Bridge inverter with single DC source by employing low frequency three-phase transformers, pp. 1981–1986 (2010). https://doi.org/10.1109/IECON.2010.5675291
10. Barros, L.A., Tanta, M., Martins, A.P., Afonso, J.L., Pinto, J.: Opportunities and challenges of power electronics systems in future railway electrification. In: 2020 IEEE 14th International Conference on Compatibility, Power Electronics and Power Engineering (CPE-POWERENG), vol. 1, pp. 530–537 (2020). https://doi.org/10.1109/CPE-POWERENG48600. 2020.9161695. ISSN 2166-9545
11. Xu, Q., et al.: Analysis and comparison of modular railway power conditioner for high-speed railway traction system. IEEE Trans. Power Electron. **32**(8), 6031–6048 (2016). https://doi.org/10.1109/TPEL.2016.2616721. ISSN 0885-8993
12. Dekka, A., Wu, B., Fuentes, R.L., Perez, M., Zargari, N.R.: Evolution of topologies, modeling, control schemes, and applications of modular multilevel converters. IEEE J. Emerg. Sel. Top. Power Electron. **5**(4), 1631–1656 (2017). https://doi.org/10.1109/JESTPE.2017.274 2938. ISSN 2168-6785
13. Wang, Y., Aksoz, A., Geury, T., Ozturk, S.B., Kivanc, O.C., Hegazy, O.: A review of modular multilevel converters for stationary applications. Appl. Sci. **10**(21), 7719 (2020). https://doi.org/10.3390/app10217719

14. Feng, J., Chu, W., Zhang, Z., Zhu, Z.: Power electronic transformer-based railway traction systems: challenges and opportunities. IEEE J. Emerg. Sel. Top. Power Electron. **5**(3), 1237–1253 (2017). https://doi.org/10.1109/JESTPE.2017.2685464. ISSN 2168-6777

15. Tanta, M., Barros, L.A., Pinto, J., Martins, A.P., Afonso, J.L.: Modular multilevel converter in electrified railway systems: applications of rail static frequency converters and rail power conditioners. In: 2020 International Young Engineers Forum (YEF-ECE), pp. 55–60 (2020). https://doi.org/10.1109/YEF-ECE49388.2020.9171814. ISBN 978-1-7281-5679-8

16. Latran, M.B., Teke, A.: Investigation of multilevel multifunctional grid connected inverter topologies and control strategies used in photovoltaic systems. Renew. Sustain. Energy Rev. **42**, 361–376 (2015). https://doi.org/10.1016/j.rser.2014.10.030

17. Cao, W., Xu, Y., Han, Y., Ren, B.: Comparison of cascaded multilevel and modular multilevel converters with energy storage system. In: 2016 IEEE 11th Conference on Industrial Electronics and Applications (ICIEA), pp. 290–294 (2016). https://doi.org/10.1109/ICIEA.2016. 7603596. ISBN 978-1-4673-8645-6

18. Antonio-Ferreira, A., Collados-Rodriguez, C., Gomis-Bellmunt, O.: Modulation techniques applied to medium voltage modular multilevel converters for renewable energy integration: a review. Electr. Power Syst. Res. **155**, 21–39 (2018). https://doi.org/10.1016/j.epsr.2017. 08.015

19. Lu, S., Yuan, L., Li, K., Zhao, Z.: An improved phase-shifted carrier modulation scheme for a hybrid modular multilevel converter. IEEE Trans. Power Electron. **32**(1), 81–97 (2016). https://doi.org/10.1109/TPEL.2016.2532386. ISSN 1941-0107

20. Marquez, A., Leon, J.I., Vazquez, S., Franquelo, L.G., Perez, M.: A comprehensive comparison of modulation methods for MMC converters. In: IECON 2017–43rd Annual Conference of the IEEE Industrial Electronics Society, pp. 4459–4464 (2017). https://doi.org/10.1109/ IECON.2017.8216768. ISBN 978-1-5386-1127-2

21. Song, S.G., Kang, F.S., Park, S.-J.: Cascaded multilevel inverter employing three-phase transformers and single DC input. IEEE Trans. Industr. Electron. **56**(6), 2005–2014 (2009). https:// doi.org/10.1109/TIE.2009.2013846. ISSN 1557-9948

22. Kang, F.-S., Park, S.-J., Lee, M.H., Kim, C.-U.: An efficient multilevel-synthesis approach and its application to a 27-level inverter. IEEE Trans. Industr. Electron. **52**(6), 1600–1606 (2005). https://doi.org/10.1109/TIE.2005.858715. ISSN 1557-9948

23. Ortúzar, M.E., Carmi, R.E., Dixon, J.W., Morán, L.: Voltage-source active power filter based on multilevel converter and ultracapacitor DC link. IEEE Trans. Industr. Electron. **53**(2), 477–485 (2006). https://doi.org/10.1109/TIE.2006.870656. ISSN 1557-9948

24. Flores, P., Dixon, J., Ortúzar, M., Carmi, R., Barriuso, P., Morán, L.: Static var compensator and active power filter with power injection capability, using 27-level inverters and photovoltaic cells. IEEE Trans. Industr. Electron. **56**(1), 130–138 (2008). https://doi.org/10.1109/ ISIE.2006.295791,ISBN:1-4244-0497-5

25. Zhou, L., Fu, Q., Li, X., Liu, C.: A novel Multilevel Power Quality Compensator for electrified railway, pp. 1141–1147 (2009). https://doi.org/10.1109/IPEMC.2009.5157555

26. ElGebaly, A.E., Hassan, A.E.-W., El-Nemr, M.K.: Reactive power compensation by multilevel inverter STATCOM for railways power grid. In: 2019 IEEE Conference of Russian Young Researchers in Electrical and Electronic Engineering (EIConRus), pp. 2094–2099 (2019). https://doi.org/10.1109/EIConRus.2019.8657058. ISBN 978-1-7281-0339-6

27. Zhou, L., Fu, Q., Li, X., Liu, C.: A novel photovoltaic grid-connected power conditioner employing hybrid multilevel inverter. In: 2009 International Conference on Sustainable Power Generation and Supply, pp. 1–7 (2009). https://doi.org/10.1109/SUPERGEN.2009.5348154. ISSN 2156-9681

28. Park, S.-J., Kang, F.-S., Cho, S.E., Moon, C.-J., Nam, H.-K.: A novel switching strategy for improving modularity and manufacturability of cascaded-transformer-based multilevel inverters. Electric Power Syst. Res. **74**(3), 409–416 (2005). https://doi.org/10.1016/j.epsr.2005. 01.005. ISSN 0378-7796. https://www.sciencedirect.com/science/article/pii/S03787796050 00751

29. Jahan, H., Naseri, M., Haji Esmaeili, M., Abapour, M., Zare, K.: Low component merged cells cascaded-transformer multilevel inverter featuring an enhanced reliability. IET Power Electronics **10** (2017). https://doi.org/10.1049/iet-pel.2016.0787

30. Diaz Rodriguez, J., Pabon, L., Peñaranda, E.: Novel methodology for the calculation of transformers in power multilevel converters **17**, 121–132 (2015)

31. Miura, Y., Mizutani, T., Ito, M., Ise, T.: A novel space vector control with capacitor voltage balancing for a multilevel modular matrix converter. In: 2013 IEEE ECCE Asia Downunder, pp. 442–448 (2013). https://doi.org/10.1109/ECCE-Asia.2013.6579134. ISBN 978-1-4799-0482-2

32. Nami, A., Liang, J., Dijkhuizen, F., Demetriades, G.D.: Modular multilevel converters for HVDC applications: review on converter cells and functionalities. IEEE Trans. Power Electron. **30**(1), 18–36 (2014). https://doi.org/10.1109/TPEL.2014.2327641. ISSN 0885-8993

33. Karimi-Ghartemani, M., Iravani, M.R.: A method for synchronization of power electronic converters in polluted and variable-frequency environments. IEEE Trans. Power Syst. **19**(3), 1263–1270 (2004). https://doi.org/10.1109/TPWRS.2004.831280,ISSN:1558-0679

34. Barros, L.A., Tanta, M., Sousa, T.J., Afonso, J.L., Pinto, J.: New multifunctional isolated microinverter with integrated energy storage system for PV applications. Energies **13**(15), 4016 (2020). https://doi.org/10.3390/en13154016,ISSN:1996-1073

35. Pinto, J., Monteiro, V., Gonçalves, H., Afonso, J.L.: Onboard reconfigurable battery charger for electric vehicles with traction-to-auxiliary mode. IEEE Trans. Veh. Technol. **63**(3), 1104–1116 (2013). https://doi.org/10.1109/TVT.2013.2283531,ISSN:1939-9359

36. Rogers, J.W., Plett, C.: Radio Frequency Integrated Circuit Design. Artech House (2010). ISBN 978-1580535021

37. Barros, L.A., Tanta, M., Martins, A.P., Afonso, J.L., Pinto, J.: STATCOM evaluation in electrified railway using V/V and Scott power transformers. In: International Conference on Sustainable Energy for Smart Cities, pp. 18–32 (2019). https://doi.org/10.1007/978-3-030-45694-8_2. ISBN 978-3-030-45693-1

Energy; Demand Response; Technical-Economic Analysis

Standard Energy Renovation at the Urban Scale in the Moroccan Context

Khalid Echlouchi[1(✉)], Mustapha Ouardouz[1], and Abdes-samed Bernoussi[2]

[1] MMC, FSTT, Abdelmalek Essaadi University, Tangier, Morocco
[2] GAT, FSTT, Abdelmalek Essaadi University, Tangier, Morocco

Abstract. As part of a participatory and pluralist approach towards the implementation of future energy policy, this study aims to address the lack of studies on urban-scale energy renovation in Morocco. We aim to provide a methodological framework to support decision-making processes related to energy-conscious urban planning strategies. The proposed methodological framework is based on a bottom-up approach in a multi-scale GIS environment. It combines physical and statistical methods to split up the building stock market into different archetypes. Simulating a dozen archetypes instead of thousands of buildings presents a good compromise of accuracy and low cost. The results of this simulation can subsequently be generalized to the entirety of the rest of the buildings. The town of M'diq in Northern Morocco is the case study for the present article, and it has shown that the implementation of large scale energy renovation can achieve an energy saving up to 52.72% in the standard of Thermal Building Regulations in Morocco (RTCM) scenario.

Keywords: Archetype · Energical simulation · Energy retrofit · GIS · Urban modelisation · RTCM

1 Introduction and Context

Morocco has set up a proactive national energy strategy in order to support strong economic growth within a sustainable development framework. Given that the country imports over 90% of its steadily increasing energy needs, the main objective of the national strategy is therefore to reduce this heavy energy dependency on imports by achieving 15% energy savings by 2030 [1].

The urbanization rate has reached 63.9% in the last 50 years [2], population growth and urban sprawl have led to an increase in energy consumption, which is up by 33% in this sector (7% and 26% for the tertiary and residential sectors, respectively). Faced with these challenges, the construction sector alone can attain energy savings of up to 40% [3].

Newly constructed buildings account for an annual rate of 1.5–2% for the entire building stock, indicating that the renewal of all existing buildings will take roughly 50–100 years or more. This implies that the current building stock will continue to be part of the urban construction environment for decades [4]. In terms of policy, there is

J. L. Afonso et al. (Eds.): SESC 2021, LNICST 425, pp. 53–72, 2022.
https://doi.org/10.1007/978-3-030-97027-7_4

no national renovation strategy in the works apart from the "Green Mosques" initiative [5] and the 2019 policy of mandatory energy audits in the industrial sector [6, 7] which recommends ISO 50001 compliant energy efficiency measures. This highlights the necessity of initiating large scale energy renovation strategies for buildings in order to support the energy transition and reduce energy consumption and greenhouse gas emissions in the urban sector.

In terms of regulation, the decree of general construction establishing building performance standards (RTCM) was passed and approved in 2015. Buildings have to fulfill minimum efficiency and performance thresholds (thermal insulation, building orientation, construction materials etc.) according to their geographic location in order to achieve the following objectives: 1) Reduce heating and air-conditioning requirements 2) Improve thermal comfort 3) Reduce the national energy bill 4) Reduce greenhouse gas emissions [8].

The decree stipulates that these thermal regulations should be considered during the process of granting construction permits. It is only being partially applied, however [9], due to the fact that its implementation is not being backed up by any legislation or definition of the procedures for carrying out technical inspections or measures taken to penalize non-compliance with the decree [10]. The 2020 joint order of the interior and urban planning ministries requires that the technical note of the energy performance regulations becomes the centerpiece of any construction permit application. An architect is therefore required to provide the note in order to confirm the building's conformity to the regulations. Nevertheless, the current energy efficiency measures are not sufficient to reach the energy and climate objectives that were set [11].

The issue of energy efficiency of existing buildings is a major factor given the size of building stock. Yet, the thermal regulations only apply to new buildings [12]. Consequently, its impact will be relatively limited in spite of the urgency of regulating the existing building stock as well [13].

In light of this situation, public policy is called upon to expand the existing thermal regulations to all types of buildings, whether newly constructed or not, to set up a roadmap for the energy renovation of these buildings, to simplify the modernization process of the building stock and increase the prevalence of renewable energies in the urban environment.

Thus, this work is motivated by the considerable lack of large scale urban energy renovation strategies within the country's energy policies. Consequently, it is necessary to support the development of new approaches and urban modernization methods by laying the groundwork for future additions or amendments to the existing regulations.

This paper seeks to explore answers for the following question: How can one evaluate the impact of large scale (district or city-level) energy retrofit strategies on heating and air-conditioning demand? What savings should be expected in a scenario of renovations based on the Moroccan Thermal Construction Regulations (RTCM)?

2 Problem Statement

Energy renovation is the modification of different aspects of a building in order to improve its energy efficiency [14]. It is one of the main methods used to reduce energy consumption and greenhouse gas emissions in the construction sector. It is considered as one of the essential pillars of the 2050 transition towards sustainable buildings (International Energy Agency, 2013) [15].

In this paper, a literature review was conducted on the scientific database Google Scholar and Scopus for the period of 2018–2020 using combinations of keywords related to the subject of large-scale energy renovation/retrofit of buildings in morocco. Mainly RTCM, Energy retrofit, archetype, Energy simulation, GIS, Urban modelling, energy planning ...

In the following paragraph, we present an overview of the most relevant research work that was carried out in Morocco:

In Ref [16] the authors used a single house in different climates as a typology for the energy performance analysis. They propose three scenarios, two of which are based on the RTCM. The results obtained show that the third scenario is the most favorable. It records the best indicators in terms of thermal performance, while the other two are more optimal for cold climates. In [17], the authors propose an energy simulation of a building with RTCM requirements in order to evaluate its impact on savings and energy bill. Their results show the effectiveness of RTCM and prove that its cost can be overcome in all climate zones and for some categories of buildings. In Ref. [18], the impact of thermal insulation on a typical Moroccan building and on its energy self-sufficiency was studied. TRNSYS was used to perform the simulation under a platform associating a hybrid system of two renewable energies (Wind and photovoltaic) to the thermal loads of the building. The results indicate that the impact of thermal isolation on self-sufficiency in all climates is very significant. For a different type of residence, the work in [19] presents a study of the energy efficiency of social residency buildings in Morocco. The objective being to compare active and passive solutions. The study was carried out in TRNSYS on a reference building in all six Moroccan climatic zones. The comparison shows that solar water heating solutions are more economical than thermally insulating the exterior building envelope from an energy point of view. For tertiary buildings, the authors of Ref [20] present a parametric study of thermal renovations of an administrative building in the region of Chefchaouen, Morocco. The authors performed a TRNSYS simulation of the multi-zones of the building envelope according to several different scenarios of occupation, insulation as well as integration of passive techniques. The results show that the optimal solution that follows RTCM regulations costs around MAD 391,31/m^2 ($39,73/$m^2$), or 154 MAD 022,26 ($15 640,60) excluding VAT for the entire building of 393,6 m^2. In Ref [21], the authors studied the impact of several energy efficiency measures (thermal insulation, building orientation, floor level, ventilation etc.) on energy performance and thermal comfort in an apartment located in Marrakesh using TRNSYS. The results show that a correct dimensioning of the thermal insulation of the walls ensures the prevention of summer overheating and consequently an optimal thermal comfort level. On the other hand, an oversized thermal insulation of the walls implies a rate of 18% for all climates of the thermal load during the summer overheating. Ref. [22] studies multiple thermal insulation scenarios using the BINAYATE software for a residential building located in Zaouiat Sidi Abdeslam, in order to choose the best scenario of insulation. They conclude from their results that glass wool leads to the best outcome, with 63% energy reduction and a payback period of 4.3 years. In Ref [23], the authors analyze the influence of the building envelope parameters on heating and air-conditioning demand using thermal simulations in TRNSYS for a building in the northern city of Tetouan. They proposed an improvement of its energy efficiency using passive techniques. Ref [24] studies a combination of building envelope parameters that allow for the lowest energy demand in heating and ventilation. In this case, DesignBuilder is the software that's been used on a typical building in the region of Casablanca. Results show a significant decrease in demand by up to 30% of the total consumption and that the parameters of thermal insulation have the greatest influence on the building's performance. In Ref [25], the authors performed a thermal study and a comparative analysis between a conventional house and two small low-energy consumption buildings in the climate of the town of Ben Guerir using DesignBuilder. The results show that combining appropriate construction materials with passive strategies allows for the reduction of thermal loads of houses. Ref [26] studies the thermal performance of two buildings located in two different climates (namely Midelt and Marrakech) constructed according to bioclimatic principles such as orientation and compactness. The authors then analyzed their architecture, relationship with the climate, use, thermal comfort, as well as performance related to RTCM. In Ref. [27], the authors carried out a study to evaluate the parameters of the envelope (orientation and insulation) on energy consumption. The TRNSYS simulation of a reference building in different climate zones in Morocco shows that the orientation plays a significant role in reducing the total load and affects the efficiency of insulation.

The literature review has shown that the majority of works related to energy retrofit in Morocco are concerned with the individual building level, and that there is a significant lack of studies evaluating energy retrofit at a larger scale (i.e. District, City) based on the RTCM regulations. We also note that there are three main software suites that were used: TRNSYS [28], BINAYATE [29] and DESIGN BUILDER [30]. The energy efficiency measures that were most popular are thermal insulation [18, 20, 22, 23] of the building envelope, orientation, and outdoor shading [26, 27].

In other side, urban energy retrofitting strategies can be categorized by the energy modelling approach that is used [13, 14, 31] (into top-down or bottom-up methods), by the nature of the models (physical-statistical) into white, gray or black-box models. This is due to the fact that energy modeling is an essential tool that is shared by most energy-related studies for renovation, building integration, energy planning of new districts/neighborhoods, or for comparative studies [32].

The main contribution of this paper is to propose a methodological framework for the evaluation of energy retrofit strategies not only at the single building scale, but also on the urban scale (district, city). The method is based on the extraction of archetypes from the urban environment, performing a simple energy simulation using the BINAYATE software which was designed to meet RTCM standards, as well as using the GIS tool to extrapolate the results on the whole studied area. On the other hand, the model allows for the evaluation of the impact and energy gains obtained from reducing the heating and air-conditioning loads in a future large-scale, RTCM-compliant energy retrofit strategy.

3   Problem Approach

The proposed methodological framework is based on a bottom-up approach in a multi-scale GIS environment. It combines physical and statistical methods to split up the building stock market into different archetypes.

In figure Fig. 1, the methodology that is used comprises 4 main phases, each phase is divided into a number of steps to be performed. The specifics of each phase and step are detailed in the following subsections.

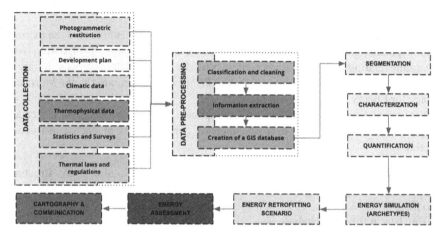

Fig. 1. Workflow

3.1   Data and Geometric Modeling

Data Collection: This phase consists mainly of gathering data of various types (geometric or non-geometric) about the building stock from various sources.

This data will then be stored in a geographic database that is supported by a GIS that simplifies the bottom-up mapping of the results at the end of the process.

The GIS tool is very useful at this stage, it provides a framework for data acquisition and sorting onto overlaying layers, thereby simplifying the management and analysis of energy renovation in a specific geographical location at the city-scale.

Data Preprocessing: This step allows one to filter, classify, and improve the quality of the collected data by detecting and filtering outliers and anomalies. Similarly, it allows one to extract the implicit information that is behind the raw data of the building stock, and to transform this data into a more comprehensible format. For example, extracting the morphological parameters from the urban form from photogrammetric restitution and city layout plans.

Segmentation of the Building Stock: The goal of this step is to group the buildings into the same class when they are as similar as possible using the clustering method.

The variables of the building stock are used to classify the buildings according to their similarities into groups of archetypes. These archetypes summarize similar buildings into a single representative building [33], and they collectively represent the characteristics of the whole building stock.

To ensure that no particular weight is given to any specific characteristic over another, and given that the clusters are calculated in terms of the distances between the data points, the variables with the highest values dominate the variables with lower ones. In order to solve this problem, a normalization and standardization step is necessary [34] to equalize the scale of values. The normalization is performed by weighing the differences between orders of magnitude in the values of the urban database [35].

Characterization: In this phase, we define the construction materials and the thermodynamic parameters of the parts constituting the envelopes of buildings. Existing work in literature relating to the Moroccan context is used, along with the materials' library of building energy simulation software "BINAYATE" [29], that is curated by the Moroccan Agency for Energy Efficiency (AMEE).

Next, we define the U-values of each component of the envelopes (roofs, facades, windows, ground floors etc.) from the thermal conductivities of each construction material.

Quantification: The goal of this phase is to analyze the distribution of the structural and dimensional characteristics of the archetypes (reference buildings) throughout the town [36].

The data in the GIS database is accessed and processed using queries. The spatial analysis allows us to classify each building according to its corresponding archetype. This will simplify the process of extrapolating the results of the energy simulation over all the buildings of the town.

3.2 Energy Simulations

Energy simulations at the urban scale are performed through the simulation of the aforementioned representative archetypes of the building stock. This considerably reduces the modelling and simulation time required for each individual building. Simulating a few dozen archetypes instead of thousands of buildings seems like a good cost-saving solution.

A number of simulation software suites can be used for the evaluation of the energy performance of buildings. In fact, in order to adapt as much as possible to the Moroccan context of the study, these energy simulations of the archetypes are performed using the AMEE developed software BINAYATE. It's a diagnostics tool for buildings to control their performance and assess their compliance with the RTCM. Furthermore, it can be used to calculate the annual energy needs of buildings according to their location, insulation envelope and other characteristics.

The BINAYATE software consists of three applications:

- BINAYATE 3D uses the BIM (Building Information Modeling) tool allowing the 3D modelling of the building's envelope elements.

- BINAYATE Performantielle calculates the annual energy requirements for heating and air-conditioning according to the climatic zone and the nature of the building (residential or tertiary). The calculations meet the Moroccan norms NM EN 15265: Performances thermiques des bâtiments - Calcul des besoins d'énergie pour le chauffage et le refroidissement des locaux - Critères généraux et procédures de validation; NM EN 12831: Systèmes de chauffage dans les bâtiments - Méthode de calcul des déperditions calorifiques de base; et ANSI/ASHRAE/ACCA Standard 183–2007 Peak Cooling and Heating Load Calculations in Buildings Except Low-rise Residential Buildings [37]
- BINAYATE Prescriptive: evaluates the technical specification given for each building and each climate zone. It does so in the form of maximum values for the coefficients of surface heat transmission of the various elements of the envelope as well as the solar factor.

BINAYATE is based on RTCM which is itself based on the parametric study that was performed in 2014 [38]. In this study, the authors carried out a sensitivity analysis of the influence of different envelope parameters of a building (residential and tertiary) on its heating and air-conditioning requirements.

Other norms are also used for the development of BINAYATE, namely (Table 1):

Table 1. Interior conditions of BINAYATE taken during energy simulations based on [38]

Interior condition	Week		Weekend	
Horaires	7:30–17:00	17:00–7:30	7:30–17:00	17:00–7:30
Type of activity	Residential			
Occupancy (person)	2	5	5	5
Ventilation rateincluding infiltration	30 m^3/h per person			
Interior gains sum up	2500 kwh/year per dwelling			
External shading (by summer) from 15 May to 15 September	50%	-	50%	-
Set point temperature heating	20 °C			
Set point temperature cooling	24 °C			

Other norms are also used for the development of BINAYATE, namely:

- NM ISO 13786: Thermal performance of building components—Dynamic thermal characteristics—Calculation methods.
- NM ISO 6946: Building components and building elements—Thermal resistance and thermal transmittance—Calculation methods;
- NM ISO 13789: Thermal performance of buildings—Transmission and ventilation heat transfer coefficients—Calculation method;
- NM ISO 13370: Thermal performance of buildings—Heat transfer via the ground—Calculation methods; [39]

3.3 Assessment of the Energy Gain

The objective of this step is to evaluate the impact of the heating and cooling needs of the building on its energy performance. The energy savings gained by implementing the standard renovation scenario (RTCM) on an urban scale are also estimated in this step.

The estimated energy gain can be calculated by the following ratio:

$$\text{Gain (\%)} = (\text{BE\_exist} - \text{BE\_rtcm})/\text{BE\_exist} \tag{1}$$

- **Gain:** *Estimated energy gain*
- **BE_exist:** *Current state energy needs*
- **BE_rtcm:** *Energy needs after the RTCM-compliant renovation scenario*

The estimated energy gain can be used as a performance indicator when making large-scale energy renovation projects. It allows one to recognize the most suitable energy efficiency measures and evaluate different large-scale retrofit strategies for implementation on a given building stock environment by ranking them according to the energy savings achieved with the highest performance scenarios.

3.4 Mapping and Outreach

Mapping the standard energy renovation scenarios of all the building stock can represent, on the one hand, a valuable tool for stakeholders and decision makers in energy planning studies, allowing to identify geographical priority zones for renovation, to target specific types of buildings, to calculate the surfaces of envelope areas, to estimate the energetic and economic gains of each scenario, to spatially analyze the impact of retrofit scenarios, and to know the initial and final states of each building, district or urban zone (Fig. 2).

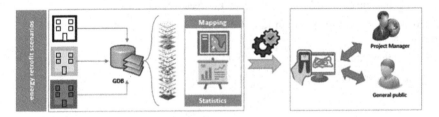

Fig. 2. Mapping and outreach

4 Study Area

To demonstrate the applicability of the proposed methodological framework and its implementation, a study on the residential building stock domain of the town of M'diq will be presented in the following section.

The town of M'diq (35.6853 North, −5.32744 East), located in Northern Morocco, has a mountainous terrain, rugged topography and a Mediterranean climate.

In terms of demography, the town has undergone significant demographic growth, with 56,227 inhabitants in 2014, an increase of 19,631 since 2004, which corresponds to an annual growth rate of 5.3%, ranking it among the highest in the country. Furthermore, the average household size is around 4.1 (Fig. 3).

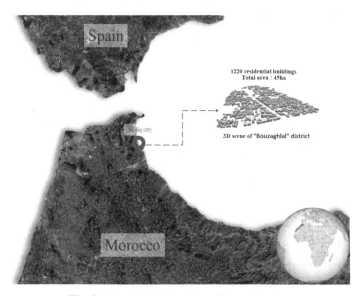

Fig. 3. Geographical location of the study zone

In terms of space, the city has a fragmented urban morphology. This is due, on one hand, to the rugged terrain itself (with slopes greater than 15°), and to poorly structured peripheral urbanization with ill-defined urban margins, on the other. The macro-form of the town is characterized by different homogeneous zones: The coast line, the seaport, the Cabo Negro forest, the mountain front, and the residential areas (Fig. 4).

In terms of age, the building stock of M'diq is relatively old, assuming an amortization period of 50 years. According to RGPH, around 39.7% of residential buildings are aged between 20 and 50 years, 35% between 10 and 20 years, 22.4% below 10 years and 2.8% are over 50 years old. It is clear that the vast majority of buildings were built before the implementation of the RTCM.

This methodological approach has been applied to the modern Moroccan dwelling, seeing as it constitutes the dominant building type in the Moroccan building stock. The case study was performed in the "Bouzaghlal" district towards the north of "M'diq", a town classified in the second climate zone "Z2" (Fig. 5).

The "Bouzaghlal" district is a recent neighborhood located in the outskirts of the town and covers a total area of 45ha. 10,73ha of which are occupied by 1220 residential buildings, most of which are modern Moroccan apartment-buildings. The density of these varies quite significantly from very dense regions to sparse, but growing ones which will also become more densely populated if current trends continue.

Fig. 4. 3D scene of M'diq city

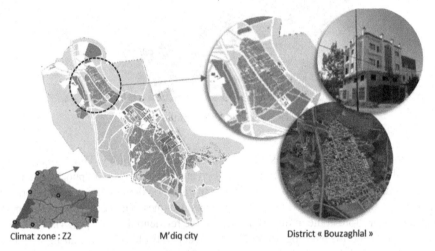

Climat zone : Z2   M'diq city   District « Bouzaghlal »

Fig. 5. Study area

5   Results and Discussion

Urban Geodatabase: The first phase of our methodology has allowed us to extract and sort the available data on the buildings of the district. The variables acquired in this phase will be used in the next phase where we divide the set of buildings into archetypical groups.

Results of the Segmentation Phase: Using the urban geographical database, we consider that buildings with similar data points are likely to have similar characteristics, construction techniques, insulating envelope quality and general geometry [35]. The proposed method for the segmentation of the building stock is broken into two steps:

- A "macro-segmentation" step based on the general segmentation criteria such as: Climate zone, type, construction date.
- A "micro-segmentation" step based on morphological factors and contiguity for more fine-grained results.

In our case study, all the buildings belong to the same climate zone "Z2", which is characterized by a Mediterranean climate. A comparison of historical imagery from Google Earth indicates that the majority of buildings are recent constructions between 2003 and 2021. Moreover, the dominant building type is, as expected, the modern Moroccan dwelling. This allows us to make the assumption that "Bouzaghlal" district is fairly homogeneous in terms of climate, age and building types (Fig. 6).

2003

2021

Fig. 6. Historical satellite imagery of the concerned district in the case study (2003 and 2021)

For the micro-segmentation of the district, the clustering technique used consists of classifying buildings in the same group when they're as similar as possible [40]. The most well-known methods are Hierarchical Clustering, k-means and k-medoids, with the k-means algorithm being the most widely used. The k-means method groups buildings using the displacement of instances between clusters, starting from an initial partitioning, in such a way that within-cluster variations are minimized. This is achieved by minimizing the sum of euclidean distances between the points and their centroids [40, 41]. The results of clustering are summarized in the following Table 2:

Table 2. Results of the clustering of the buildings of the "Bouzaghlal" district

Cluster	Building area (m^2)	Building height (m)	% Adjacency	Building orientation (°)
C1	96.35	8.76	29.65	−24.24
C2	100.55	8.27	16.90	64.38
C3	85.96	9.51	54.27	54.53
C4	194.71	9.02	19.78	25.25

Each aggregate and centroid value from the clustering represents the characteristics of an individual archetypical building.

Archetype Characterization: In morocco, floor construction techniques using full slabs has been mostly replaced by floor hourdis since the 1990s. For walls, current construction techniques generally consist of double walls [42] (Table 3).

Table 3. Thermophysical properties of the constituent elements of the envelope elements for the building type: modern Moroccan house based on [18, 23, 43]

Building envelope	Materials	Thickness (cm)	Density kg/m^3	Conductivity W/m k	Specific heat J/kg k
Facades	Plaster	1	1350	0.560	1000
	Cement	1.5	2500	1.8	1000
	Brick	10	918	0.241	741
	Air layer	10	R = 0.18 m^2 K /W		
	Brick	7	938	0.247	741
	Cement	1.5	2500	1.8	1000
	Plaster	1	1350	0.560	1000
Side wall (adjacent buildings)	Plaster	1	1350	0.560	1000
	Cement	1.5	2500	1.8	1000
	Brick	10	918	0.241	741
	Brick	10	918	0.241	741
	Cement	1.5	2500	1.8	1000
	Plaster	1	1350	0.560	1000
Exterior wall	Plaster	1	1350	0.560	1000
	Cement	1.5	2500	1.8	1000
	Brick	10	918	0.241	741
	Cement	1.5	2500	1.8	1000
Interior wall	Plaster	1	1350	0.560	1000
	Cement	1.5	2500	1.8	1000
	Brick	10	918	0.241	741
	Cement	1.5	2500	1.8	1000
	Plaster	1	1350	0.560	1000
Roof	Tiles	2	2300	1.3	840
	Screed	10	2500	1.8	1000
	Hourdis	20	1456.7	1.176	1000
	Cement	1.5	2500	1.8	1000
	Plaster	1	1350	0.560	1000

(continued)

Table 3. (*continued*)

Building envelope	Materials	Thickness (cm)	Density kg/m³	Conductivity W/m k	Specific heat J/kg k
Floor	Tiles	2	2300	1.3	840
	Screed	10	2500	1.8	1000
	Concrete	20	1456.7	1.176	1000
	Sand and gravel	15	1950	2	1000
Windows	Single glazing	U = 4.88 W/m²k, Solar factor: 0.52			

The U-values of each component of the envelope (roofing, facade, windows, floors) are defined using these thermophysical properties which are based on the construction materials. They are assumed to be similar for every building given that construction techniques and materials have not significantly changed since 2003 when the district was first created. It should also be noted that no buildings were subject to energy retrofitting in the district.

3D Modeling: 3D modeling of the previously discussed building archetypes is necessary before an energy simulation can be performed, and it is done based on architectural designs. The results of the 3D modeling step are shown below for each building archetype (Fig. 7):

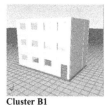  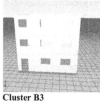 

Cluster B1
-Area : 96.35 m
-Height : 8.76 m
-% Adjacency : 29.65%
Orientation :114°

Cluster B2
-Area : 100.55 m
-Height : 8.27 m
-% Adjacency: 16.90%
-Orientation :25.62°

Cluster B3
-Area : 85.96 m
-Height : 9.51 m
-% Adjacency : 54.27%
-Orientation :35.47°

Cluster B4
-Area : 194.71 m
-Height : 9.02 m
-% Adjacency : 19.78%
-Orientation :64.75°

Fig. 7. 3D models of the building archetypes

Results of the Energy Simulation: The previously 3D-modeled archetypes are used as inputs for the energy simulation in the BINAYATE software. Below are the heating and air-conditioning needs of each archetype building (Table 4):

Table 4. Simulation results for the archetype buildings

Archetype	Conditioned floor area m^2	Heating		Cooling		Total	
		kWh/y	kWh/(m^2.y)	kWh/y	kWh/(m^2.y)	kWh/y	kWh/(m^2.y)
C1	248.06	14179.82	57.16	9499.70	38.30	23679.52	95.46
C2	233.27	13958.75	59.84	10598.08	45.43	24556.84	105.27
C3	207.82	11834.67	56.95	7855.88	37.80	19690.55	94.75
C4	516.38	25901.34	50.16	19759.83	38.27	45661.17	88.43

These archetypes are generalized using the GIS over the enter district to calculate its yearly energy balance.

Quantification: The GIS operations, specifically the queries and spatial joint, allow us to classify each building in this zone according to its corresponding archetype, simplifying spatial identification and data extrapolation. As a result, the computation of the total energy requirements of the district becomes a simple addition operation.

In this step, each building is labelled by its matching archetype as indicated in the following map.

To estimate the energy requirements for the whole district, we calculate for each building the net conditioned floor surface which does not consider hallways, stairways, cupboards, interior wall widths. This is because information related to cupboards or hallways is difficult to obtain and collect. We only estimated the surface occupied by stairways and exterior walls, and that is, therefore, the only surface that is subtracted from the total floor area.

Fig. 8. Distribution of buildings in the "Bouzaghlal" district by archetypes

We suppose that the wall thickness is 0.25 m and that the average stairway surface area is (2,60 m * 2.40 m). The net heated/air-conditioned floor surface is estimated by the following equation (Fig. 8):

$$SP\_NET = SP\_gross - S\_stairs \times N - (P\_buil \times 0.25 \times N) \qquad (2)$$

- **SP_NET:** *net heated/air-conditioned floor surface of building.*
- **SP_gross:** *Gross Surface area of the building's floors*
- **S_stairs:** *Average stairway surface (2,60 m × 2.40 = 6,24 m^2)*
- **P_buil:** *Building Perimeter*

- **N**: *Number of floors*
- **0.25**: *Thickness of the exterior walls(m)*

Afterwards, the total yearly energy requirements for thermal comfort in each building in the district is calculated with the following equation (Fig. 9):

$$BE\ (Bi) = SP\_NET(Bi) \times BE\ (Ci) \tag{3}$$

- **BE (Bi):** *Yearly energy requirements for thermal comfort in a building of archetype Ci.*
- **BE (Ci):** *Yearly energy requirements per surface (m^2) for thermal comfort in a building of archetype Ci.*
- **SP_NET:** *Net heated/air-conditioned floor surface of building Bi* (Table 5).

Table 5. Annual energy balance for heating and cooling the "Bouzaghlal" district

Heating energy needs (MWh/year)	Cooling energy needs (MWh/year)	Total energy needs (MWh/year)
14881,08	10527,58	25408,66

Fig. 9. Spatial distribution of the calculated energy demand for the "Bouzaghlal" district

The results of the energy balance calculation show that the heating demand is higher than the cooling one for the "Bouzaghlal" district. This is due to the Mediterranean climate that is typically characterized by hot, dry summers and mild winters. This, in turn, means that savings can be made in heating more so than in cooling, which is also the case for the rest of the country, except in very hot climate zones.

Evaluation and Performances: In this section, we present the results of the evaluation that was performed on the impact of implementing the RTCM thermal regulations on heating/cooling requirements in the district.

According to the RTCM, the technical specifications of the thermal performance of residential buildings are mainly related to heating/air-conditioning requirements, which are capped at 46 kwh/m²/year for zone Z2.

In a standard RTCM-compliant renovation scenario applied to the district in the future, the estimated energy savings can be calculated using the Eq. (1).

The total energy savings of each building and the energy that can be saved for the district is summarized in the following Table 6:

Table 6. Energy requirements and total energy savings for an RTCM-compliant renovation scenario for the "Bouzaghlal" district.

Current energy needs (MWh/year)	Energy needs after the RTCM-compliant renovation scenario (MWh/year)	Estimated energy savings (MWh/year)	Gain (%)
25408,66	12089,19	13319,46	52,72

Implementing the RTCM through an energy renovation scenario at the scale of "Bouzaghlal" district leads to a significant reduction in heating and air conditioning requirements, with total annual savings of 52.72% relative to the current situation. This result reflects the rate of energy savings that can be achieved in an urban environment.

Mapping and Outreach: The maps that we obtained can be included in the municipal geoportal [44], in solar cadastres [45], or for outreach and communication of the results before and after the renovation scenario to citizens. This would help them with decision-making and allow them to study the feasibility of their renovation projects (Fig. 10).

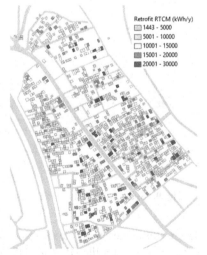

Fig. 10. Distribution of annual energy needs in the case of a standard renovation RTCM

6   Conclusion and Perspectives

During the last decade, developed countries made significant efforts to improve energy efficiency and retrofit of their building stock. This is not the case, however, for developing countries, including Morocco, due to financial difficulties and lack of skilled labor. Hence, public authorities need simple approaches, operational methods and flexible tools to simplify the identification and efficient evaluation of the scope of energy efficiency. This would help with and accelerate the mastery of the process of strategic energy renovation planning.

In this paper, we proposed a methodological framework to support decision-making processes in terms of energy planning at the urban scale by evaluating the impact of energy renovation strategies of heating and air-conditioning demand. Similarly, the model allows the estimation of the energy savings that can be achieved in an RTCM based energy renovation scenario.

The proposed methodological framework is based on a bottom-up approach in a multi-scale GIS environment. It combines physical and statistical methods to divide the set of buildings into different archetypes that represent the main physical and geomet rical characteristics of the studied area. The archetypes are subsequently analyzed and their performance assessed by an energy simulation using the BINAYATE software in order to estimate the heating and air-conditioning demand before and after the implementation of an RTCM based energy retrofit scenario. The results of the simulation are then generalized and extrapolated on the entire set of buildings using the GIS tool that gives the possibility to aggregate them at different scales. Thus, we can calculate the estimated energy savings that are used as a performance indicator for the evaluation and prioritization of different renovation strategies and energy efficiency measures that are to be applied in a given building stock domain.

This methodological framework was applied to a typical modern Moroccan residential building. The case study was carried out in the «Bouzaghlal» district in the north of M'diq, which is a town in the Z2 climate zone. The implementation of an RTCM-based energy retrofit scenario at the district scale has achieved significant energy savings of up to 52.72%. This mapping of different energy renovation scenarios for the entire urban environment will present, on one hand, a supportive decision-making tool for energy planning studies, and a tool to encourage citizens to join and adhere to the energy renovation process on the other.

In this work, this method was considered for the typical building of a modern Moroccan apartment-building, which is very widespread and is the dominant type of building in the country. However, it should be noted that this framework can be used for other types of buildings.

Future research will pertain to the application of the study to all the districts and neighborhoods of the M'diq town with an energetic analysis of other building typologies in local housing.

Acknowledgments. This work has been supported by MESRSFC and CNRST under the project PR2-OGI-Env, reference PPR2/2016/79.

References

1. ADEREE: Tendance de l'efficacité énergétique au Maroc (2012). https://www.amee.ma/sites/default/files/inline-files/Rapport_indicateurs_EE_Medener.pdf. Accessed 27 July 2021
2. "Taux d'urbanisation (en %) par année : 1960–2050. https://www.hcp.ma/Taux-d-urbanisation-en-par-annee-1960-2050_a682.html. Accessed 27 July 2021
3. AMEE: Efficacité énergétique dans le bâtiment. https://www.amee.ma/fr/expertise/batiment. Accessed 27 July 2021

4. Jagarajan, R., Asmoni, M.N.A.M., Mohammed, A.H., Jaafar, M.N., Mei, J.L.Y., Baba, M.: Green retrofitting – a review of current status, implementations and challenges. Renew. Sustain. Energy Rev. **67**, 1360–1368 (2017). https://doi.org/10.1016/j.rser.2016.09.091
5. GIZ: Mosquées et bâtiments verts. https://www.giz.de/en/worldwide/33674.html. Accessed 27 July 2021
6. "Efficacité énergétique dans le secteur de l'industrie. https://www.amee.ma/fr/expertise/ind ustrie. Accessed 27 July 2021
7. AMEE: Audit Énergétique Obligatoire : recueil juridique (2020). https://www.mem.gov. ma/Lists/Lst_Textes_Reglementaires/Attachments/201/AEO-RecueilJuridique201120.pdf. Accessed 27 July 2021
8. B. d'études ALGEES: EFFICACITÉ ÉNERGÉTIQUE DANS LES BÂTIMENTS AU MAROC Support de sensibilisation (2019)
9. M'lahfi, B., Amegouz, D., El Qandil, M.: A new approach for the mandatory application of the thermal regulation of construction (RTCM) in the future moroccan buildings. SN Appl. Sci. **2**(10), 1–16 (2020). https://doi.org/10.1007/s42452-020-03367-w
10. Maroc, L.: Rapport annuel de la Cour des comptes au titre de l'année 2018 (2020)
11. International Energy Agency and OECD: Energy policies beyond IEA countries. Russia 2014, p. 309 (2014)
12. AMEE: Le Règlement Thermique de Construction au Maroc Version simplifiée Guide pratique destiné aux professionnels
13. Ma, Z., Cooper, P., Daly, D., Ledo, L.: Existing building retrofits: methodology and state-of-the-art. Energy Build. **55**, 889–902 (2012). https://doi.org/10.1016/j.enbuild.2012.08.018
14. Ahmed, W., Asif, M.: A critical review of energy retrofitting trends in residential buildings with particular focus on the GCC countries. Renew. Sustain. Energy Rev. **144**, 111000 (2021). https://doi.org/10.1016/j.rser.2021.111000
15. Sibilla, M., Kurul, E.: Transdisciplinarity in energy retrofit. a conceptual framework. J. Cleaner Prod. **250**, 119461 (2020). https://doi.org/10.1016/j.jclepro.2019.119461
16. Sobhy, I., Benhamou, B., Brakez, A.: Effect of retrofit scenarios on energy performance and indoor thermal comfort of a typical single-family house in different climates of Morocco. ASME J. Eng. Sustain. Build. Cities **2**(2), 1–14 (2021). https://doi.org/10.1115/1.4051051
17. M'lahfi, B., Amegouz, D., El Qandil, M.: RTCM's role in green building and the green economy. In: Saka, A., et al. (eds.) CPI 2019. LNME, pp. 305–321. Springer, Cham (2019). https://doi.org/10.1007/978-3-030-62199-5_28
18. Chegari, B., Tabaa, M., Moutaouakkil, F., Simeu, E., Medromi, H.: Local energy self-sufficiency for passive buildings: case study of a typical Moroccan building. J. Build. Eng. **29**, 101164 (2020). https://doi.org/10.1016/j.jobe.2019.101164
19. Gargab, F.Z., Allouhi, A., Kousksou, T., El-Houari, H., Jamil, A., Benbassou, A.: Energy efficiency for social buildings in Morocco, comparative (2E) study: active VS. Passive solutions Via TRNsys. Inventions **6**(1), 4 (2020). https://doi.org/10.3390/inventions6010004
20. Lamrani, A., Rougui, M.: Parametric study of thermal renovation of an administrative building envelope in region of Chefchaouen (Morocco). In: 2018 6th International Renewable and Sustainable Energy Conference (IRSEC), December 2018, pp. 1–5 (2018). https://doi.org/ 10.1109/IRSEC.2018.8702919
21. Drissi Lamrhari, E.-H., Benhamou, B.: Thermal behavior and energy saving analysis of a flat with different energy efficiency measures in six climates. Build. Simul. **11**(6), 1123–1144 (2018). https://doi.org/10.1007/s12273-018-0467-3
22. Saidi, E.M., El Baraka, A., Limami, H., Khaldoun, A.: Design of an efficient insulation system for a house in Zaouiat Sidi Abdeslam. In: 2019 7th International Renewable and Sustainable Energy Conference (IRSEC), November, pp. 1–6 (2019). https://doi.org/10.1109/IRSEC4 8032.2019.9078177

23. Lebied, M., Sick, F., Choulli, Z., El Bouardi, A.: Improving the passive building energy efficiency through numerical simulation–a case study for Tetouan climate in northern of Morocco. Case Stud. Therm. Eng. **11**, 125–134 (2018). https://doi.org/10.1016/j.csite.2018. 01.007

24. El Azhary, K., Laaroussi, N., Garoum, M., El Harrouni, K., Mansour, M.: A dynamic thermal simulation in new residential housing of Lakhiayta City in Morocco. In: Fırat, S., Kinuthia, J., Abu-Tair, A. (eds.) Proceedings of 3rd International Sustainable Buildings Symposium (ISBS 2017), pp. 26–35. Springer International Publishing, Cham (2018). https://doi.org/10. 1007/978-3-319-64349-6_3

25. El Kadiri, S., Kaitouni, S.I., Ikkcn, B., El Otmani, R.: Thermal performance of a residential building in Ben Guerir city: a comparative evaluation for an optimized thermal load needs. In: 2018 6th International Renewable and Sustainable Energy Conference (IRSEC), December 2018, pp. 1–8 (2018). https://doi.org/10.1109/IRSEC.2018.8703011

26. Harrouni, K.E., et al.: [IEEE 2018 6th International Renewable and Sustainable Energy Conference (IRSEC) - Rabat, Morocco (2018.12.5–2018.12.8)] 2018 6th International Renewable and Sustainable Energy Conference (IRSEC) - Energy Efficient Houses Meeting both Bioclimatic Architecture Principles and Moroccan Thermal Regulation, pp. 1–8 (2018). https:// doi.org/10.1109/IRSEC.2018.8702273

27. Srhayri, I., Bah, A.: Impact of building's orientation and insulation on energy consumption: case study in different thermal zones of Morrocco using TRNSYS Software. In: 2018 6th International Renewable and Sustainable Energy Conference (IRSEC), pp. 1–5 (2018). https:// doi.org/10.1109/IRSEC.2018.8702937

28. TRNSYS: Transient system simulation tool. http://www.trnsys.com/. Accessed 27 July 2021

29. Binayate BINAYATE Software, par AMEE: Assessment of the buildings energy performance and control of the conformity with the Moroccan Thermal Regulation for Construction (2015). http://www.amee.ma/index.php/fr/expertise/efficacite-energetique/bat iment. Accessed 27 July 2021

30. DesignBuilder simulation tool. DesignBuilder Software Ltd, UK (2020). https://designbui lder.co.uk. Accessed 27 July 2021

31. Deb, C., Schlueter, A.: Review of data-driven energy modelling techniques for building retrofit. Renew. Sustain. Energy Rev. **144**, 110990 (2021). https://doi.org/10.1016/j.rser.2021. 110990

32. Ang, Y.Q., Berzolla, Z.M., Reinhart, C.F.: From concept to application: a review of use cases in urban building energy modeling. Appl. Energy **279**, 115738 (2020). https://doi.org/10. 1016/j.apenergy.2020.115738

33. Carnieletto, L.: Italian prototype building models for urban scale building performance simulation. Build. Environ. **192**, 107590 (2021). https://doi.org/10.1016/j.buildenv.2021. 107590

34. De Jaeger, I., Reynders, G., Callebaut, C., Saelens, D.: A building clustering approach for urban energy simulations. Energy Build. **208**, 109671 (2020). https://doi.org/10.1016/j.enb uild.2019.109671

35. Tardioli, G., Kerrigan, R., Oates, M., O'Donnell, J., Finn, D.P.: Identification of representative buildings and building groups in urban datasets using a novel pre-processing, classification, clustering and predictive modelling approach. Build. Environ. **140**, 90–106 (2018). https:// doi.org/10.1016/j.buildenv.2018.05.035

36. Delmastro, C., Mutani, G., Corgnati, S.P.: A supporting method for selecting cost-optimal energy retrofit policies for residential buildings at the urban scale. Energy Policy **99**, 42–56 (2016). https://doi.org/10.1016/j.enpol.2016.09.051

37. Romani, Z.: Développement d'une méthode d'aide à la décision multicritère pour la conception des bâtiments neufs et la réhabilitation des bâtiments existants à haute efficacité énergétique. Génie civil. Université de La Rochelle ; Université Abdelmalek Essaâdi (Tétouan, Maroc), 2015. Français. ffNNT : 2015LAROS034ff. fftel-01373443f (2015)

38. Sick, F., Schade, S., Mourtada, A., Dieter, U., Grausam, M.: Dynamic building simulations for the establishment of a Moroccan thermal regulation for buildings. J. Green Build. **9**(1), 145–165 (2014). https://doi.org/10.3992/1943-4618-9.1.145

39. Merini, I., Molina-García, A., García-Cascales, M.S., Ahachad, M.: Energy efficiency regulation and requirements: comparison between Morocco and Spain. In: Ezziyyani, M. (ed.) Advanced Intelligent Systems for Sustainable Development (AI2SD'2018). AISC, vol. 912, pp. 197–209. Springer, Cham (2019). https://doi.org/10.1007/978-3-030-12065-8_19

40. Re Cecconi, F., Moretti, N., Tagliabue, L.C.: Application of artificial neutral network and geographic information system to evaluate retrofit potential in public school buildings. Renew. Sustain. Energy Rev. **110**, 266–277 (2019). https://doi.org/10.1016/j.rser.2019.04.073

41. Ali, U., Shamsi, M.H., Hoare, C., Mangina, E., O'Donnell, J.: A data-driven approach for multi-scale building archetypes development. Energy. Build. **202**, 109364 (2019). https://doi.org/10.1016/j.enbuild.2019.109364

42. ADEREE: Guide technique sur l'isolation thermique du bâtiment au maroc, p. 114 (2016)

43. AMEE Giz: propriétés thermodynamique des materiaux de construction locaux vers un batiment performant et durable. RABAT (2020). https://fr.calameo.com/read/006261459c736fd 0af644

44. Echlouchi, K., Ouardouz, M., Bernoussi, A.-S., Boulaassal, H.: Smart geoportal for efficient governance: a case study municipality of M'diq. In: Ezziyyani, M. (ed.) Advanced Intelligent Systems for Sustainable Development (AI2SD 2019). LNNS, vol. 92, pp. 237–245. Springer, Cham (2020). https://doi.org/10.1007/978-3-030-33103-0_24

45. Echlouchi, K., Ouardouz, M., Bernoussi, A.S.: Urban solar cadaster: application in North Morocco. In: Proceedings of 2017 International Renewable and Sustainable Energy Conference IRSEC 2017, Mmc (2018). https://doi.org/10.1109/IRSEC.2017.8477342

Technical-Economic Analysis of a Power Supply System for Electric Vehicle Charging Stations Using Photovoltaic Energy and Electrical Energy Storage System

Lucélio M. da Costa[1]($\boxtimes$) (iD) and Paulo G. Pereirinha[1,2]($\boxtimes$) (iD)

[1] Department of Electrical Engineering, Coimbra Polytechnic, ISEC, Coimbra, Portugal
luceliocosta1994@hotmail.com, ppereiri@isec.pt
[2] INESC Coimbra, Coimbra, Portugal

Abstract. Electrical energy storage can reduce energy consumption at the time of greatest demand on the grid, thereby reducing the cost of fast charging electric vehicles (EVs). With storage, it is also possible to store mainly energy from renewable sources or to limit the power requested by Public Power Grid (PPG), allowing charging of EVs in areas where power supply is limited via PPG. In this paper, to meet the requirements of an EV charging station and the management of the energy storage system, a lithium-ion battery system with second life batteries is proposed and compared with new batteries. A photovoltaic system that will allow the use of solar energy is also proposed. HOMER Grid software was used to simulate and analyze the different systems from a technical and economic point of view for different cases. It was concluded that HOMER is a powerful tool but some drawbacks are also pointed out.

Keywords: Electric vehicles · Charging station · Energy storage · Lithium-ion battery · Second-life batteries · Photovoltaic system · Homer grid

1 Introduction

The world's demand for energy is increasing rapidly, putting a great strain on existing energy resources, and having a negative impact on the environment and global warming. As governments strive for a green energy economy, electric vehicles (EVs) are playing an increasingly important role in helping to reduce emissions from the transport sector. Electrification of the transport sector is an important step towards a sustainable society. This will bring several benefits, such as reducing oil consumption, reducing emissions and integrating renewable energy sources into the grid [1–3].

The foreseen massive deployment of EVs is driving the solution to the challenge of combating climate change and urban pollution, with the aim of providing a balanced and sustainable response. Nowadays, using an EV to get around a city center is one way to reduce urban pollution and to contribute to the sustainability of our planet.

© ICST Institute for Computer Sciences, Social Informatics and Telecommunications Engineering 2022
Published by Springer Nature Switzerland AG 2022. All Rights Reserved
J. L. Afonso et al. (Eds.): SESC 2021, LNICST 425, pp. 73–86, 2022.
https://doi.org/10.1007/978-3-030-97027-7_5

The installation of fast charging stations for EVs is essential to encourage widespread adoption of EVs, as this will reduce concerns about "range anxiety" regarding the range of the EV before the battery runs out [2, 4, 5]. Combining the use of EVs and renewable energy sources such as solar and wind power to support EV charging stations should be considered to ensure economical and environmentally friendly charging [6, 7].

Sales of electric cars have increased significantly over the last 10 years, and an important question arises: what to do with EV batteries after they reach the end of their life? [8]. Several solutions have been studied to find a sustainable answer to the question posed. Several electrical energy storage studies have been developed by researchers and major automobile manufacturers like Nissan and others [9–14], bringing up the concept of giving these batteries a new life, i.e., a second-life, reusing them for stationary applications. In this way, it is possible to store a significant amount of energy that can later be injected into the power grid or into consumer devices to support the power grid and be used to charge an electric vehicle [15]. Consequently, energy storage can reduce the peak power consumption of the grid and thus the cost of fast charging of electric vehicles. It can also enable electric vehicle charging in areas where the power grid does not allow it [16]. Furthermore, it is possible to use this type of solution in a smart system where the energy sources are mainly renewable.

So, this work aims to investigate the possibility of incorporating another fast or semi-fast charger into an existing system without having to increase the power contracted with the public grid. For this, it is investigated the technical and economic feasibility of installing a photovoltaic system and a battery storage system, comparing the usage of used lithium-ion batteries (2nd life utilization) or new lithium-ion batteries, for different case studies. Finally, based on the results, to meet the need for fast charging infrastructure and to enable the reutilization of used batteries, photovoltaic panels and energy storage based on second life batteries for fast charging systems for electric vehicles is proposed.

2 Methodology

The methodology is implemented in the software HOMER (Hybrid Optimization Model for Electric Renewables) Grid. The software, HOMER Grid, is a robust optimization model developed by NREL (National Renewable Energy Laboratory) that can be used to simulate various power system configurations or mixes of components, optimize design options for cost efficiency, or perform sensitivity analysis based on inputs of loads, components, and resources [17, 18].

The software HOMER Grid consists of three main operational phases, specifically simulation, optimization, and sensitivity analysis. In the simulation phase, the selection of system components and sizes is presented. The simulations are based on estimates of installation, operation and maintenance costs and electricity tariffs. In the optimization phases, an optimal system is determined after several simulations of configurations of the hybrid system. The final phase is the sensitivity analysis, which is achieved for each system configuration based on the parameters of the sensitivity analysis [17].

The optimal solution is centered on the Net Present Cost (NPC). After all, HOMER Grid also provides feasible simulation results that allow the user to compare configurations and evaluate them according to their economic, technical, and environmental interest [18, 19].

The total NPC is the main economic output of HOMER, the value by which all system configurations are ranked in the optimization results, and the basis for calculating the total annual cost and the levelized cost of energy. The total NPC of a system is the present value of all the costs the system incurs over its lifetime minus the present value of all the revenues it generates over its lifetime. Costs include capital costs, replacement costs, operation and maintenance costs, fuel costs, emission penalties, and the cost of purchasing electricity from the grid. Revenues include the residual value and sales revenue from the electricity grid [24].

3 Theorical Background: Hybrid System Modeling

The considered system consists of the following components: PV systems, power converter, battery storage, fast charging station for electric vehicles, load profile and grid connection. To evaluate the performance of the different systems and scenarios, HOMER Grid simulates and optimizes the same load profile with the different system components. In the following sections, each component is analyzed individually [20, 21].

3.1 PV Systems

The power output of the PV system is expressed in Eq. 1,

$$P_{PV} = P_{PV,STC} f_{PV} \left(\frac{G}{G_{STC}} \right) \left[1 + \alpha_P \left(T_C - T_{C,STC} \right) \right] \tag{1}$$

where, $P_{PV,STC}$ is the output power at standard test conditions (STC), f_{PV} is the PV derating factor (power losses due to factors such as panel soiling, wiring losses, shading, snow cover, aging, etc.), G is the current irradiance, G_{STC} is the irradiance at STC, α_P is the temperature coefficient of power, T_C is the PV module temperature, $T_{C,STC}$ is the temperature of the PV module under STC, and STC (standard test conditions: $G_{STC} = 1000\,W/m$, $T_{C,STC} = 25\,°C$) [21].

The PV array has the configuration of PV modules such as:

$$P_{PV,STC} = (N_S \times N_P) P_{m,STC} \tag{2}$$

where $P_{m,STC}$ is the output power of the PV modules under standard test conditions, N_S is the number of modules connected in series, and N_P is the number of strings connected in parallel [21].

3.2 Solar Energy Sources

The solar irradiance and clearness index data are retrieved from the website HOMER Grid. Entering a specific location into the software, the data from NASA will be recovered from the website. The full solar data is based on the latitude and longitude of the selected area. Figure 1 below shows the clearness index and monthly average solar global horizontal irradiance from the NASA Prediction of Worldwide Energy Resource database via the HOMER Grid software [25].

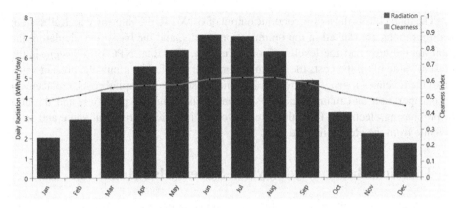

Fig. 1. Monthly average solar global horizontal irradiance data

3.3 Converter

The converter is coupled between the DC bus and the AC bus, as shown in Fig. 2. The converter works bidirectionally depending on the energy flow and acts as an inverter for transferring energy between the PV system and the load AC and as a rectifier for charging the battery bank from the grid.

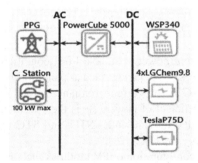

Fig. 2. System model

For this study, the bidirectional Huawei Power Cube 5000 converter with a capacity of 60 kW (2 modules) and a rated output voltage of 380/400/415 AC, available on HOMER database, was initially selected. The investment cost for this converter is 1500 €/kW and the replacement cost per year is the same. However, since this model is quite expensive, looking at the current market, other solutions were considered, and finally it was selected and manually added to the database, the SMA America STP24000-US-10 (480 V) bidirectional converter, which can be connected to get the same capacity, and at a much lower price (139.58 €/kW) according to the present price list of a Portuguese company FF SOLAR [27]. The number of inverters is optimized based on HOMER Grid optimizer. The efficiency of the Huawei Power Cube 5000 is 96% with a lifetime of 15 years and the efficiency of the SMA America STP24000-US-10 is 98% with a lifetime of 15 years.

3.4 Battery Storage

Battery charging helps store excess generation from mixed sources for use later when consumption is higher than generation.

The charging or discharging power of the battery is regulated by the output power of the power system (PV and grid) and the load demand at a given time. At any given hour, the state of charge of the battery (SOC) is expressed as follows:

$$SOC(t) = SOC(0) + \eta_c \sum\nolimits_{k=0}^{t} P_c(k) + \eta_d \sum\nolimits_{k=0}^{t} P_d(k) \qquad (3)$$

where, $SOC(0)$ is the initial SOC of the battery, P_c is the charged power, P_d is the discharged power, η_c is the charge efficiency, η_d is the discharge efficiency.

The available capacity of the battery bank shall not be less than the minimum allowable capacity B_{min} and not greater than the maximum allowable capacity B_{max} [22],

$$\begin{cases} B_{min} \leq SOC \leq B_{max} \\ B_{min} \leq (1 - DOD \leq B_{max} \end{cases} \qquad (4)$$

where B_{min} and B_{max} are the minimum and maximum power limits, respectively, and DOD is the depth of discharge.

Moreover, the discharged power of the battery should satisfy the condition [22]

$$0 \leq P_d(k) \leq P_{max} \qquad (5)$$

where P_{max} is the maximum hourly discharge.

3.5 Grid Connection

The electric vehicle charging station under investigation is connected to the public power grid (PPG). The connection between the electric vehicle charging station and the PPG is made in low voltage (three-phase, 400 V), with a three-phase 75 kW connection [26]. The rate of consumption is shown in Fig. 3 as a function of the time of day and the day of the year.

In Portugal, the price of energy varies throughout the day, the month, and the year. Figure 3 shows a variation of the energy price over the year by color band. For example, the red color band means that the energy price varies between 0.07 and 0.14 €/kWh.

3.6 Load Profile

It was modeled a daily energy profile in the HOMER Grid software as can be seen in Fig. 4. This profile is based on one-month data from the electric vehicle charging station in Coimbra. The average daily energy is equivalent to 320 kWh, and by extension this value was considered for the remaining months.

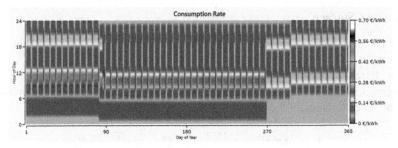

Fig. 3. Consumption rate

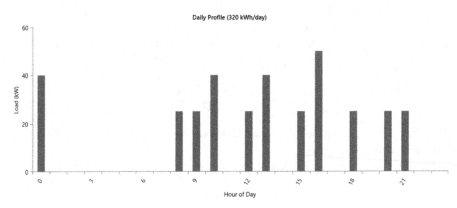

Fig. 4. Daily profile

3.7 Dispatch Algorithm

The dispatch algorithm is responsible for deciding at each time step how the electric load should be served by the available generation sources. One of the many decisions it makes is whether to charge the EV from storage battery, from the grid, or from both. It worth noting that dispatching in HOMER Grid has "perfect prediction", which means that it knows [23]:

- The electric demand for each time step in the future;
- The utility rate schedule;
- PV production for each time step in the future.

HOMER Grid optimizes and finds the least cost system by lowering demand charges and doing energy arbitrage if feasible. If this system is feasible, i.e., the electric demand can be served at each time step without exceeding the peak load limit, the economic efficiency of the system is calculated. In the final results table, the system is ranked in the order of NPC [23].

4   Case of Study

The present case concerns a real EV charging station in Coimbra, Portugal. The charging station has a 50 kW charger of the Portuguese company Efacec, model QC50. This charger has three different sockets, namely the CCS2, CHAdeMO and Mennekes sockets, but can only charge one vehicle at a time. Analyzing in detail the charging events of August 2020, several occasions were detected where there was at least one EV waiting for the charger to be freed to be able to charge, so at least one more charger would be needed. However, the connection to the PPG has limitations. So, in order to expand the system, and thus increase the availability of services without increasing the contracted power to the PPG, other solutions would have to be considered, such as energy storage and solar panels.

5   Simulation and Optimization Results

5.1   Proposed Scenario

The system shown in Fig. 2 was modeled in Homer Grid software, keeping the connection to the PPG (75 kW), and including a photovoltaic panel system and a battery storage system. The proposed scenario allows simultaneous charging of two electric vehicles, as an additional 50 kW charger has been added, for a total of 100 kW. Table 1 shows the characteristics of the proposed scenario.

Table 1. Characteristics of the proposed scenario

Charger output power (kW)	Mean time connected (hr)	Number of chargers	Scaled Avg Sessions/day
2 × 50	0.6	2	15

Figure 5 shows the new annual energy profile based on the proposed scenario modeled in the HOMER Grid software. In the figure, the vertical bar on the right side represents the charging power of the electric vehicles, in kW, where the warmer colors (orange, red) represent the higher power, and the colder colors (blue, black) represent the lower power. This means that several vehicles can be charged at the same time, as the warmest color range corresponds to the power range between 70 kW and 100 kW.

Based on the characteristics of the electric vehicles visiting the charging station in Coimbra, two types of generic EVs were modelled taking August of 2020 as a reference. Generic EV 1 corresponds to 76% of the EV population visiting the charging station and generic EV 2 corresponds to 24%. Both have different energy requirements. The first one requires 15 kWh and can be charged with a power of up to 26 kW, while the second one requires 24 kWh and can be charged with a power of up to 50 kW. For a better illustration, Table 2 can be seen.

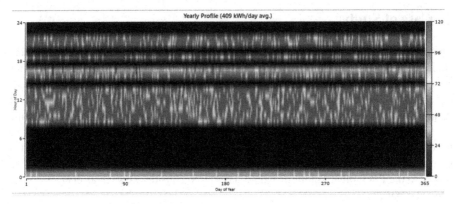

Fig. 5. Annual profile of the proposed scenario

Table 2. EV features

Name	Proportion of EV population (%)	Max. charging power per EV (kW)	Required charge energy per EV (kWh)
Generic EV 1	76	26	15
Generic EV2	24	50	24

5.2 Results

The software HOMER Grid simulated 137 solutions, omitting 22 solutions due to lack of a converter and 1 solution due to an unnecessary converter, and of the 137 solutions, all were feasible. The four cases which have been considered are as follows:

1. PV + Energy Storage System (Tesla: Second Life Battery) + Converter + Grid;
2. PV + Energy Storage System (LGChem: New Battery) + Converter + Grid;
3. PV + Converter + Grid;
4. Grid (base case).

For simplicity, it was considered a nominal discount rate (the rate at which one could borrow money) and an expected inflation rate both equal to 0%. Electricity costs in the base case (highlighted) amount to 0.212 € per load unit (kWh), while they decrease by 26.42% in the winner case (1. PV + Energy Storage System (Tesla Second Life Battery) + Converter + Grid) as shown in Table 3.

The cheapest case is the one in which the EV is charged with the help of solar panel, storage system, converter, and grid. In this case, the unit cost of electricity is 0.156 €/ kWh. The comparison can also be seen in Table 4 and Table 5.

The IRR (Internal Rate of Return) for this system is 22% and the simple payback period is 4.2 years. Also, the ROI (Return on Investment) is 17%.

The cash flow diagram for the winning system can be found in Fig. 6. We can see that at the beginning of the project, the PV system, the energy storage systems and the

Table 3. Architectural combination

Architecture											Cost					Compare Economics
							WSP340 (kW)	4xLGChem9.8	TeslaP75D	PPG (kW)	SMA24.1 (kW)	NPC (€)	COE (€)	Operating cost (€/yr)	Initial capital (€)	Simple Payback (yr)
							23.0		1	75	25.0	€349,357	€0.156	€12,761	€30,324	4.2
							23.0	1		75	25.0	€359,219	€0.161	€12,988	€34,512	4.8
							23.0			75	25.0	€368,176	€0.165	€14,071	€16,404	3.3
											75	€474,966	€0.212	€18,999	€0.00	

Table 4. Cost summary

	Base Case	Lowest Cost System
NPC 🛈	€474,966	€349,357
Initial Capital	€0.00	€30,324
O&M 🛈	€18,999/yr	€12,761/yr
LCOE 🛈	€0.212/kWh	€0.156/kWh

Table 5. Savings

Annualized Utility Bill Savings	€7,539/yr
Net Present Utility Bill Savings	€188,467
Annualized Demand Charge Savings	€0.00
Annualized Energy Charge Savings	€7,539

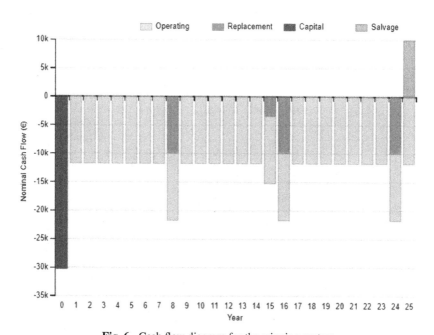

Fig. 6. Cash flow diagram for the winning system

inverter will incur in capital costs of 30,324 euros, while in years 8, 16 and 24, the batteries of the storage system and in year 15, the inverter will also incur in replacement costs. During the project lifetime of 25 years, the system will also incur in operation and maintenance costs.

The HOMER Grid software also simulated energy exchange with the grid. The plots in Fig. 7 and Fig. 8 show the energy exchange with the grid for the first 7 days of a typical summer and winter month in Portugal, respectively.

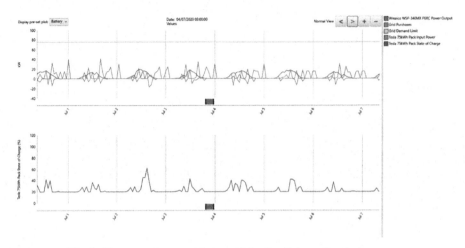

Fig. 7. Energy exchange with the grid for first 7 days of typical summer

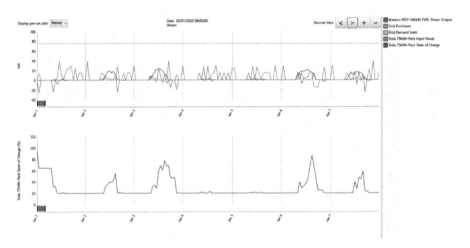

Fig. 8. Energy exchange with the grid for first 7 day of typical winter

6   Discussion

The software HOMER Grid proved to be a very powerful tool, able to economically and technically evaluate all possible combinations of the proposed system and select a winning system in less than 15 s.

As presented, the winning system consists of a photovoltaic panel, a storage system with second-life lithium batteries from Tesla's EVs, a converter and a 75 kW power grid connection. The initial capital of this system is equal to 30,324 €, a return on investment of 17%, an internal rate of return of 22%, and with an investment recovery from the 4.2th year. The annual savings of this system are 7,539 € per year.

The second winning case is similar to the first case, but uses new lithium batteries (LG Chem), making this solution less economically viable than the first case, with an initial capital of 34,512 €, a return on investment of 13.4%, an internal rate of return of 18.3%, and a simple payback of 4.8 years.

The third winning case considers only the photovoltaic panels, the inverter, and the connection to the grid, but not the storage system. This results in an initial capital reduction of 13,920 €, which is almost half of the initial investment of the first case. This shows that the storage system makes the solution more expensive in the first case. The third winning case has a return on investment of 26%, an internal rate of return of 30.4%, and obviously a lower simple payback (3.27 years), since in this case the initial investment was reduced by almost half (16,404 €).

The fourth winning system, which corresponds to the base case (currently installed), consists only of connection to the power grid. This system cannot meet the load when two EVs want to charge at 50 kW at the same time, which limits the availability of the service (75 kW).

The software HOMER Grid also simulated power exchange with the grid and ensured that most of the load was met. It made forecasts and predictions of solar power generation and load to make the best decision on when to charge the batteries and buy power from the grid.

Finally, from what was seen, HOMER software is a very powerful and usefully tool. However at least two important drawbacks have to be pointed out:

First, HOMER Grid software operates as a black box, i.e., users do not have access to the internal decision system. For loads such as a charging station in the HOMER Grid, we are limited to the internal strategies of the software, i.e., with this version 1.8 of the software HOMER Grid, it is, for example, not yet possible to force the battery to charge when power is available from the grid, in particular during the night, to ensure power availability (more than the PPG allowed) for next EV's charging events.

Second, the best case using the HOMER's database proposed Huawei Power Cube 5000 inverter would lead to a simple payback of 11 years instead of 4.2 years. So, even if using HOMER's database components is very easy and convenient, it is very advisable to check the present market components and costs, and manually introduce new models/prices as they can have dramatic impact on the economic indicators obtained.

7   Conclusion

The presented work shows the result of a project development, in which a photovoltaic energy generation system and a battery storage system were considered that can cover most of the needs of a charging station for EVs connected to the grid. Despite the limitations of the software HOMER Grid, which does not allow to create our own strategy where the user can decide when to charge the batteries from the grid or not, it proved to be a very powerful tool to analyze the economic viability of a system, if proper care is taken as pointed out, namely checking the currently available models and prices of the considered components. HOMER Grid has also shown that a system consisting of a storage system with second-life batteries can be an advantage over new batteries because of the latters' higher cost. This study also suggests that with the use of PV and a storage system, it is possible to increase the available power beyond the contracted power.

Acknowledgements. The authors would like to thank Prio Energy (www.prio.pt/pt/) for the partnership in this project. This work is partially funded by Portuguese National Funds through the FCT -Foundation for Science and Technology, I.P., within the scope of the projects UIDB/00308/2020 and MANaGER (POCI-01-0145-FEDER-028040).

References

1. Hafez, O., Bhattacharya, K.: Optimal design of electric vehicle charging stations considering various energy resources. Renew. Energy **107**, 576–589 (2017). https://doi.org/10.1016/j.ren ene.2017.01.066
2. Aldhanhani, T., Al-Durra, A., El-Saadany, E.F.: Optimal design of electric vehicle charging stations integrated with renewable DG. In: IEEE Innovative Smart Grid Technologies - Asia (ISGT-Asia), Dez. 2017, pp. 1–6. doi: https://doi.org/10.1109/ISGT-Asia.2017.8378428
3. Abd Alla, S., Bianco, V., Tagliafico, L. A., Scarpa, F.: Pathways to electric mobility integration in the Italian automotive sector. Energy **221**, 119882 (2021). https://doi.org/10.1016/j.energy. 2021.119882
4. Yoon, S.-G., Kang, S.-G.: Economic Microgrid planning algorithm with electric vehicle charging demands. Energies **10**(10), 1487 (2017). https://doi.org/10.3390/en10101487
5. Biresselioglu, M.E., Kaplan, M.D., Yilmaz, B.K.: Electric mobility in Europe: a comprehensive review of motivators and barriers in decision making processes. Transp. Res. Part A Policy and Pract. **109**, 1–13 (2018). https://doi.org/10.1016/j.tra.2018.01.017
6. Jhala, K., Natarajan, B., Pahwa, A., Erickson, L.: Coordinated electric vehicle charging for commercial parking lot with renewable energy sources. Electr. Power Compon. Sys. **45**(3), 344–353 (2017). https://doi.org/10.1080/15325008.2016.1248253
7. Khan, S., Ahmad, A., Ahmad, F., Shafaati Shemami, M., Saad Alam, M., Khateeb, S.: A Comprehensive Review on Solar Powered Electric Vehicle Charging System. Smart Sci. **6**(1), 54–79 (2018). https://doi.org/10.1080/23080477.2017.1419054
8. Hossain, E., Murtaugh, D., Mody, J., Faruque, H.M.R., Haque Sunny, Md.S., Mohammad, N.: A comprehensive review on second-life batteries: current state, manufacturing considerations, applications, impacts, barriers potential solutions, business strategies, and policies. IEEE Access **7**, 73215–73252 (2019) https://doi.org/10.1109/ACCESS.2019.2917859

9. Venkatapathy, K., Tazelaar, E., Veenhuizen, B.: A systematic identification of first to second life shift-point of lithium-ion batteries. In: 2015 IEEE Vehicle Power and Propulsion Conference (VPPC), pp. 1–4 (2015). https://doi.org/10.1109/VPPC.2015.7352885

10. Gohla-Neudecker, B., Maiyappan, V.S., Juraschek, S., Mohr, S.: Battery 2nd life: Presenting a benchmark stationary storage system as enabler for the global energy transition. In: 6th International Conference on Clean Electrical Power (ICCEP), pp. 103–109 (2017). https://doi.org/10.1109/ICCEP.2017.8004799

11. Martinez-Laserna, E., et al.: Battery second life: Hype, hope or reality? A critical review of the state of the art. Renew. Sustain. Energy Rev. **93**, 701–718 (2018). https://doi.org/10.1016/j.rser.2018.04.035

12. Jiao, N., Evans, S.: Business models for sustainability: the case of second-life electric vehicle batteries. Procedia CIRP **40**, 250–255 (2016). https://doi.org/10.1016/j.procir.2016.01.114

13. Saez-de-Ibarra, A., Martinez-Laserna, E., Koch-Ciobotaru, C., Rodriguez, P., Stroe, D., Swierczynski, M.: Second life battery energy storage system for residential demand response service. In: 2015 IEEE International Conference on Industrial Technology (ICIT), pp. 2941–2948 (2015). https://doi.org/10.1109/ICIT.2015.7125532

14. Nissan gives EV batteries a second life. In: Nissan gives EV batteries a second life. https://global.nissanstories.com/en/releases/4r (2021). Accessed 9 Oct 2021

15. The importance of second life batteries for energy storage. https://airqualitynews.com/2020/12/01/the-importance-of-second-life-batteries-for-energy-storage/ (2021). Accessed 9 Oct 2021

16. Kamath, D., Arsenault, R., Kim, H.C., Anctil, A.: Economic and environmental feasibility of second-life lithium-ion batteries as fast-charging energy storage. Environ. Sci. Technol. **54**(11), 6878–6887 (2020). https://doi.org/10.1021/acs.est.9b05883

17. Al-Janahi, S.A., Ellabban, O., Al-Ghamdi, S.G.: Technoeconomic feasibility study of grid-connected building-integrated photovoltaics system for clean electrification: a case study of Doha metro. Energy Rep. **6**, 407–414 (2020). https://doi.org/10.1016/j.egyr.2020.11.192

18. Ma, W., Xue, X., Liu, G.: Techno-economic evaluation for hybrid renewable energy system: application and merits. Energy **159**, 385–409 (2018). https://doi.org/10.1016/j.energy.2018.06.101

19. Makwana, V., Kotwal, C., Arora, K.: Optimum Sharing of Solar Power and Grid for an Academic Institute using HOMER. In: 2019 IEEE 5th International Conference for Convergence in Technology (I2CT), pp. 1–5 (2019). https://doi.org/10.1109/I2CT45611.2019.9033648

20. Ekren, O., Canbaz, C.H., Güvel, Ç.B.: Sizing of a solar-wind hybrid electric vehicle charging station by using HOMER software. J. Clean. Prod. **279**, 123615 (2021). https://doi.org/10.1016/j.jclepro.2020.123615

21. Raveena, B., Rao, B.V., Gouthamkumar, N.: Optimization of Hybrid off Grid Power System Using HOMER software. In: 2018 3rd IEEE International Conference on Recent Trends in Electronics, Information Communication Technology (RTEICT), pp. 696–700 (2018). https://doi.org/10.1109/RTEICT42901.2018.9012219

22. Tazvinga, H., Xia, X., Zhang, J.: Minimum cost solution of photovoltaic–diesel–battery hybrid power systems for remote consumers. Sol. Energy **96**, 292–299 (2013). https://doi.org/10.1016/j.solener.2013.07.030

23. HOMER Grid Dispatch Strategy. https://www.homerenergy.com/products/grid/docs/1.1/homer_grid_dispatch_strategy.html. Accessed 5 Oct 2021

24. Total Net Present Cost. https://www.homerenergy.com/products/grid/docs/latest/total_net_present_cost.html. Accessed 10 Oct 2021

25. NASA. http://eosweb.larc.nasa.gov

26. Ligação de baixa tensão: Negócios | E-REDES. https://www.e-redes.pt/pt-pt/empresas/neg ocios/baixa-tensao. Accessed 9 Nov 2021 (in Portuguese)

27. Products | FF Solar. http://www.ffsolar.com/index.php?lang=EN&page=products. Accessed 9 Nov 2021

Assessing Household Electricity Consumers' Willingness to Load Shift

Paula Ferreira$^{(\boxtimes)}$ ⓘ, Ana Rocha ⓘ, and Madalena Araújo ⓘ

ALGORITMI Research Center, University of Minho, Guimarães, Portugal
paulaf@dps.uminho.pt

Abstract. This paper focuses on the acceptance and motivations towards load shifting programs in the household sector. The research is based on a questionnaire addressing the Portuguese population and aiming to better understand the willingness to engage in load shifting, the main motivations for this, and the acceptance of automatic control systems to improve responsiveness to prices changes. The willingness to load shift electricity was then assumed as a proxy for the availability of the respondents to engage in a demand response (DR) program. The results show that most respondents would consider the engagement in DR and that the economic benefits are still the main driver. However, environmental concerns and even contribution towards reducing importations for the country emerge also as important motivations in particular for younger respondents. The study concludes also on the need to improve communication on DR programs and overcome the consumers' inertia that still exists and prevent more effective participation in the electricity market.

Keywords: Demand response · Survey · Portugal · Flexibility · Consumers' inertia

1 Introduction

The energy supply grid system is currently undergoing a transition from a centralized and non-participating end-user model towards a decentralized and highly participative model. The former is mostly associated with non-renewable and fossil fuel supply, while the latter has been increasingly related to a greater share of renewable energy supply across the world and by the increase of small-scale energy producers. This entails a significant change in pre-existing models as consumers become also energy producers, i.e. transition to prosumers status as agents that both consume and produce energy [1]. Although this will create new opportunities for consumers to participate in electricity markets, the abovementioned change is characterized by the increasing concerns over intermittency and increased grid complexity, which poses a challenge in meeting a balance between the supply and demand sides. Among the challenges associated with this new energy supply model, is that the potential burden costs have to be ensured by the final consumer through the energy bill. The envisioned solutions to overcome these challenges are based

© ICST Institute for Computer Sciences, Social Informatics and Telecommunications Engineering 2022
Published by Springer Nature Switzerland AG 2022. All Rights Reserved
J. L. Afonso et al. (Eds.): SESC 2021, LNICST 425, pp. 87–98, 2022.
https://doi.org/10.1007/978-3-030-97027-7_6

on technological progress and innovation, as well as improved communication systems that enable the deployment of smart grids. Fostering the development of Smart Grids could facilitate the transition from a traditional to a new model: (i) removing of existing barriers between the energy producers and end-users, thereby establishing microgrids; and (ii) through Demand Side Management (DSM), which comprises energy efficiency, energy storage, and Demand Response (DR) strategies. DSM aims then to implement amendments in demand for electricity through different measures such as providing better and on-time information about electricity tariffs or changing the existing tariff structure [2], promoting the use of smart devices (e.g. smart meter), thereby supporting the end-users on the energy management [3] and reducing overall energy demand.

In a power system, the demand side was a huge potential for flexibility requirements and have an important role in the transition towards renewable energy systems [4]. The flexibility potential is uncertain, once their potential is mainly affected by the consumer energy behaviour, i.e., if the consumers are willing to shift their energy usage from peak (high price) to off-peak period (low price) [5]. However, to increase the flexibility is remarkably necessary a massive investment in a new power system. As an example, heat pumps that connected with the district heating system and heat storage could promise flexibility [6], the Electric Vehicles (EVs) through of charging and discharging of their battery, could be used as a flexibility source, in which the V2G (Vehicle to Grid) technology enables the end-user to manage the electricity use, charging the vehicle in off-peak hours, storing the energy to be used at peak times [7]. Another relevant option to benefit from the consumers' flexibility is the DR that usually is related to changes in energy consumption behaviour to respond to the changing of prices.

According to Federal Energy Regulatory Commission (FERC), DR can be defined as "Changes in electric usage by end-use customers from their normal consumption patterns in response changes in the price of electricity over time, or to incentive payments designed to induce lower electricity use at times of high wholesale market prices or when system reliability is jeopardized" [8].

In particular, the potential benefits of DR can be felt on both demand and supply sides: (i) end-users (demand side), allowing to reduce the electricity bill providing financial incentives to the consumers for reducing electricity consumption, when the price is high, or shifting the electricity consumption to off-peak hours; (ii) electricity market operator (supply side), providing several options for grid and electricity cost management and the system operators making the system more capable to meet contingencies [9]. As [10] stated, DR is a valuable tool to provide flexibility to the power system, to support the integration of Variable Renewable Energy resources and to manage the grid. Shifting or reducing the demand for electricity during peak hours can contribute to improving the grid, but according to [11] the potential benefit has to be enough to encourage the consumers to shift their electricity usage. The results of [4] also point to important societal benefits but modest consumers savings related to DR programs and underline the need to consider additional policy measures. In addition to the issue of private economic benefits, [1] call attention to the social and behavioural aspects of energy decision making including the reduced interest on the topic or even concerns related to privacy and sharing of data.

This paper contributes to add to the state-of-the-art by addressing the social awareness, acceptance and motivations towards DR programs. This research used a combination of literature review and questionnaires to explore the willingness to participate in these programs, main motivations factors and to estimate the consumers' flexibility. The empirical research method focused on DR programs and target the Portuguese household consumers, assessing in particular (i) the motivational factors to shift the electricity use (ii) the willingness to participate in load shifting programs (iii) the willingness to accept the automatic control of the heating and cooling system. For this study, willingness to shift electricity use was then assumed as a proxy for the availability of the respondents to engage in a DR program.

The central research questions associated with this paper are:

Are the electricity consumers willing to participate in some load shifting activities? Which motivational factors may trigger the acceptance of the shifting of electricity use? Are the electricity consumers willing to accept the automatic mode of the heating and cooling system to respond to electricity price changes?

The remainder of this study is organized as follow. The following section presents an introduction to household energy use in Portugal. Then, Sect. 3 presents the research method applied in this study. Section 4 discloses the results and their discussion, and Sect. 5 presents the conclusions of this paper.

2   Household Energy Use in Portugal

The electricity consumption of the household sector in Portugal still lags behind the industrial and tertiary sectors, but even so, it represents close to 27% of the total demand in 2019 (source www.dgge.pt, consulted September 2021). Electricity plays a fundamental role in household activities and according to the last survey on energy consumption in households, published in 2020, electricity is the main source of energy consumed in households representing 46.4% of the total energy consumption against 42.6% in 2010. The report demonstrates the increasing importance of electricity for the household sector, related to the increasing demand for comfort and the growth of electricity appliances [12]. However, biomass is still the dominant heating system which can affect the consumers' sensitiveness to electricity price changes. For example, [13] argue that rural households in Portugal are more sensitive to price changes than urban ones and this may happen because rural populations can more easily use biomass for heating or even cooking.

As [14] recalls, electricity tariff price structures should always be borne in mind the supply marginal cost to foster the efficient use of electricity and the recourses involved in the value chain of the power system. Namely, the production marginal cost differs from hour to hour, during the month or even throughout the year, motivated by the different cost functions of the entire value chain of the power system, production, system, distribution, distribution, and retail. Another relevant point is that the demand is stochastic, this will have repercussions on production cost that could be vastly affected by external factors such as changes in fossil fuel prices and weather conditions [14].

In Portugal, the electricity tariff can have different values, depending on the timeframe and different seasons (summer and winter periods). Time schedules for the free time-of-day tariff intervals and tariffs for the last resource supplier are determined once a year by the regulator (ERSE) for the coming year [14]. Therefore, considering the afore-mentioned background, different time-of-day tariff schemes are available to the con-sumers (e.g. weekly vs daily). The last regulation published by ERSE [15] established the following intervals for the daily scheme for the household low voltage consumers:

(i)   Low – period of low electricity consumption and low price corresponding to 4 h/day;
(ii) (ii) Full – period of high electricity consumption and high price corresponding to 10 h/day;
(iii) Peak – period of very high electricity consumption and very high price correspond-ing to 10 h/day.

The possibility of dynamic tariffs is also being considered in this regulation, although still focusing on industrial consumers.

3   Research Method

3.1   Survey Design and Implementation

Data was collected by a company specialized in CATI (computer-assisted telephone interview). The sample was randomly taken from 278 municipalities, in geographic terms, the above analysis only considers Continental Portugal (i.e. excluding Azores and Madeira Islands). The questionnaire was drafted in Portuguese, and the time taken for answering all questions reached about five minutes.

For the preparation of the questionnaire, an analysis of the household electricity consumption and the tariff was conducted as described in the previous section. To define the final questionnaire's formats a pre-test was conducted using a face-to-face approach with a small group of residential electricity consumers. This pre-test enabled us to get a better feel of the difficulties the respondents could have in understanding the vocabulary used and the time needed to fill the questionnaire. Lastly, a pilot project with university students through web-survey was conducted to evaluate their electricity perception about electricity use and refine the questions [16].

The survey was conducted during May and June of 2018. To ensure at least a confident interval of 95%, with a marginal error of 5%, the sample size was calculated using the Eq. (1).

$$s = \frac{Z^2 \times (p) \times (1 - p)}{c^2} \tag{1}$$

where z is equal to 1.96 (since the confidence level is 95%); p is a percentage picking a choice, expressed as a decimal (in which, 0.5 was used for the sample size needed) and c is the confidence interval (5%) that needed to be expressed as a decimal (0.05).

3.2 Survey Description

The questionnaire included four parts:

- Part I, related to sociodemographic characteristics of respondents and included 5 questions concerning gender, age, education, professional activity and household size.
- Part II, addressing the issues related to consumers inertia/knowledge about electricity use and bill, and included 4 questions addressing regularly reading the electricity consumption on the meter, actively looking for different electricity suppliers, awareness about ToU tariffs and ownership of electricity monitoring devices.
- Part III, on possible motivational factors to engage in DR programs, with 4 questions adressing environmental, cost, country importations or acquaintances advice. If the respondent was not interested in participating in DR programs, a fifth question was asked about the motivations for rejection.
- Part IV, on flexibility on electricity use, with 1 question about the possibility of engaging in an automatic control program for the heating or cooling system.

The respondents were asked about their agreement with some presented sentences. This agreement was measured by the scale "totally disagree"; "tend to disagree"; "tend to agree"; "totally agree" and "does not know/does not answer". A summary of the statistics regarding the respondents' sociodemographic characteristics is presented in Table 1.

The sample is composed of 410 respondents, of which 225 female and 185 male. Results on educational characterization show that 38.8% of the respondents have a higher education level (university), while about 34.4% of the respondents have studied less than 12 years in school. About 64% of the respondents are aged between 25 and 64. The majority of respondents is engaged in professional activity (53.7%), of which about 10%% are self-employed. The remaining respondents are students (4.6%), retired (27.3%), unemployed (10.3%) or households (4.1%). The average household size (number of occupants) is approximately 2.7. The majority (52.73%) of the respondents claimed that their monthly electricity bill would be in the range of 26 €–55€ and only 2.6% of the respondents claimed to pay more than 150 €/month.

After collecting the data a descriptive analysis was performed employing the Fisher's exact test and Chi-square test. These tests were used according to the nature of the variables and based on the methodologies described in [17]. Results were considered statistically significant when the p-value was less than 0.05. Statistical analysis was conducted using the software STATA 15.1.

Table 1. Sociodemographic characteristics of respondents

	N	%
Gender		
Male	185	45.12
Female	225	54.88
Age		
18–24	38	9.27
25–44	136	33.17
45–64	128	31.22
Above 65 years old	108	26.34
Education		
No education	4	0.98
4th grades of school	53	12.93
6th grades of school	44	10.73
High school	40	9.76
Secondary school	110	26.83
Graduate or bachelor	125	30.49
Master's degree	33	8.05
PhD	1	0.24
Professional activity		
Unemployed	42	10.24
Student	19	4.63
Posted worker	179	43.66
Self-employed worker	41	10.00
Retired	112	27.32
Domestic (stay-at-home)	17	4.15
Household size		
1 member	54	13.17
2 members	145	33.37
3 members	119	29.02
4 members	65	15.85
5 members	19	4.63
Above 5 members	8	1.95
Monthly electricity bill value		

(*continued*)

Table 1. (*continued*)

	N	%
DA – 25€ or less	30	7.79
DB – 26€–55€	203	52.73
DC – 56€–100€	118	30.65
DD – 101–150€	24	6.23
DE – more than 150€	10	2.60
Urban/Rural		
Urban	268	65.37
Rural	142	34.63

Note: the attribution of rural and urban classification for each parish is based on (PRODER, http://www.proder.pt/). A municipality is considered rural or urban if 50% of parishes are included within the former or the latter category. Hence, the predominance of the rural category (>50%) implies a rural "concelho" and vice-versa.

4   Results and Discussion

This section is divided into three subsections according to the structure of the questionnaire.

4.1   Consumers Inertia and Knowledge on Electricity Consumption

After collecting the data about sociodemographic characteristics, the respondents were asked about their knowledge about time of use (ToU) tariffs, in which the terms "*bi-horário*" (two-tier tariffs) and "*tri-horário*" (three-tier tariffs) were used to facilitate a better understanding of the respondents. For this question, respondents were presented with two options "yes" or "no" to assess whether the respondents were familiar with these terms. To assess the inertia of the respondents three proxy questions were formulated:

– Do you regularly communicate (around every two months) the reading of your electricity meter to your electricity supplier?
– Have you changed to another electricity supplier in the last two years?
– Do you own/use any electricity monitoring device (other than the electricity supplier meter)?

The options for answering these three questions were "yes" and "no". Figure 1 summarizes the obtained results.

According to the results, about 85% of the respondents are familiar with the ToUs tariffs. Over half of the respondents regularly communicate their electricity consumption to the electricity supplier, and 22.2% of them showed to be proactive in switching electricity suppliers. However, only a minority of the respondents (about, 11.1%), indicate that they own an electricity monitoring device.

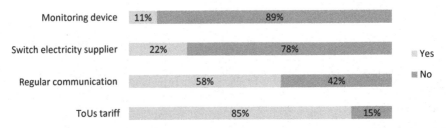

Fig. 1. Knowledge and inertia of the respondents

Using Fisher's exact test, the results indicate that gender seems not to be statistically correlated to all these four questions: familiarity with ToUs tariffs (p = 0.891), regular communication (p = 0.548), switching electricity supplier (p = 0.282) and ownership of monitoring device (p = 0.543). This suggests the inertia and the knowledge of the respondents are not correlated with gender.

To understand the extent of the significance of age on the knowledge and inertia of the respondents, the Chi-square test was used. The results showed that the respondents between 25 and 44 years old are better-informed about ToUs tariff (p = 0.004). The respondents included in this category also tend to indicate that they communicate regularly the reading of the electricity meter to the electricity supplier (p = 0.018). This is not an expected result, given that these respondents categories tend to be in charge of electricity bill payment [18]. Although the ownership of smart meters was in general limited, age is statistically significant with young participants showing higher ownership rates (between1 8–24 years old, p = 0.000). As expected, technology acceptance is correlated with age [19]. However, according to the Chi-square test, age does not seem to be correlated to the interest in switching electricity suppliers (p = 0.422).

The Chi-square test showed that the education level is statistically significant for familiarity with ToUs tariffs (p = 0.012), regular communication of the reading of the electricity meter (p = 0.025) and ownership of the monitoring device (p = 0.001). In general, the respondents with a high educational level tend to be more well informed and active. However, once again the variable education is not statistically significant for switching electricity supplier (p = 0.415).

Using the Chi-square test, it is possible to state that the professional activity of the respondents is associated with the knowledge and the inertia ($p_{\text{toUs tariff}} = 0.015$; $p_{\text{regular communication}} = 0.025$; $p_{\text{monitoring devise}} = 0.001$), while again not statically significant for the case of switching of electricity supplier. Nevertheless, some important trends can be drawn: respondents whose professional activity can benefit from spending more time at home, such as, retired, domestic or unemployed, tend to be less active and less well informed.

This study also takes into consideration the level of electricity consumption between the rural and urban areas. Using Fisher's exact test, it is possible to conclude that people who are living in urban areas are more prone to regularly communicate electricity consumption to the supplier. This finding is in line with [20], as the authors suggest that in urban areas the chance of success to implement DR is higher due to higher population density and higher energy and environmental concerns.

4.2 Motivational Factors for Load Shifting

In the survey, respondents were also asked about their motivation to shift electricity usage. To address this, the respondents should answer using the scale "totally disagree"; "tend to disagree"; "tend to agree"; "totally agree" and "does not know/does not answer" whether they are willing to shift their daily electricity usage: (1) to contribute to benefit the environment, (2) to contribute to reducing the dependence on imported energy, (3) to reduce their electricity bill or (4) to follow acquaintances advice.

Only 6% of the respondents were not willing to shift their electricity use for whatever motivational factor. When asked about the main reasons not to make, the principal motives reported were the possibility of reducing the comfort of the household (32%) and lack of time (24%). Two other important reasons were mentioned: the feeling that they were not well-informed on the theme (16%) and believing that shifting electricity consumption will not be enough to reduce significantly the electricity bill (20%).

However, an overwhelming majority (94%) of the respondents show some degree of willingness to shift the electricity use. As shown in Fig. 2, the reduction of the electricity bill is a determinant factor for respondents to shift their electricity usage. This result suggests that the monetary benefits would be key to deploy the DR programs as debated in other studies [21, 22]. In addition, a large percentage of respondents said that they "totally agree" or "tend to agree" to shift the electricity usage whether it would benefit the environment (66%) or reduce the percentage of imported energy (61%). It is also interesting to notice the social effect measured by the recommendations seems to play a less important role in the decision-making process of the participants.

Using the Chi-square test it was possible to conclude that the environmental factors are statistically associated with the education level ($p = 0.001$), and professional activity ($p = 0.003$). This result suggests that people with a high level of education and students tend to be more aware of environmental problems. Younger respondents ($p = 0.001$) are more willing to shift their electricity usage if it benefits the environment. This result demonstrates that the variable "environmental factors" may contribute to boosting DR programs and associated technologies, as discussed in a survey sponsored by the Eurobarometer [23]. This report [23] concluded that the majority of the European respondents (35%) agree that a potentially effective way of tackling environmental problems is investing in research and development to find technological solutions. It should also be noted that the variable "gender" is not statistically significant for any of the motivational factors (environmental; reducing energy imports, reducing the electricity bill and recommendation).

Fig. 2. Motivational factors to shift electricity usage

As for the cost savings motivation, the Chi-square test indicated statistical significance to the education level (p = 0.044) and professional activity (p = 0.000). People with higher education levels and domestic are more willing to shift their electricity usage to reduce the bill. The same also goes for age, as respondents aged between 24–44 years old (p = 0.000) are more willing to shift their electricity usage.

4.3 Flexibility on Electricity Use

In the survey, participants were also asked whether they would accept the automatic adjustment of the heating or cooling system to respond to higher electricity prices. This question aimed to assess the willingness to participate in a future dynamic tariffs scheme.

The results presented in Fig. 3 indicate that more than half of the respondents are willing to accept some automatic control system. Nevertheless, there is a significant share (24% of respondents) who answered, "does not know/does not answer" or that "totally disagree" and "tend to disagree" (17%). This result suggests that the respondents feel that they are still not well-informed of the potential benefits, of the mechanisms to implement this system or may even have concerns about data privacy.

■ Totally agree   Tend to agree ■ Tend to disagree   Totally disagree ■ Does not know/ does not answer

Fig. 3. Willingness to accept the automatic control of the heating or cooling system

The statistical tests indicate that that the sociodemographic variables do not influence the willingness to accept the load control (p-value > 0.05). However, the Chi-square showed that the value of the electricity bill of the respondents is statistically significant (p-value = 0.022), suggesting that the value that respondent's survey pays for the electricity encourage them to accept the automatic control of the heating cooling. Namely, respondents paying higher electricity bills are more open to accepting this automatic control system.

5   Conclusions

Using a large, nationally representative sample of 410 household respondents, this work aims to contribute to better understand the public acceptance of possible DR programs, possible concerns and main motivational factors. In general, Portuguese citizens are well informed about ToUs tariff. A large share (85%) of the respondents are aware of the possibility of switching from flat rate to ToUs tariff. Moreover, most of the energy consumers would consider the possibility of engaging in some load shifting scheme. Only 6% of the consumers refused the idea of shifting their electricity use and this was mainly due to concerns related to household comfort. The lack of information to make a decision is also mentioned by the respondents and reflects an important barrier for DR uptake.

The results indicate that the economic incentives still play a decisive role in the consumers' decision-making process. This is particularly evident for respondents with higher education levels and staying at home (domestic). However, the results also show that the retired and domestic groups are the less active ones on changing electricity suppliers and tend to be less informed about ToU tariffs. The environmental factors and contribution for reducing the dependency on energy imports are also significant for the decision to shift electricity use. The results confirm that younger respondents tend to be more sensitive to these environmental aspects. This shows the importance of designing information campaigns directed towards different consumers and acknowledging their different concerns and motivation. This should also contribute to overcoming the low consumer awareness or interest to participate in the electricity market.

The majority of the respondents would be willing to accept the automatic control for the heating or cooling systems. This result suggests that the automatic mode should be considered in the development of DR programs. There is still a lot of undecided consumers which once more calls for additional information to reduce the consumers' inertia and increase their trust in the system.

The results of this work could provide important insights for energy policies and energy companies to design policies and strategies towards the development of future power grids and influence the final consumers to be more flexible. For this, future work should address the range of the energy flexibility as this may be limited by the building characteristics [24], socio-economics conditions and everyday routines [25]. Moreover, new DR programs well fitted to different consumers should be established along with effective communication strategies.

References

1. Parag, Y., Sovacool, B.K.: Electricity market design for the prosumer era. Nat. Energy 1(4), 16032 (2016). https://doi.org/10.1038/nenergy.2016.32
2. Weck, M.H.J., Van Hooff, J., Van Sark, W.G.J.H.M.: Review of barriers to the introduction of residential demand response: a case study in the Netherlands, pp. 790–816 (2017). https://doi.org/10.1002/er.3683
3. Goulden, M., Bedwell, B., Rennick-Egglestone, S., Rodden, T., Spence, A.: Smart grids, smart users? The role of the user in demand side management. Energy Res. Soc. Sci. 2, 21–29 (2014). https://doi.org/10.1016/j.erss.2014.04.008
4. Tveten, I., Bolkesjø, A.S., Ilieva, T.F.: Increased demand-side flexibility: market effects and impacts on variable renewable energy integration. Int. J. Sustain. Energy Plan. Manag. 11, 33–50 (2016). https://doi.org/10.5278/ijsepm.2016.11.4
5. Cruz, M.R.M., Fitiwi, D.Z., Santos, S.F., Catalão, J.P.S.: A comprehensive survey of flexibility options for supporting the low-carbon energy future. Renew. Sustain. Energy Rev. 97, 338–353 (2018). https://doi.org/10.1016/j.rser.2018.08.028
6. Paiho, S., et al.: Increasing flexibility of Finnish energy systems — A review of potential technologies and means. Sustain. Cities Soc. 43, 509–523 (2018). https://doi.org/10.1016/j.scs.2018.09.015
7. Gay, D., Rogers, T., Shirley, R.: Small island developing states and their suitability for electric vehicles and vehicle-to-grid services. Util. Policy 55, 69–78 (2018). https://doi.org/10.1016/j.jup.2018.09.006

8. Federal Energy Regulatory Commission: Federal Energy Regulatory Commission Survey on Demand Response, Time-Based Rate Programs/Tariffs and Advanced Metering Infrastructure Glossary, FERC-727 a (2008)
9. U.S. Department of Energy: Benefits of Demand Response in Electricity Markets and Recommendations for Achieving Them. A report to the United States Congress Pursuant to Section 1252 of the Energy Policy Act of 2005, February, pp. 1–122 (2006)
10. Dranka, G.G., Ferreira, P.: Review and assessment of the different categories of demand response potentials. Energy **179**, 280–294 (2019). https://doi.org/10.1016/j.energy.2019.05.009
11. Alparslan, M., Batman, A., Bagriyanik, M.: Review and comparison of demand response options for more effective use of renewable energy at consumer level. Renew. Sustain. Energy Rev. **56**, 631–642 (2016). https://doi.org/10.1016/j.rser.2015.11.082
12. Instituto Nacional de Estatística: Resultados preliminares do Inquérito ao Consumo de Energia no Sector Doméstico 2020 (2021)
13. Silva, S., Soares, I., Pinho, C.: Electricity residential demand elasticities: urban versus rural areas in Portugal. Energy **144**, 627–632 (2018). https://doi.org/10.1016/j.energy.2017.12.070
14. Apolinario, I., Felizardo, N., Garcia, A.L., Oliveira, P., Trinidad, A., Verdelho, P.: Determination of time-of-day schedules in the Portuguese electric sector. In: 2006 IEEE Power Engineering Society General Meeting, p. 8 (2006). https://doi.org/10.1109/PES.2006.1709487
15. Entidade Reguladora dos Serviços Energéticos (ERSE): Reformulação do Regulamento Tarifário do setor elétrico (2021)
16. Ferreira, P., Rocha, A., Araujo, M.: Awareness and attitudes towards demand response programs – a pilot study. In: 2018 International Conference on Smart Energy Systems and Technologies (SEST), pp. 1–6, September 2018. https://doi.org/10.1109/SEST.2018.8495804
17. Dalgleish, T., et al.: Handbook of biolological statistics. J. Exp. Psychol. Gen. **136**(1), 23–42 (2007)
18. Weber, S., Puddu, S., Pacheco, D.: Move it! How an electric contest motivates households to shift their load profile. Energy Econ. **68**, 255–270 (2017). https://doi.org/10.1016/j.eneco.2017.10.010
19. Arning, K., Ziefle, M.: Understanding age differences in PDA acceptance and performance. Comput. Human Behav. **23**(6), 2904–2927 (2007). https://doi.org/10.1016/j.chb.2006.06.005
20. Srivastava, A., Van Passel, S., Laes, E.: Assessing the success of electricity demand response programs: a meta-analysis. Energy Res. Soc. Sci. **40**, 110–117 (2018). https://doi.org/10.1016/j.erss.2017.12.005
21. Boogen, N., Datta, S., Filippini, M.: Demand-side management by electric utilities in Switzerland: analyzing its impact on residential electricity demand. Energy Econ. **64**, 402–414 (2017). https://doi.org/10.1016/j.eneco.2017.04.006
22. Conchado, A., Linares, P., Lago, O., Santamaría, A.: An estimation of the economic and environmental benefits of a demand-response electricity program for Spain. Sustain. Prod. Consum. **8**, 108–119 (2016). https://doi.org/10.1016/j.spc.2016.09.004
23. European Commission: Special Eurobarometer 468 Report Attitudes of European citizens towards the environment Fieldwork September-October 2017 November 2017 Survey requested by the European Commission, Special Eurobarometer 468 Report Attitudes of European citizens towards th (2017)
24. Majdalani, N., Aelenei, D., Lopes, R.A., Silva, C.A.S.: The potential of energy flexibility of space heating and cooling in Portugal. Util. Policy **66**, 101086 (2020). https://doi.org/10.1016/j.jup.2020.101086
25. Foulds, C., Christensen, T.H.: Funding pathways to a low-carbon transition. Nat. Energy **1**(7), 16087 (2016). https://doi.org/10.1038/nenergy.2016.87

A Feature and Classifier Study
for Appliance Event Classification

Benjamin Völker$^{(\boxtimes)}$ ⓘ, Philipp M. Scholl ⓘ, and Bernd Becker ⓘ

Computer Architecture, University of Freiburg, Freiburg im Breisgau, Germany
{voelkerb,pscholl,becker}@informatik.uni-freiburg.de

Abstract. The shift towards advanced electricity metering infrastructure gained traction because of several smart meter roll-outs during the last decade. This increased the interest in Non-Intrusive Load Monitoring. Nevertheless, adoption is low, not least because the algorithms cannot simply be integrated into the existing smart meters due to the resource constraints of the embedded systems. We evaluated 27 features and four classifiers regarding their suitability for event-based NILM in a standalone and combined feature analysis. Active power was found to be the best scalar and WaveForm Approximation the best multidimensional feature. We propose the feature set $[P, cos\,\Phi, TRI, WFA]$ in combination with a Random Forest classifier. Together, these lead to F_1-scores of up to 0.98 on average across four publicly available datasets. Still, feature extraction and classification remains computationally lightweight and allows processing on resource constrained embedded systems.

Keywords: NILM · Non-Intrusive Load Monitoring · Feature evaluation · Appliance classification

1 Introduction

Reducing our electricity consumption is a vital step to achieve the goal of saving earth's energy resources. In the residential or industrial domain energy monitoring and eco-feedback help by raising the awareness of an unnecessary electricity consumption of particular devices. To pinpoint user to specific appliances that consume too much energy, appliance specific consumption data are required. These can be retrospectively provided by utilizing existing smart meter infrastructure with Non-Intrusive Load Monitoring (NILM). NILM methods disaggregate the composite load into the load of each electrical consumer by incorporating machine learning approaches. These approaches can be classified into event-based and event-less methods. The latter apply disaggregation for each new data entry, while event-based approaches apply disaggregation whenever a new appliance event was recognized in the aggregated load. After identifying events, a classifier is typically used to determine to what appliances these events belong to. The generated list of events is finally used to reconstruct the load profile of the appliance, e.g. by grouping *switch-on* and *switch-off* events and

© ICST Institute for Computer Sciences, Social Informatics and Telecommunications Engineering 2022
Published by Springer Nature Switzerland AG 2022. All Rights Reserved
J. L. Afonso et al. (Eds.): SESC 2021, LNICST 425, pp. 99–116, 2022.
https://doi.org/10.1007/978-3-030-97027-7_7

assigning a known average consumption to times an appliance was switched on. The steps to detect and classify an appliance event include the extraction and pre-processing of the event, feature extraction, and finally classification. Classification algorithms working with a large number of features may achieve high classification performances (F_1-score > 0.9 such as proposed in [14]). However, the deployment on smart meters is hindered by the amount of features due to the required computational resources to calculate them and a typically linear increase in complexity for most classifiers.

The contributions of this work mainly include: (1) An evaluation of 27 features and four classifiers regarding their suitability for the task of appliance classification. (2) An evaluation of several combinations of these features with the goal to find a trade-off between feature dimensionality and classification performance. (3) The proposition of the feature set $[P, cos\Phi, TRI, WFA]$ with a Random Forest classifier for the task of appliance classification on resource constrained systems.

The remainder of this paper is organized as follows: Sect. 2 provides an overview of the NILM pipeline and lists state-of-the-art features and classifiers for event-based NILM as well as existing datasets for NILM. Section 3 introduces the event detector used to generate the training data, the features and classifiers as well as the evaluation strategy. Section 4 presents the results of the standalone feature analysis. The feature selection scheme for the combined analysis is explained in Sect. 5 and the results of the analysis are presented and discussed in Sect. 6. Finally, concluding remarks are provided in Sect. 7.

2   Related Work

The general NILM process can be divided into the two steps (1) *Data Acquisition* and (2) *Disaggregation* as shown in Fig. 1. *Data Acquisition* is comprised of measuring the required attributes (such as active- and reactive power) and performing general pre-processing steps while the *Disaggregation* step is a specially designed and often individually trained algorithm. Most of the disaggregation algorithms that have been proposed by researchers can be categorized into *event-based* and *event-less* approaches (e.g. according to [27,33]).

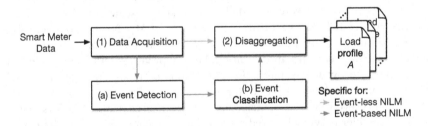

Fig. 1. General pipeline of event-less and event-based NILM systems

Event-less approaches optimize an overall system state using individually trained appliance models. These models are typically based on Hidden Markov Model (HMM) [21,25] or Artificial Neural Network (ANN) [6,19]. As the optimization step is recalculated for each new data input, event-less approaches typically suffer from high computational complexity and can, therefore, only be applied to lower sampling rates (<1 Hz). According to Anderson et al. [2] the *event-based* NILM process introduces two additional sub-steps as depicted in Fig. 1: (a) *Event Detection* and (b) *Event Classification*. *Event Detection* relies on the concept of the Switch Continuity Principle (SCP). The SCP was introduced by Hart [10] in 1992 and states that at a specific point in time only a single event, i.e. appliance state change, can occur and that overall, the number of events is small. This allows to treat events as signal anomalies, which need to be detected during event detection. *Event Classification* (also called appliance classification) follows the pattern recognition paradigm. Features, which are typically handcrafted by domain experts, are extracted from each event and are fed into a classifier, which outputs more details about the type of event (e.g. a specific appliance turning on). As the classification step is only applied to events, which are typically rare, event-based NILM systems are computational less expensive compared to *event-less* approaches, which perform the inference step for each new sample. The *Disaggregation* step uses the generated list of appliance events to extract estimated load profiles for each appliance (e.g. by recognizing the appliance's state transitions such as from *on* to *off* and mapping a known average consumption to each state).

2.1   Event Classification

Over the years, several hand-crafted features, for the task of event classification, have been introduced by various researchers. The most frequently used features are surveyed e.g. by Liang et al. [24]. Kahl et al. [17] evaluated 36 features in a stand-alone feature analysis as well as their combination using a feature forward selection technique. The authors found that across all used datasets, the phase angle difference between voltage and current ($cos\Phi$) was the best scalar feature ($F_1 = 0.49$) while Current Over Time (COT) achieved the best multi-dimensional feature performance ($F_1 = 0.8$). Different classification algorithms have been evaluated for the task of appliance classification such as Random Forests (RF) [4,8,26] Support Vector Machines (SVM) [16], k-Nearest Neighbour (kNN) [8,16,32] and more recently Artificial Neural Networks (ANN) [4,5,14]. Hubert et al. [13] and Kahl et al. [17] surveyed several algorithms for appliance classification. Hubert et al. [13] focused on Deep Neural Networks (DNNs) and identified higher sampling rates, the use of larger receptive fields, and an ensemble of input features, amongst others, as promising techniques to improve the performance of such networks. Kahl et al. [17] directed their focus on standard machine learning algorithms and identified that kNN performs quite well for the task of appliance classification despite its comparable low computational complexity. It is further noted that the training of ANNs constitutes a large burden for resource constrained embedded systems such as smart meters. Depending on the system's restrictions, a computationally lightweight algorithm such as kNN may be better suited.

2.2 Datasets

To achieve comparable results, experiments are typically carried out using pre-recorded datasets. In the domain of event-based NILM, several high-frequency datasets exist such as WHITED [15], PLAID [7], REDD [20], BLUED [1], UK-DALE [18], BLOND [22], and FIRED [28]. They mainly differ in the used Data Acquisition System (DAQ). The data sampling frequencies range from 8 kHz for FIRED up to 250 kHz for BLOND-250. While WHITED and PLAID include isolated appliance events recorded in a laboratory setup, the remaining datasets include aggregated data of real world deployments.

3   Background

This section details the event detection algorithm, the extracted features, and the basic classifiers used throughout this work.

3.1   Event Detection

Event detection, often referred to as edge detection, describes the process of identifying relevant changes in a signal. We use an event definition for electrical power signals, which has been proposed by Wild et al.: "*An event is a transition from one steady state to another steady state, which definitely differs from the previous one [...] [or] a so-called active section where the signal is somehow deviating from the previous steady state*" [31]. As appliance event detection is a research field on its own (see e.g. [2,27,31]) and a deeper evaluation would go beyond the scope of this paper, we choose a relatively simple expert heuristic event detector based on work by Weiss et al. [30]. It uses a threshold-based setup, which is applied on the apparent power signal (S). At first, the signal is filtered using the combination of a median filter to remove outliers and a mean filter to further smooth the signal. Both filters have a width of 3 s. Afterwards, the absolute difference between adjacent samples of the apparent power signal is calculated (ΔS). Next, a 3 VA filter is applied to the signal, which sets all values below 3 VA to zero as

$$\Delta S_{filtered}(i) = \begin{cases} 0 & \text{if } \Delta S(i) < 3\,VA, \\ \Delta S(i) & \text{else.} \end{cases} \tag{1}$$

Each non-zero portion in the filtered signal is regarded as an event (*up* or *down*). If multiple events happen within a time window of 3 s, we only keep the first one. This ensures that fluctuations after an event are not regarded as a new event. Figure 2 shows the different stages of the event detection process for the apparent power signal of an espresso machine.

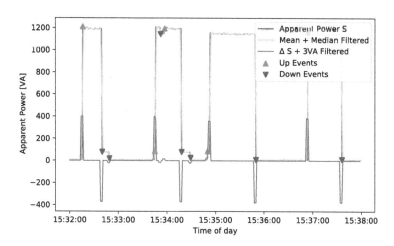

Fig. 2. Event detection applied to the 1 Hz apparent power signal of the *espresso machine* from the FIRED [28] dataset.

All significant events are clearly visible as peaks after the filtering process (green signal). The times, which are finally considered as events, are highlighted by red and blue triangles.

To be able to calculate high-frequency features for a detected event, we extract voltage and current waveforms 500 ms prior till 1 s after the timestamp of the event. We refer to this 1.5 s time interval as the Region of Interest (ROI) in the following. We further force each ROI to begin with a positive zero-crossing of the voltage measurements. All 27 features explained in the following can be extracted for each event from its corresponding ROI data.

For this evaluation, we solely use start-up events taken from individual device profiles. This means that no current is drawn in the first 500 ms. Figure 3 shows the current drawn in the ROI during a start-up event of two different appliances from the PLAID dataset.

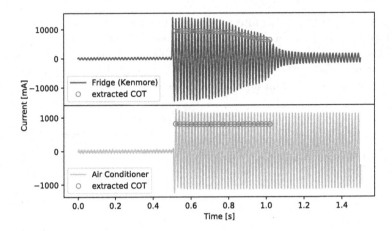

Fig. 3. Start-up transient ROI of a fridge and an air conditioner extracted from the PLAID [7] datasets. The red circles show the COT feature. (Color figure online)

3.2   Feature Selection

We have selected a set of 27 features, which have been introduced by various domain experts in related works [17,24,26]. All used features are summarized in Table 2 and can be extracted from the time or frequency domain of the ROI of an event. According to the Nyquist-Shannon theorem, current and voltage waveforms with a sampling rate f_s of more than $2 \cdot (18 + 1) \cdot f_0$ are required, as we analyze the signals for frequency components up to the 18th harmonic f_{18} of the grid line frequency f_0, so $f_s > 1900\,\text{Hz}$ for $f_0 = 50\,\text{Hz}$. To avoid aliasing artifacts, we apply a *Butterworth* low-pass filter (order = 6, $f_{\text{cutoff}} = 1\,\text{kHz}$) to the current and voltage waveforms to suppress higher frequencies before extracting any feature. The feature set includes both transient and steady state features. Steady state features include several electrical measurands such as phase angle between voltage and current ($cos\Phi$), resistance (R), admittance (Y) or active (P), reactive (Q), and apparent power (S), which can be calculated on the basis of a single main cycle. Transient features such as Current Over Time (COT) or Temporal Centroid (TC) describe the change of certain electrical characteristics (such as the current) over a certain time window. The set further includes features, which stem from excessive feature engineering such as the V-I Trajectory (VIT). The VIT was first introduced by Lam et al. [23] in 2007. The authors state that it shows a very high discriminative power, which has been proven by other researchers such as [12,17,29]. To calculate the VIT, the first ten periods of the current and voltage waveforms after the event are averaged and normalized. Afterwards, the averaged period is sub-sampled to 20 samples resulting in a feature vector of size 40 if voltage and current are linked together. Figure 4 shows the VIT of six different appliances from the FIRED [28] dataset. While we can assume that most of these can be distinguished quite well (e.g. *television, fridge, vacuum cleaner, smartphone charger*), some devices like the *espresso machine* and the *kettle* may be difficult to keep apart using VIT as the exclusive feature.

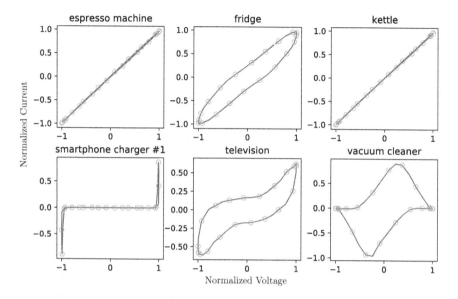

Fig. 4. Averaged and normalized VIT of six different appliances from the FIRED [28] dataset. The red dots show the sub-sampled values used in the feature vector. (Color figure online)

A second feature that stems from feature engineering is the relative Harmonic Energy Distribution (HED). The HED is a vector containing the first 18 harmonic current components normalized by the magnitude of the fundamental frequency as

$$HED = \frac{1}{x_{f_0}} \cdot [x_{f_1}, x_{f_2}, \ldots, x_{f_{18}}]. \tag{2}$$

Figure 5 shows the normalized spectrum of two appliances with a strong odd-even harmonic imbalance from the BLOND [22] dataset. The extracted HED is marked with red circles.

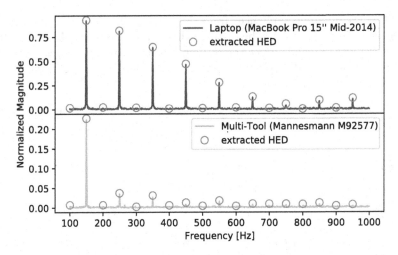

Fig. 5. The spectra of a notebook and a rotary multi-tool included in the BLOND [22] dataset, normalized to their fundamental frequency f_0. Both devices induce a strong odd-even harmonic imbalance. The extracted HED is highlighted by red circles. (Color figure online)

The feature Current Over Time (COT) describes the amount of Root Mean Square (RMS) current in the first 25 consecutive mains cycles after an event. The mains cycle in which the event happens is not included, as its corresponding RMS current depends on the specific time the event occurred within the cycle.

$$COT = \left[I_{RMS(1)}, I_{RMS(2)}, \ldots, I_{RMS(25)} \right]. \tag{3}$$

Figure 3 shows the current signal (ROI) of two appliances from the PLAID [7] dataset and the extracted COT.

For the corresponding formulas to calculate the remaining features used in this work (see Table 2), we refer to Kahl et al. [17] and Liang et al. [24]. Since we use feature combinations with different ranges, we apply feature scaling to prevent undesired feature weighting. Each dimension x in the feature space is scaled using z-score normalization by $x_{\text{scaled}} = \frac{x - \mu}{\sigma}$ with μ being the mean of all training samples and σ being the standard deviation.

3.3 Classifiers

We used four different classifiers in this work: (1) SVM, (2) kNN, (3) RF, and (4) XGBoost. These have been specifically selected for the following reasons: As will become apparent in the following, the number of training samples, i.e. appliance events, is comparably low. The used classifiers generally work quite well on smaller training sets ($< 50k$ samples) compared to e.g. ANN. The number of events differ depending on the appliance type (e.g. more fridge events than iron events) resulting in imbalanced training sets. While kNN is generally invariant to imbalanced data, RF, SVM, and XGBoost can be adapted using class weighting or resampling strategies. Furthermore, all classifiers can be easily adapted to multi-class classification tasks and, due to their low hyper-parameter space, allow a comparably fast retraining. We applied a grid search technique to tune the parameters of each classifier based on the parameter sets listed in Table 1. For all remaining hyper-parameters, the standard values of the *scikit-learn* library are used.

Table 1. Hyper-parameter grid used while tuning each classifier.

Classifier	Parameters	Combinations
*k*NN	$k \in [1, 2, \ldots, 20]$	20
SVM	$C \in [0.01, 0.1, 1, 10, 100, 1000]$	84
	$\gamma \in [10000, 1000, 100, 10, 1, 0.1, 0.01]$	
	$kernel \in [RBF, linear]$	
RF	$max_{depth} \in [10, 20, \ldots, 100]$	40
	$n_{estimators} \in [10, 50, 100, 1000]$	
XGBoost	$\gamma \in [0.5, 1, 1.5]$	9
	$n_{estimators} \in [100, 200, 1000]$	

3.4 Metrics and Cross Validation

For each dataset, all events were shuffled and split into 80% training and 20% test samples (stratified). This allows to estimate the classification score when picking events at random as a potential NILM system would be exposed to. During grid search we applied a 5-fold random stratified split Cross Validation (CV) and averaged the results for an improved generalization estimate. During CV and for the reported scores, the confusion matrix notation in terms of True Positives (TP), True Negatives (TN), False Positives (FP) and False Negatives (FN) is used to calculate Accuracy (Acc), Precision (Pre), Recall (Rec) and F_1 score (F_1) as:

$$Acc = \frac{TP + TN}{TP + TN + FP + FN} \quad (4) \qquad Pre = \frac{TP}{TP + FP} \quad (5)$$

$$Rec = \frac{TP}{TP + FN} \quad (6) \qquad F_1 = \frac{TP}{TP + 0.5 \cdot (FP + FN)} \quad (7)$$

We use macro-averaging and calculate the unweighted means of each metric. Therefore, all classes contribute equally to the average of each metric ensuring that a class with more support in terms of the available number of samples (i.e. events) is not preferred. To simplify evaluation, we treat two different appliances of the same type (e.g. two monitors) as the same target class ($\rightarrow$monitor). Classes with a support of less than 5 samples are removed from the evaluation.

4   Standalone Analysis

In a first step, each feature is evaluated individually by training each classifier solely on a single feature. As Hyper-Parameter Optimization (HPO) is performed for each classifier, each dataset, and each feature individually, a total of $4 \cdot 4 \cdot 27 = 432$ different grid search instances are evaluated. The final results are reported in Table 2 and represent the F_1-scores of the selected models applied to the test set. The results show that some features alone (e.g. VIT, WFA, COT, or HED) already show decent classification capabilities (F_1-score > 0.8) while other features like Positive-Negative half cycle Ratio (PNR) or Periods to Steady State (PSS) stand out with exceptionally poor F_1-scores. As found by Kahl et al. [17] among others, these features may be bad at discerning different appliances but can be used to recognize specific appliances, which exhibit certain electrical characteristics. In the time domain, e.g., the VIT already reached an F_1-score of 0.99 and 0.95 on the laboratory datasets WHITED and PLAID, respectively. Those high scores could not be matched for the FIRED and BLOND datasets, which represent data closer to a real-world scenario. In the spectral domain, the HED achieves comparatively high scores of 0.97 on WHITED and PLAID while again not matching such performance on FIRED (0.89) and BLOND (0.8). Log Attack Time (LAT), PNR, Max-Min Ratio (MAMI), Max-Inrush Ratio (MIR), PSS, and Spectral Flatness (SPF) show a very low average F_1-score ($\oslash < 0.2$). As found by Kahl et al. [17] among others, these features may be bad at distinguishing a larger set of different appliances but can be used to recognize specific appliances, which exhibit certain electrical characteristics. Interestingly, those features (except MAMI) show consistent better results on BLOND and PLAID compared to FIRED and WHITED. Both BLOND and PLAID have a larger inner-class variability compared to FIRED and WHITED indicating that these features might still improve classification performance if more data are available for training.

Table 2. Classification results of a single feature applied to each dataset (WHITED, PLAID, FIRED, and BLOND) using four classifiers (kNN, SVM, RF, and XGBoost (xgb)). HPO using grid search and 5-fold CV has been applied. The features with the highest F_1-scores for each dataset are highlighted bold in the time and spectral domain, respectively.

Feature	Dim.	WHITED				PLAID				FIRED				BLOND				$\oslash$
		knn	svm	rf	xgb	knn	svm	rf	xgb	knn	svm	rf	xgb	knn	svm	rf	xgb	
Time domain																		
Active power (P)	1	0.49	0.45	0.48	0.51	0.58	0.53	0.56	0.57	0.65	0.62	0.63	0.66	0.5	0.49	0.49	0.49	0.54
Reactive power (Q)	1	0.29	0.3	0.31	0.32	0.37	0.41	0.43	0.34	0.47	0.53	0.54	0.52	0.36	0.32	0.36	0.34	0.39
Apparent power (S)	1	0.53	0.49	0.48	0.5	0.45	0.46	0.43	0.43	0.59	0.62	0.62	0.6	0.41	0.42	0.41	0.43	0.49
Resistance (R)	1	0.52	0.5	0.49	0.55	0.43	0.4	0.44	0.46	0.68	0.55	0.66	0.65	0.41	0.42	0.4	0.42	0.5
Admittance (Y)	1	0.51	0.5	0.49	0.55	0.43	0.43	0.44	0.46	0.68	0.63	0.66	0.65	0.41	0.41	0.39	0.42	0.5
Crest factor (CF)	1	0.15	0.17	0.17	0.18	0.38	0.36	0.32	0.39	0.33	0.33	0.32	0.31	0.42	0.31	0.41	0.42	0.31
Form factor (FF)	1	0.27	0.22	0.26	0.26	0.44	0.44	0.43	0.46	0.36	0.3	0.37	0.37	0.34	0.34	0.35	0.33	0.35

(continued)

Table 2. (*continued*)

Feature	Dim.	WHITED				PLAID				FIRED				BLOND				∅
		knn	svm	rf	xgb	knn	svm	rf	xgb	knn	svm	rf	xgb	knn	svm	rf	xgb	
Log attack time (LAT)	1	0.05	0.05	0.05	0.05	0.12	0.16	0.15	0.15	0.1	0.09	0.09	0.09	0.19	0.22	0.23	0.19	0.12
Temporal centroid (TC)	1	0.15	0.17	0.15	0.15	0.38	0.42	0.37	0.42	0.3	0.22	0.23	0.22	0.25	0.23	0.27	0.25	0.26
Positive-negative half cycle ratio (PNR)	1	0.04	0.03	0.09	0.05	0.19	0.18	0.16	0.19	0.19	0.19	0.2	0.19	0.18	0.15	0.18	0.12	0.14
Max-min ratio (MAMI)	1	0.06	0.06	0.06	0.07	0.28	0.26	0.18	0.25	0.28	0.3	0.29	0.32	0.13	0.11	0.12	0.11	0.18
Peak mean ratio (PMR)	1	0.2	0.19	0.16	0.19	0.4	0.3	0.43	0.37	0.38	0.37	0.37	0.39	0.4	0.38	0.42	0.38	0.33
Max-inrush ratio (MIR)	1	0.07	0.04	0.07	0.06	0.16	0.17	0.16	0.14	0.12	0.12	0.11	0.1	0.13	0.13	0.14	0.12	0.12
Mean-variance ratio (MVR)	1	0.21	0.24	0.3	0.28	0.41	0.34	0.36	0.38	0.42	0.41	0.4	0.4	0.33	0.34	0.35	0.32	0.34
Waveform distortion (WFD)	1	0.27	0.24	0.24	0.23	0.35	0.36	0.38	0.39	0.44	0.44	0.43	0.45	0.3	0.31	0.28	0.3	0.34
Period to steady state (PSS)	1	0.01	0.03	0.03	0.03	0.11	0.12	0.12	0.12	0.09	0.12	0.12	0.12	0.11	0.12	0.12	0.12	0.09
Phase angle (cosΦ)	1	0.26	0.24	0.26	0.27	0.48	0.46	0.42	0.49	0.45	0.45	0.43	0.44	0.43	0.44	0.38	0.44	0.4
Inrush current ratio (ICR)	1	0.17	0.07	0.15	0.16	0.27	0.23	0.27	0.36	0.41	0.22	0.44	0.37	0.27	0.25	0.26	0.25	0.26
Waveform approximation (WFA)	20	0.92	0.91	0.93	0.83	0.93	0.92	0.9	0.9	0.91	0.93	0.88	0.84	0.84	0.82	0.75	0.8	**0.88**
Current over time (COT)	25	0.8	0.84	0.93	0.86	0.81	0.72	0.86	0.87	0.88	0.93	**0.95**	0.94	0.8	0.81	0.83	0.83	0.85
V-I Trajectory (VIT)	40	0.93	**0.99**	0.95	0.89	0.91	0.93	**0.95**	0.88	0.7	0.82	0.77	0.72	0.82	**0.85**	0.71	0.78	0.85
Spectral domain																		
Total harmonic distortion (THD)	1	0.37	0.39	0.34	0.37	0.49	0.5	0.48	0.51	0.42	0.4	0.43	0.41	0.38	0.34	0.39	0.38	0.41
Spectral flatness (SPF)	1	0.06	0.07	0.09	0.1	0.2	0.19	0.21	0.22	0.17	0.17	0.15	0.18	0.23	0.21	0.19	0.21	0.17
Odd-even harmonics ratio (OER)	1	0.09	0.09	0.12	0.09	0.26	0.28	0.26	0.3	0.28	0.25	0.26	0.25	0.29	0.25	0.3	0.21	0.22
Spectral centroid (SC)	1	0.12	0.12	0.13	0.14	0.31	0.3	0.25	0.26	0.22	0.2	0.22	0.23	0.33	0.31	0.29	0.3	0.23
Tristimulus (TRI)	3	0.89	0.86	0.86	0.79	0.87	0.82	0.82	0.79	0.77	0.81	0.84	0.77	0.61	0.64	0.63	0.59	0.77
Harmonic energy distribution (HED)	18	0.97	0.93	**0.97**	0.83	**0.97**	0.88	0.94	0.93	0.85	0.85	**0.89**	0.88	0.7	**0.8**	0.77	0.77	**0.87**

Unsurprisingly, features showing better performance have the drawback of a high dimensionality (e.g., 40 for VIT and 20 for WFA). If the focus is shifted towards the best performing scalar features (F_1-score > 0.4), classical electrical features such as P, S, R, Y, $cos\Phi$, and Total Harmonic Distortion (THD) can be identified. It is argued that these features may be of choice for lightweight NILM algorithms deployed on resource constrained systems such as smart meters.

5   Feature Selection

Some of the features already performed quite well in the standalone analysis. However, it can be assumed that the combination of multiple features leads to even better classification scores. While combining all 27 features may result in better classification performance, the number of dimensions should be held small to save computational resources and to prevent performance degradation, which stem from larger feature spaces also known as *the curse of dimensionality.* Therefore, in a second analysis several feature combinations are evaluated based not only on their final classification score but also on their overall dimensionality. While the standalone feature VIT already reaches an F_1-score of up to 0.99 in the experiments, its large dimensionality may hamper a possible application. Furthermore, it might be possible that a combination of multiple features of smaller dimensionality even outperforms VIT. Consequently, a second analysis is conducted for which the combination of several features up to a maximum dimensionality N is examined.

While Principal Component Analysis (PCA) can deliver valuable information about the expressiveness of a certain feature, it does look at each feature dimension individually and, therefore, does not account that other dimensions are already calculated for certain multidimensional features such as e.g. HED. Since an excessive evaluation that considers all possible feature combinations is not feasible ($\sum_{k=0}^{27} \binom{27}{k}$), a simple greedy heuristic i.e. a sequential selection algorithm is used. The algorithm starts by adding the best performing scalar feature ($feat^x$) to a feature set ($F_0 = \{feat^x\}$ with dimensionality $N_0 = 1$). It then evaluates all combinations of F_i with another scalar feature $feat^j$. The best performing combined set ($F_{i+1} = F_i \cup \{feat^j\}$) is stored resulting in a dimensionality of $N_{i+1} = N_i + 1$. It is then checked if any of the possible combinations of non-scalar features (F_{i+1}^{NS}), which result in the same dimensionality N_{i+1}, outperforms F_{i+1}. If this is not the case, the algorithm continues with F_{i+1}, otherwise F_{i+1}^{NS} is used. This process is repeated until a maximum dimensionality N_{max} is reached. The performance of each tested feature set is stored.

6   Combined Analysis

The selection scheme is executed for all 27 features on all datasets with a kNN, SVM, and RF classifier. XGBoost was left out due to its extensive computational requirements and comparable low performance on the standalone feature evaluation (see Table 2). The results of this experiment, which are visualized in Fig. 6, highlight that feature combinations with rather low dimensionality ($N < 10$) already lead to classification scores of over 0.98 on WHITED and PLAID. The evaluation further highlights that the performance on recordings in laboratory setups (PLAID and WHITED) is generally better and more consistent compared to more representative real-world data (FIRED and BLOND). This is, however, expected due to the lower noise-level in laboratory environments.

In this evaluation, all classifiers performed equally well. Only for the BLOND dataset, SVM classifiers outperform the others by quite a margin. Table 3 shows

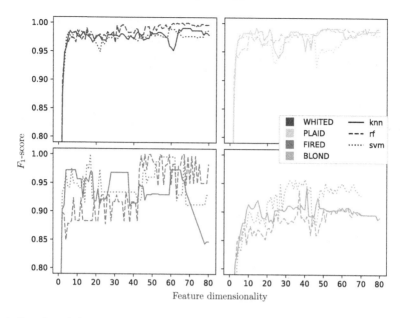

Fig. 6. Results of the proposed feature selection strategy for all classifiers (line styles) and all datasets (line colors).

the specific feature sets that have been chosen by the selection scheme for different dimensionalities N. As a tradeoff between dimensionality, performance, and computational effort, it is proposed to use features up to a dimensionality of 25. The feature set, which has been proposed by the algorithm for $N = 25$ (see Table 3), depends on the used classifier. However, it always includes the features WFA and Tristimulus (TRI). It is decided to supplement these features with P and $cos\Phi$ resulting in the proposed feature set $[P, cos\Phi, TRI, WFA]$. P has already been evaluated in Table 2 as being the best scalar feature with an average F_1-score of 0.54. $cos\Phi$ reoccurs in nearly all feature sets (see Table 3) and is added to accommodate the reactive component, which may be introduced by an appliance. TRI further showed high classification results in Table 2 and represents the only frequency domain feature in the set. TRI is preferred over the actually better performing HED (see Table 2), as it requires only three dimensions instead of 18. From the corresponding formulas, it can be seen that TRI also represents a compressed form of the HED feature. While WFA (with a dimensionality of 20) did not outperform 20 scalar features, its simple calculation and the overall best results obtained in the standalone feature analysis (see Table 2) justifies its inclusion in the set that is finally proposed.

With these four features, the proposed set is of comparatively small dimensionality, computationally lightweight enough for resource constrained systems, and still delivers decent classification results. To emphasize this, the proposed set and the combination of all 27 features was evaluated on all classifiers and datasets. The results are shown in Table 4. A slight performance increase can even be identified if the proposed feature set is used instead of all features due to the *course of dimensionality*. With a dimension reduction from 128 to 25, the proposed set still outperforms the combination of all features, highlighting the effectiveness of the proposed feature set.

Table 3. Used features for selected dimensionalities N of the proposed feature selection strategy. The F_1-scores for each dataset and classifier (Clf.) are shown in addition to the F_1-scores averaged over all datasets.

N	Clf.	Featureset	WHITED	PLAID	FIRED	BLOND	$\varnothing F_1$
5	knn	$P, Y, THD, cos\Phi, OER$	0.98	0.97	0.94	0.82	0.93
5	rf	$P, Y, THD, cos\Phi, MVR$	0.96	0.96	0.93	0.77	0.91
5	svm	$P, Y, THD, cos\Phi, MVR$	0.96	0.98	1.0	0.81	0.93
22	knn	$P, Y, THD, cos\Phi, OER, FF, R, S,$ $PMR, WFD, TC, ICR, MVR, SC, Q, CF,$ $PNR, MAMI, SPF, LAT, PSS, MIR$	0.87	0.96	0.91	0.89	0.91
22	rf	$P, Y, THD, cos\Phi, MVR, WFD, SC,$ $LAT, OER, SPF, ICR, CF, S, PSS,$ $MIR, PNR, R, MAMI, Q, TC, PMR, FF$	0.98	0.97	0.92	0.87	0.93
22	svm	$P, Y, THD, cos\Phi, MVR, CF, R,$ $OER, FF, SC, Q, PMR, S, WFD, SPF,$ $ICR, TC, PNR, MAMI, LAT, PSS, MIR$	0.95	0.96	0.97	0.88	0.94
25	knn	$WFA, TRI, cos\Phi, Y$	0.99	1.0	0.92	0.9	0.95
25	rf	WFA, TRI, LAT, S	0.98	0.98	0.91	0.88	0.94
25	svm	WFA, TRI, S, THD	0.98	0.95	0.93	0.95	0.95
32	knn	$WFA, TRI, cos\Phi, Y, R, OER,$ MVR, THD, P, S, SC	0.99	1.0	0.93	0.89	0.95
32	svm	$WFA, TRI, S, THD, R, CF, Y,$ $cos\Phi, MVR, FF, OER$	0.98	0.97	0.93	0.96	0.96
32	rf	$WFA, TRI, LAT, S, CF, Y, MAMI,$ SC, SPF, MIR, OER	0.98	0.97	0.91	0.89	0.94

The average F_1-scores of the proposed set over all datasets exceed 0.94 independent of the used classifier. The RF classifier performs best with an average F_1-score of 0.98. It is, however, noted that a computationally fairly simple kNN classifier with $k = 1$ already achieves a rather high F_1-score of 0.97 on WHITED and 0.98 on PLAID. kNN is a so called *lazy learning* algorithm that requires no internal parameter tuning except for the choice of the number of neighbors (k) to consider. During training, the complete training set is stored. During inference, a new sample is assigned to the most common class within its k-nearest neighbors. To reduce the required memory of a kNN classifier, which linearly increases with the number of training samples, the Condensed Nearest Neighbor Rule [11] can be applied. Because of its simple training and the ability to reduce the required memory, it is argued that kNN should be the classifier of choice if deployed (including training) on systems with small computational resources such as typical smart meters. However, for systems with sufficient computational power, SVM and RF should be the classifiers of choice. XGBoost has shown enormous potential by leading many machine learning competitions during the recent years [9]. Even though it exhibits the worst performance across all classifiers in the analysis at hand, it is argued that XGBoost might still outperform RF and SVM

Table 4. Classification results for all 27 features and for the proposed feature combination $[P, cos\Phi, TRI, WFA]$. The best results are highlighted in bold.

Clf.	WHITED				PLAID				FIRED				BLOND				$\oslash F_1$
	Pr	Re	Ac	F_1	Pr	Re	Ac	F_1	Pr	Re	Ac	F_1	Pr	Re	Ac	F_1	
Using all 27 feature; overall vector dimension: 128																	
knn	0.97	0.97	0.96	0.97	0.98	0.97	0.97	0.97	0.89	0.87	0.99	0.86	0.94	0.94	0.99	**0.94**	0.93
svm	0.99	0.99	0.99	0.99	0.99	0.98	0.98	0.98	0.91	0.94	1.0	0.92	0.96	0.88	0.99	0.91	0.95
rf	1.0	1.0	0.99	**1.0**	0.99	0.98	0.98	0.98	1.0	0.98	1.0	**0.98**	0.97	0.88	0.99	0.91	**0.97**
xgb	0.97	0.96	0.97	0.96	0.97	0.96	0.97	0.97	0.9	0.87	0.99	0.87	0.95	0.86	0.99	0.89	0.92
Using the feature set $[P, cos\Phi, TRI, WFA]$; overall vector dimension: 25																	
knn	0.97	0.97	0.96	0.97	0.98	0.98	0.98	0.98	0.91	0.92	0.99	0.91	0.95	0.89	0.99	0.91	0.94
svm	0.98	0.97	0.97	0.97	0.96	0.96	0.95	0.96	0.92	0.95	1.0	0.93	0.94	0.96	0.99	0.95	0.95
rf	0.99	0.99	0.98	**0.99**	1.0	0.99	0.99	**0.99**	1.0	0.98	1.0	**0.98**	0.96	0.95	0.99	**0.95**	**0.98**
xgb	0.94	0.91	0.93	0.91	0.97	0.96	0.97	0.97	1.0	0.97	1.0	0.98	0.95	0.86	0.98	0.89	0.94

for other hyperparameter choices as the ones tested during these evaluations (see the used grid search parameters in Table 1). However, due to its large hyperparameter space and, therefore, extensive training time, RF and SVM were selected in favor, representing a tradeoff between the required training time and possible gain in classification performance. Figure 7 shows the confusion matrix of the RF classifier using the proposed feature set on the PLAID dataset (the corresponding performance metrics are shown in Table 4. Despite the overall F_1-score of 0.98, only some appliances with rotary motors (fan, heater, and air conditioner) are confused with one another. Due to the outstanding performance of

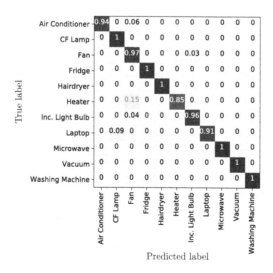

Fig. 7. Confusion matrix of a RF classifier with the feature set $[P, cos\Phi, TRI, WFA]$ applied to the PLAID dataset.

the RF classifier with the feature set $[P, cos\Phi, TRI, WFA]$, it is proposed to use their combination as a benchmarking algorithm when comparing novel appliance classification algorithms, similar to the low-frequency disaggregation algorithms that have been implemented as benchmarks in NILMTK [3].

7 Conclusion

In this work, we used four electricity datasets recorded at higher sampling rates to evaluate 27 features and four classifiers for the task of event classification. The best standalone features are P and WFA with corresponding F_1-scores of 0.54 and 0.88, respectively. A feature selection algorithm revealed the feature set $[P, cos\Phi, TRI, WFA]$ for a desired dimensionality of 25. This set achieved F_1-scores of 0.98 on average using a RF classifier. As all classifiers appeared to be suitable, the performance of classifier ensembles should be investigated in future work.

References

1. Anderson, K., et al.: BLUED: a fully labeled public dataset for event-based non-intrusive load monitoring research. In: Proceedings of the 2nd KDD Workshop on Data Mining Applications in Sustainability (SustKDD), vol. 7. ACM (2012)
2. Anderson, K.D., Berges, M.E., Ocneanu, A., Benitez, D., Moura, J.M.: Event detection for Non Intrusive load monitoring. IECON Proceedings (Industrial Electronics Conference), pp. 3312–3317 (2012). https://doi.org/10.1109/IECON.2012.6389367
3. Batra, N., et al.: NILMTK: an open source toolkit for non-intrusive load monitoring. In: Proceedings of the 5th International Conference on Future Energy Systems, pp. 265–276. ACM (2014)
4. Davies, P., Dennis, J., Hansom, J., Martin, W., Stankevicius, A., Ward, L.: Deep neural networks for appliance transient classification. In: IEEE International Conference on Acoustics, Speech and Signal Processing (ICASSP) (2019)
5. De Baets, L., Ruyssinck, J., Develder, C., Dhaene, T., Deschrijver, D.: Appliance classification using vi trajectories and convolutional neural networks. Energy Build. **158**, 32–36 (2018)
6. Faustine, A., et al.: UNet-NILM: a deep neural network for multi-tasks appliances state detection and power estimation in NILM. In: Proceedings of the 5th International Workshop on Non-Intrusive Load Monitoring (2020)
7. Gao, J., Giri, S., Kara, E.C., Bergés, M.: Plaid: a public dataset of high-resolution electrical appliance measurements for load identification research. In: proceedings of the 1st ACM Conference on Embedded Systems for Energy-Efficient Buildings (2014)
8. Gao, J., Kara, E.C., Giri, S., Bergés, M.: A feasibility study of automated plug-load identification from high-frequency measurements. In: IEEE Global Conference on Signal and Information Processing (GlobalSIP) (2015)
9. GitHub: Xgboost - extreme gradient boosting (2020). https://github.com/dmlc/xgboost/tree/master/demo#machine-learning-challenge-winning-solutions. List of Machine Learning Challenge Winners based on XGBoost

10. Hart, G.W.: Nonintrusive appliance load monitoring. Proc. IEEE **80**(12), 1870–1891 (1992)
11. Hart, P.: The condensed nearest neighbor rule (CORRESP). IEEE Trans. Inf. Theory. **14**(3), 515–516 (1968)
12. Hassan, T., Javed, F., Arshad, N.: An empirical investigation of VI trajectory based load signatures for non-intrusive load monitoring. IEEE Trans. Smart Grid **5**(2), 870–878 (2013)
13. Huber, P., Calatroni, A., Rumsch, A., Paice, A.: Review on deep neural networks applied to low-frequency NILM. Energies **14**(9), 2390 (2021). https://doi.org/10.3390/en14092390
14. Jorde, D., Kriechbaumer, T., Jacobsen, H.A.: Electrical appliance classification using deep convolutional neural networks on high frequency current measurements. In: IEEE International Conference on Communications, Control, and Computing Technologies for Smart Grids (SmartGridComm) (2018)
15. Kahl, M., Haq, A.U., Kriechbaumer, T., Jacobsen, H.A.: WHITED - A worldwide household and industry transient energy data set. In: 3rd International Workshop on Non-Intrusive Load Monitoring (2016)
16. Kahl, M., Kriechbaumer, T., Haq, A.U., Jacobsen, H.A.: Appliance classification across multiple high frequency energy datasets. In: IEEE International Conference on Smart Grid Communications (SmartGridComm) (2017)
17. Kahl, M., Ul Haq, A., Kriechbaumer, T., Jacobsen, H.A.: A comprehensive feature study for appliance recognition on high frequency energy data. In: Proceedings of the 8th ACM International Conference on Future Energy Systems (2017)
18. Kelly, J., Knottenbelt, W.: The UK-dale dataset, domestic appliance-level electricity demand and whole-house demand from five UK homes. Sci. Data **2**, 150007 (2015)
19. Kim, J.G., Lee, B.: Appliance classification by power signal analysis based on multi-feature combination multi-layer LSTM. Energies **12**(14), 2804 (2019)
20. Kolter, J.Z., Johnson, M.J.: REDD: a public data set for energy disaggregation research. In: Workshop on Data Mining Applications in Sustainability (SIGKDD), San Diego, CA, vol. 25, pp. 59–62 (2011)
21. Kolter, Z., Jaakkola, T., Kolter, J.Z.: Approximate inference in additive factorial HMMs with application to energy disaggregation. In: Proceedings of the International Conference on Artificial Intelligence and Statistics, pp. 1472–1482 (2012). http://people.csail.mit.edu/kolter/lib/exe/fetch.php?media=pubs:kolter-aistats12.pdf
22. Kriechbaumer, T., Jacobsen, H.A.: BLOND, a building-level office environment dataset of typical electrical appliances. Sci. Data **5**, 180048 (2018)
23. Lam, H.Y., Fung, G., Lee, W.: A novel method to construct taxonomy electrical appliances based on load signatures. IEEE Trans. Consum. Electron. **53**(2), 653–660 (2007)
24. Liang, J., Ng, S.K., Kendall, G., Cheng, J.W.: Load signature study-part i: basic concept, structure, and methodology. IEEE Trans. Power. Deliv. **25**, 551–560 (2010)
25. Makonin, S., Popowich, F., Bajic, I.V., Gill, B., Bartram, L.: Exploiting HMM sparsity to perform online real-time nonintrusive load monitoring. IEEE Trans. Smart Grid (2015). https://doi.org/10.1109/TSG.2015.2494592
26. Sadeghianpourhamami, N., Ruyssinck, J., Deschrijver, D., Dhaene, T., Develder, C.: Comprehensive feature selection for appliance classification in NILM. Energy Build.? **151**, 98–106 (2017)

27. Völker, B., Pfeifer, M., Scholl, P.M., Becker, B.: Annoticity: a smart annotation tool and data browser for electricity datasets. In: Proceedings of the 5th International Workshop on Non-Intrusive Load Monitoring, pp. 1–5 (2020)
28. Völker, B., Pfeifer, M., Scholl, P.M., Becker, B.: FIRED: A fully labeled high-frequency electricity disaggregation dataset. In: Proceedings of the 7th ACM International Conference on Systems for Energy-Efficient Buildings, Cities, and Transportation (2020)
29. Wang, A.L., Chen, B.X., Wang, C.G., Hua, D.: Non-intrusive load monitoring algorithm based on features of v–i trajectory. Elect. Power Syst. Res. **157**, 134–144 (2018)
30. Weiss, M., Helfenstein, A., Mattern, F., Staake, T.: Leveraging smart meter data to recognize home appliances. In: IEEE International Conference on Pervasive Computing and Communications (2012)
31. Wild, B., Barsim, K.S., Yang, B.: A new unsupervised event detector for non-intrusive load monitoring. In: 2015 IEEE Global Conference on Signal and Information Processing (GlobalSIP), pp. 73–77 (2015)
32. Yang, C.C., Soh, C.S., Yap, V.V.: A systematic approach in appliance disaggregation using k-nearest neighbours and naive bayes classifiers for energy efficiency. Energy Effic. **11**(1), 239–259 (2018)
33. Zoha, A., Gluhak, A., Imran, M.A., Rajasegarar, S.: Non-intrusive load monitoring approaches for disaggregated energy sensing: a survey. Sensors **12**(12), 16838–16866 (2012)

Power Quality; Power Electronics

Computer Studies of the Operation of a Three-Phase Four Wire Shunt Active Power Filter Applied to the Industry

Bruno Nova, Diogo Vaz, Paulo Passos$^{(\boxtimes)}$, and Nelson Andrade

Centro ALGORITMI, University of Minho, Guimaraes, Portugal
{bruno.nova,diogo.vaz,paulo.passos}@algoritmi.uminho.pt,
nelson.andrade@pt.bosch.com

Abstract. As the industry progresses, power quality problems become more and more relevant. The increase of non-linear loads in industries, leads to higher current harmonic distortion and low power factor. In order to mitigate these problems, this paper validates a shunt active power filter (SAPF). The adopted topology and its control algorithm are analyzed through computer simulations considering real industrial load models, which were elaborated from data collected in power quality analyzers that were connected to different points of an industry.

The results achieved validate the correct operation of the applied SAPF, as well as it presents the improvements obtained of the total current distortion and neutral current.

Keywords: Industry 4.0 · Power electronics · Power quality · Shunt active power filter

1 Introduction

The evolution of the industry and the consequent increase of non-linear loads on the factory facilities, increase the associated electrical power quality problems, namely harmonic distortion and low power factor [1]. These problems translate into unbalanced currents and excessive current in the neutral conductor, which can lead to overeating and deterioration of the installation. Furthermore, the harmonics and unbalances propagate to the voltages eventually causing the equipment malfunction [2].

With the arrival of industry 4.0, which aims to increasingly integrate sensors and smart meters designed to obtain large amounts of data from different variables of the facility, there is an opportunity to carry out more detailed analyses on the operation of installed equipment as well as the impact exerted under the quality of the electrical energy of the installation [3, 4].

Supplementary Information The online version contains supplementary material available at https://doi.org/10.1007/978-3-030-97027-7_8.

J. L. Afonso et al. (Eds.): SESC 2021, LNICST 425, pp. 119–140, 2022.
https://doi.org/10.1007/978-3-030-97027-7_8

Traditionally, passive LC filters and capacitor banks are used to mitigate power quality problems. However, these solutions are usually not adaptable to dynamic loads and tend to be robust and expensive [5, 6]. Given that, today's industry is designed not to consume reactive power, capacitor banks can present themselves as harmful solutions for the system, because they can contribute to increase the harmonic distortion of the system.

The shunt active power filters (SAPF) have been increasingly adopted due to their ability to perform real-time compensation. Depending on the control theory and hardware topology, it is possible to compensate in real time the harmonic currents, current unbalances as well as the low power factor [7]. The SAPF used in this study presents a three-phase four-wire power electronics converter. The Fryze-Buchholz-Depenbrock theory is used to calculate the reference currents to carry out the correct power management of the system [8]. In order to obtain results from real factory situations, the real loads of the factory, that is, production lines and electrical switchboards, were modeled in order to understand the effectiveness and benefits of the application of the SAPF. These loads are modeled in simulation using data collected by sensors employed at the factory.

Thus, this paper is divided into 6 sections. Section 1 presents the introduction to the paper as well as the topics approached. Section 2 presents the topology of the applied SAPF and its operation. Section 3 deals with the control algorithms used to control powers and currents. Section 4 refers to the reconstruction of the loads used, which is based on data provided by the factory sensors. Section 5 presents the simulation developed as well as the results obtained. Finally, Sect. 6 presents the conclusions regarding the results obtained in simulation.

2 Shunt Active Power Filter

A shunt active power filter (SAPF) is an equipment connected in parallel to the electrical power grid functioning as a current source, used to compensate in real time, harmonics, current unbalances (in the case of three-phase installations) and power factor of an installation, through the production of reactive power and harmonic currents [9, 10]. A SAPF can be single-phase or three-phase. The purpose of a SAPF is to make the currents in the electrical power grid sinusoidal and in phase with the power grid voltages, balance the current of the three phases which leading to a practically null neutral current [8, 11]. The aim is to supply, from the electrical power grid to the loads, only the necessary active power. A SAPF allows a dynamic response, adjusting itself to the needs of the load and the conditions of the electrical power grid [12]. As a result of the operation of a SAPF, when compensating the current harmonics, it allows the decrease of the harmonic distortion of the grid voltage, as well as reducing the losses in the conductors. Since the RMS values of the currents are reduced, the losses in the conductors are also decreased.

There are several hardware topologies for the SAPF such as a three-wire converter with one dc-link, a three-wire converter with two dc-links, where the neutral is connected to the midpoint of the two dc-links, and the four-wire converter topology here the neutral conductor connects to the fourth leg [13].

The chosen SAPF topology for this study consists of a two-level four-wire voltage source inverter (VSI), which uses 08 IGBTs and a capacitor in the dc-link. The use of a four-wire topology allows to compensate for the neutral current. Figure 1 shows the block diagram of the three-phase four-wire SAPF. The inductance (L) is used to connect the inverter to the power grid.

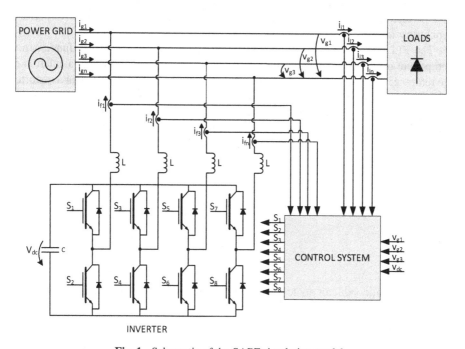

Fig. 1. Schematic of the SAPF simulation model.

By using sensors to measure the loads currents, the currents in the SAPF and the power grid voltages, the control system generates the gate signals to the switching devices, so that the currents in the grid (i_{g1}, i_{g2}, i_{g3}) are balanced and in phase with the voltages (v_{g1}, v_{g2}, v_{g3}) and the current in the neutral (i_{gn}) is practically zero.

3 Control Algorithm

The purpose of the SAPF is to compensate harmonic currents present in the load side. To calculate the compensation reference currents, the Fryze-Buchholz-Depenbrock (FBD) power theory is used. This power theory is implemented in the time domain and is based on the idea of representing a load by its conductance in parallel with a harmonic current source and a reactive element [14]. The conductance corresponds to the power component of the load that the grid must supply, i.e., the active power. To applicate this theory, it is calculated the average value of the total instantaneous power consumed by the loads, which correspond to the active power. The active power is divided by three, to be equally divided by the three phases. The explanation of the next steps of the FBD theory, will be done for one phase and for the other two phases the procedure is the same, being only replicated [15].

Knowing that the conductance is the inverse of the resistance and knowing the active power value for each phase (P_1) and the power grid RMS voltage (V_{G1}), the conductance is defined by Eq. (1). To calculate the value of the reference current (i_{g1ref}) Eq. (2) is applied, where v_g is the instantaneous value of the voltage. Since the grid voltage may be distorted, a phase locked-loop (PLL) algorithm is applied in order to perform synchronization with the grid voltage.

The PLL algorithm produces a sinusoidal signal in phase with the fundamental component of the grid voltage [16]. The produced signal is used for the calculation of the reference current, allowing the reference current to be sinusoidal even for a distorted voltage. Replacing in Eq. (2) the grid voltage by the PLL (v_{pll1}) gives Eq. (3). Knowing the reference current for the grid and the current at the loads (i_{l1}), apply Eq. (4) to calculate the reference current for the SAPF (i_{f1ref}), and this reference current is then applied on the current control.

$$G_1 = \frac{P_1}{V_{G1}^2} \tag{1}$$

$$i_{g1ref} = G_1 v_{g1} \tag{2}$$

$$i_{g1ref} = G_1 v_{pll1} \tag{3}$$

$$i_{f1ref} = i_{l1} - i_{g1ref} \tag{4}$$

For the semiconductor switching, the periodic sampling technique is applied. This technique is widely used and it is simple to implement. Figure 2 shows the block diagram. This technique defines a maximum value for switching frequency, not having a fixed switching frequency [17].

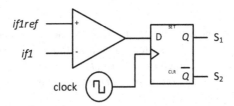

Fig. 2. Schematic of the periodic sampling switching technique.

The periodic sampling technique works as follows, when the reference current (i_{f1ref}) is higher than the SAPF current (i_{f1}), the S_1 semiconductor is switched ON and the S_2 semiconductor is switched OFF. If the reference current is lower than the current in the filter the bottom semiconductor is switched ON. The clock frequency has been set to 100 kHz, meaning that the maximum switching frequency is 50 kHz.

4   Industrial Loads

As the factory under analysis has taken a step forward into the industry 4.0, it has employed different power quality analyzers throughout its system. These analyzers (sensors), allow a more precise analysis of the installed electrical system. As such, data of the RMS values of the voltage, current and their waveforms, harmonic distortion, power factor, among others, are taken.

With this data it is possible to define the different loads both theoretically, resorting to the manufacturer's datasheets, and practically through the data recorded at regular intervals (programmed by the user). It is also possible to check the data and waveforms in real time. Thus, in the case study used for this situation, there are very different loads, but these will be divided into two groups, air conditioning system (HVAC) and line productions switchboards (electrical switchboards). Note that only these main loads are considered, as they are the ones with the highest power consumption and make the study more generic.

4.1 HVAC System

The air conditioning system consists of two switchboards where four air treatment units (ATUs) are connected in each, and five equal independent chillers. The ATUs are divided into two switchboards due to belonging to different areas of the industrial complex and the five chillers are distributed throughout the industrial complex.

Regarding the ATUs there are two types, which are presented in Table 1. The data presented are taken from the builder's plates. In one of the tables there are four type 1 ATUs and in the other table there are four type 2 ATUs. In Table 1, it is also presented the type of chiller applied as well as its characteristics.

Table 1. Characteristics of ATU of type 1, type 2 and chillers.

	Voltage (V)	Frequency (Hz)	Power (kW)	Current (A)	Power factor
Type 1	400	50	23	33.53	0.99
Type 2	400	50	24.6	–	–
Chiller	400	50	326.8	497	0.95

Through the analyzers, it was possible to extract other data about these two switchboards of the HVAC system. A complete month of the year 2021 was analyzed and the monthly average value was taken for the current consumed, apparent power, harmonic distortion of the current (THD%I) and power factor. In the case of the switchboard of ATU type 1. The Table 2 presents the summarized data for selected month. Note that in this month this switchboard presents a current unbalance between the three phases of 2.11% and that the variable L1, L2, L3 refers to the three phases of the system.

In Table 3, it is presented the same data that was shown for the Type 2 switchboard. In this type 2 switchboard an average monthly current unbalance of 1.43% was calculated.

In addition to these calculated data, it was possible to obtain the waveform of these two at specific frames, through an Excel file generated by the analyzers with several points of the current waveform. In Fig. 3 and Fig. 4, the current in the Type 1 and Type 2 switchboard is presented, where the currents of phases L1, L2 L3 and neutral (N) are shown.

Table 2. Monthly average value of current, apparent power, THD%I and power factor of the ATU type 1.

Month average	L1	L2	L3
I_{RMS} (A)	187.92	193.65	194.84
Power (kVA)	39.6	40.93	41.61
THD%I (%)	43.51	41.68	39.17
Power factor	0.90	0.91	0.91

Table 3. Monthly average value of current, apparent power, THD%I and power factor of the ATU type 2.

Month average	L1	L2	L3
I_{RMS} (A)	145.47	146.77	147.29
Power (kVA)	30.6	30.85	30.85
THD%I (%)	42.33	42.57	41.51
Power factor	0.90	0.91	0.90

For the five chillers, only one was analyzed due to the fact that they are all equal. The same happens to the two HVAC switchboards. So, through the data recorded by the analyzers, over the same month, and applying a monthly average, Table 4 is obtained. In addition to this data, the current unbalance calculated through the monthly data of the currents of the three phases resulted in 4.44% unbalance between the three phases, although the monthly average value of the current does not show this unbalance. The waveform of this chiller, in operation, can be seen in Fig. 5.

4.2 Electrical Switchboard

The electrical switchboards are used to ensure a better management and protection of the production lines throughout the case study analyzed. In general, in each switchboard it is possible to connect about four production lines, thus allowing a better protection of each line (because it can be made individual protection of machines and the application of smaller protections) and facilitating the management of them each time it is necessary to make adjustments. For this case study, an electrical switchboard is considered, which is normally the set of four production lines. For a brief contextualization, one of the production lines analyzed contains three-phase and single-phase machines. In the set of three-phase machines there is a combination of maximum theoretical power of 98.2 kVA, in the set of single-phase machines of 6.7 kVA and a THD%I between 5.5% and 6.5%.

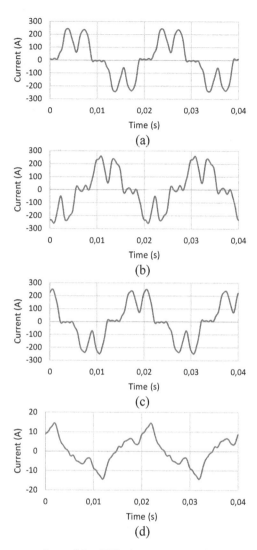

Fig. 3. Current waveform of the ATU of type 1: (a) L1 (b) L2 (c) L3 (d) neutral.

That said, and as presented in the previous section, the monthly average value of the consumed current, apparent power, harmonic distortion of the current and power factor was done through the power quality analyzers. Table 5 presents the monthly average values. It was possible to calculate the unbalance between the phases of the electric board, which resulted in an unbalance of about 7.17%.

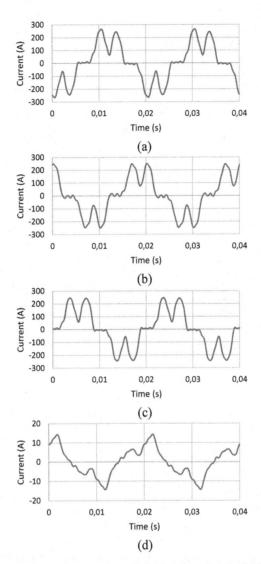

Fig. 4. Current waveform of the ATU of type 2: (a) L1 (b) L2 (c) L3 (d) neutral.

In addition to these values calculated using the data recorded by the analyzers, the waveform of the current for an instant, from the analyzed switchboard, was also taken. This waveform is shown in Fig. 6.

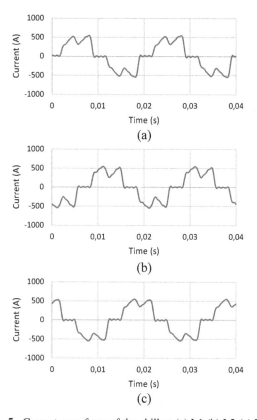

Fig. 5. Current waveform of the chiller: (a) L1 (b) L2 (c) L3.

Table 4. Monthly average value of current, apparent power, THD%I and power factor of the chiller.

Month average	L1	L2	L3
I_{RMS} (A)	41.94	42.52	43.57
Power (kW)	8.6	8.72	8.87
THD%I (%)	30.8	56.17	53.71
Power factor	0.71	0.75	0.43

Table 5. Monthly average value of current, apparent power, THD%I and power factor of the electrical switchboard.

Month average	L1	L2	L3
I_{RMS} (A)	157.6	139.98	161.51
Power (kVA)	36.89	32.08	37.39
THD%I (%)	11.63	13.12	13.62
Power factor	0.98	0.98	0.98

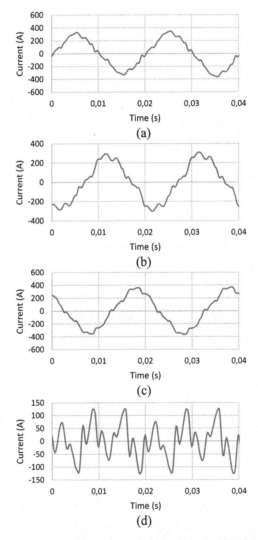

Fig. 6. Current waveform of the electrical switchboard: (a) L1 (b) L2 (c) L3 (d) neutral.

5 Simulation and Results

In Sect. 2 was presented the electrical scheme of the SAPF used in this study. In order to validate its correct functioning with the factory loads, two different situations were designed. For both situations the SAPF only starts its operation after the instant of 0.2 s and the considered loads are: 5 chiller equipment, 2 HVAC electrical switchboards and 10 electrical switchboard that provide power to the production lines.

– Scenario 1: In the first approach, it was considered that there are 5 chillers and 12 electrical switchboards in operation, however, it is considered that the 5 chillers and 2 HVAC electrical switchboards are on the load side and the remaining 10 electrical switchboards are on the grid side. This means that the 5 chillers and the 2 HVAC electrical switchboards are being compensated by the SAPF and that the remaining 10 electrical switchboards are not compensated.

– Scenario 2: In a second approach the inverse is done, that is, the 5 chillers and the 2 HVAC electrical switchboards are now on the grid side and the remaining 10 electrical switchboards are on the load side. Thus, the 10 switchboards are being compensated by the developed SAPF while the 5 chillers and HVAC switchboards are not compensated.

In order to simulate these two scenarios, it was necessary to create models of the factory loads. To do this, the data provided by the installed sensors was collected, where the Fast Fourier Transform (FFT) was applied, in order to obtain the values of magnitude and phase for each harmonic component associated to currents in the production lines, electrical switchboards and HVAC equipment and also the voltages of the transformers in parallel. The Fig. 7 presents the voltage values of transformer 1 and transformer 3 when both are operating in parallel.

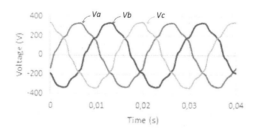

Fig. 7. Voltage waveform of the coupling point of transformer 1 and 3.

In this situation the voltage values for L1 are 231.1 V, L2 is 229.8 V and L3 is 232.7 V. It is also noted that the THD values recorded are 5.7% for L1, 6.34% for L2 and 6.35% for L3.

In Sect. 5.1 and Sect. 5.2 it is presented the results obtained for both Scenario 1 and Scenario 2 respectively.

5.1 Scenario 1

In this scenario, all the proposed loads are connected to the system, but only the 5 chillers and the 2 HVAC switchboards are being compensated. The results presented in Fig. 8 are the grid currents, when considering all the connected loads.

The Fig. 8 shows the grid currents waveforms for before and after the SAPF operation.

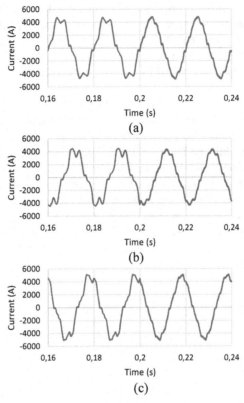

Fig. 8. Current waveform of the power grid, before and after the SAPF is turn-on in instant 0.2 s: (a) L1 (b) L2 (c) L3.

Before the SAPF operation, the grid currents present values of 3168 A at L1, 2933 A at L2 and 3370 A at L3. With regard to THD%I, it should be noted that this presents a value of 16.38% at L1, 20.59% at L2 and 16.70% at L3. Subsequently, it is possible to observe the compensation of the currents carried out by the SAPF, where a grid-side current of 3132 A at L1, 2851 A at L2 and 3328 A are recorded. The THD%I is significantly reduced to 7.8% at L1, 8.94% at L2 and 7.35% at L3. Table 6 presents these results.

Figure 9 presents the grid reference currents that are calculated by the implemented control algorithm.

Table 6. THD%I and grid current values before and after the parcial compensation of the loads.

	Before compensation		After compensation	
	THD%I	Current values (A)	THD%I	Current values (A)
L1	16.38	3168	7.8	3132
L2	20.59	2933	8.94	2851
L3	16.70	3370	7.35	3328

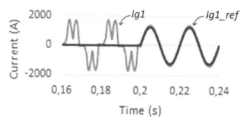

Fig. 9. Current waveform of the power grid *Ig1* and the reference *Ig1_ref* generated by the control system.

Figure 10 shows the current waveforms of the loads that will be compensated. These loads are the chiller and the 2 HVAC electrical switchboards. It can be observed that at this point the current values are 1011 A at L1, 1042 A at L2 and 1015 A at L3. Regarding the THD%I values, 46.89% is observed for L1, 45.06% for L2, and 44.68% for L3. After 0.2 s the moment when the SAPF begins to act, it can be seen that the current and THD%I values are reduced. There is a current value of 915 A at L1, 918 A at L2 and 918 A at L3. THD%I has been reduced to 3.98% for L1, 4.06% for L2 and 3.96% for L3. Such results are highlighted in Table 7.

Figure 11 shows the waveform of the reference currents produced by the control system and applied to the SAPF.

Figure 12 shows the current produced by the SAPF in order to compensate the current of the loads. In this case the loads to compensate are the chiller and HVAC electrical switchboards.

It can be seen that the values of the currents produced by the SAPF are 437.1 A at L1, 431.3 A at L2 and 419 A at L3.

Figure 13 shows the current values present in the neutral before and after the SAPF operation.

It can be seen that before the SAPF operation the neutral current value is 642 A, and that after the SAPF operation (instant 0.2 s) the neutral current value is reduced to 65.7 A.

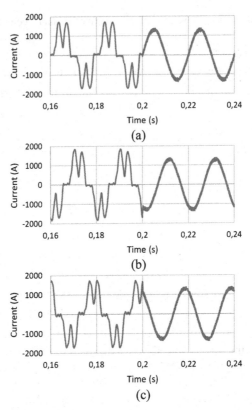

Fig. 10. Current waveforms of the combination of chillers and HVAC loads, before and after the SAPF is turned-on, in instant 0.2 s: (a) L1 (b) L2 (c) L3.

Table 7. THD%I and loads current values before and after filter's action.

	Before compensation		After compensation	
	THD%I	Current values (A)	THD%I	Current values (A)
L1	46.89	1011	3.98	915
L2	45.06	1042	4.06	918
L3	44.68	1015	3.96	918

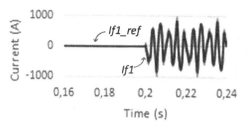

Fig. 11. Current waveform of the active power SAPF *If1* and the reference generated by control system *If1_ref*, for the chillers and HVAC system.

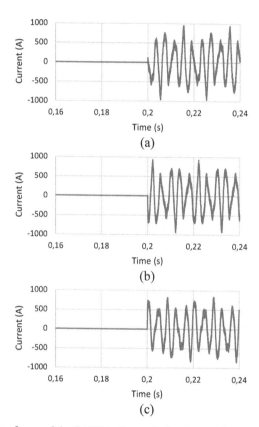

Fig. 12. Current waveforms of the SAPF, before and after it starts its compensation: (a) L1 (b) L2 (c) L3.

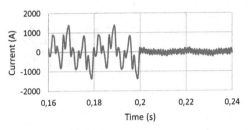

Fig. 13. Current waveform of neutral line, before and after the SAPF is turned-on in instant 0.2 s.

5.2 Scenario 2

In this second scenario, all the mentioned loads are connected to the system, but only the 10 electrical switchboards are being compensated. The results presented in Fig. 14 are the grid currents, when considering all the connected loads.

Figure 14 shows the grid-side current values before and after the SAPF operation.

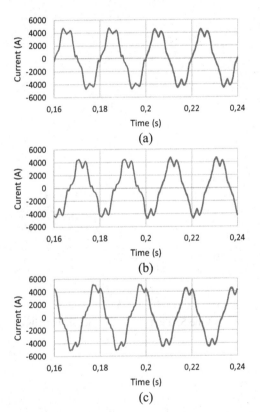

Fig. 14. Current waveform of the power grid, before and after the SAPF is turned-on in instant 0.2 s: (a) L1 (b) L2 (c) L3.

Before the SAPF operation, current values of 3168 A at L1, 2933 A at L2 and 3370 A at L3 are presented. Regarding THD%I, values of 16.38% at L1, 20.59% at L2 and 16.70% at L3 are presented. At instant 0.2 s the SAPF is active and compensating. After this instant the values of current and THD%I are reduced. It can be observed current values of 3041 A at L1, 3076 A at L2 and 3051 A at L3. Regarding THD%I, values of 14.34% at L1, 14.14% at L3 and 13.82% at L3 are presented. Table 8 presents these results.

Table 8. THD%I and grid current values before and after the filter's action.

	Before compensation		After compensation	
	THD%I	Current values (A)	THD%I	Current values (A)
L1	16.38	3168	14.34	3041
L2	20.59	2933	14.14	3076
L3	16.70	3370	13.82	3051

Figure 15 illustrates the reference current generated by the control system in order to compensate the currents on the grid side.

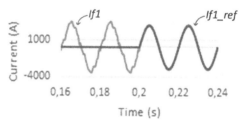

Fig. 15. Current waveform of the SAPF *If1* and the reference generated by control system *If1_ref*, for the electrical switchboard.

Figure 16 presents the current values to be compensated by the SAPF (before 0.2 s). In this case, this current refers to the electrical switchboards.

Figure 16 shows the currents before and after the operation of the SAPF. It can be seen that before the SAPF actuation, the current values are of 2225 A at L1, 1940 A at L2 and 2416 A at L3 are presented. Regarding THD%I values of 11.09% at L1, 13.36% at L2 and 10.22% at L3 are presented. At instant 0.2 s the SAPF becomes active and begins to compensate. After this instant the values of current and THD%I are reduced and current values of 2097 A at L1, 2097 A at L2 and 2097 A at L3 are observed. Regarding THD%I, values of 1.70% at L1, 1.70% at L2 and 1.70% at L3 are presented. Table 9 presents these results.

Figure 17 shows the reference current calculated by the control system and which is applied to the SAPF.

Figure 18 presents the SAPF current value which is of 346.7 A at L1, 337.8 A at L2 and 415.6 A at L3.

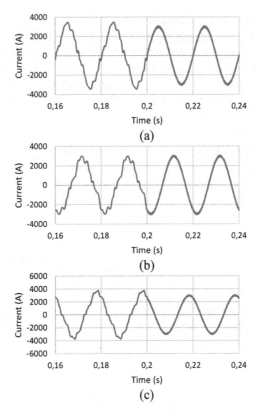

Fig. 16. Current waveforms of the electrical switchboards, before and after the SAPF is turned-on at instant 0.2 s: (a) L1 (b) L2 (c) L3.

Table 9. THD%I and loads current values before and after the filter's action.

	Before compensation		After compensation	
	THD%I	Current values (A)	THD%I	Current values (A)
L1	11.09	2225	1.70	2097
L2	13.36	1940	1.70	2097
L3	10.22	2416	1.70	2097

Figure 19 shows the neutral current before and after the SAPF operation.

It can be seen that before the SAPF actuation the current value is 640 A and that after the SAPF actuation, this current is reduced to 37.2 A.

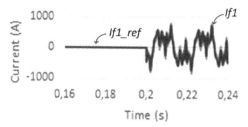

Fig. 17. Current waveform of the SAPF *If1* and the reference generated by control system *If1_ref*, for the electrical switchboards.

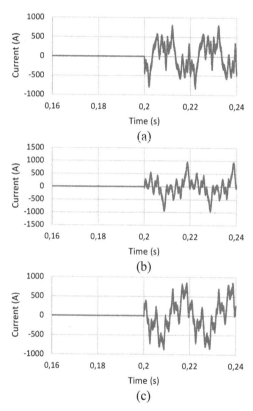

Fig. 18. Current waveforms of the SAPF, before and after it starts its compensation: (a) L1 (b) L2 (c) L3.

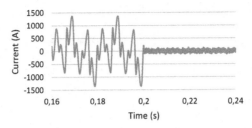

Fig. 19. Current waveform of neutral line, before and after the SAPF is turned-on in instant 0.2 s.

6   Conclusions

After analyzing the results obtained in simulation of the two different scenarios, it is possible to verify a reduction of THD%I, a reduction of the current in the neutral, as well as a balance of currents among the three phases.

In the simulation presented in Sect. 5.1, there is a reduction of about 42% of THD%I recorded after the operation of the SAPF, and a reduction of about 53.3% of the current in the neutral conductor.

Regarding the simulation presented in Sect. 5.2, there is a reduction of about 10% after the operation of the SAPF, and a reduction of about 94.2% of the current present in the neutral conductor.

It can also be seen that after the SAPF operation, the currents always present quite identical values throughout the three phases of the system, which translates into a balanced system. If two SAPF were applied, one for the production lines and another for the HVAC system, it is assumed that the reduction of THD%I and neutral current would be even higher.

Thus, with the reduction of THD%I and consequent reduction of the neutral current, problems associated with the malfunction of the machines in the factory will be avoided. Also, since there is less current circulating in the neutral conductor, it's overheating is avoid.

There will also be monetary savings associated with the cost of electricity. Even though the active power is maintained, the overall system's current is decreased. This results in fewer losses in the conductors and transformers. So, according to the results presented, the installation of the SAPF brings technical benefits to the electrical installation of the industrial complex.

In summary, this article aims to present the benefits that a SAPF can bring to the plant installation, in order to prevent problems derived from harmonics and unbalances.

Acknowledgment. This work is supported by: European Structural and Investment Funds in the FEDER component, through the Operational Competitiveness and Internationalization Programme (COMPETE 2020) [Project n° 39479; Funding Reference: POCI-01-0247-FEDER-39479].

References

1. Akagi, H.: New trends in active filters for improving power quality. In: Proceedings of IEEE International Conference on Power Electronics, Drives and Energy Systems for Industrial Growth, PEDES, vol. 1, pp. 417–425 (1996). https://doi.org/10.1109/pedes.1996.539652
2. Lin, Z., Li, G., Zhou, M., Lo, K.L.: Economic evaluation of real-time power quality cost. In: Proceedings of Universities Power Engineering Conference, pp. 11–15 (2010)
3. Shrouf, F., Ordieres, J., Miragliotta, G.: Smart factories in Industry 4.0: a review of the concept and of energy management approached in production based on the Internet of Things paradigm. In: IEEE International Conference on Industrial Engineering and Engineering Management, pp. 697–701, January 2015. https://doi.org/10.1109/IEEM.2014.7058728
4. Mohamed, N., Al-Jaroodi, J., Lazarova-Molnar, S.: Industry 4.0: opportunities for enhancing energy efficiency in smart factories. In: SysCon 2019 - 13th Annual IEEE International Systems Conference Proceedings (2019). https://doi.org/10.1109/SYSCON.2019.8836751
5. Archana, K., Sumukha, M.S., Mohammed, T.M.: Power quality improvement using shunt active filter. In: International Conference on Current Trends in Computer, Electrical, Electronics and Communication, CTCEEC 2017, no. 1, pp. 622–626 (2018). https://doi.org/10.1109/CTCEEC.2017.8455197
6. Lu, W., Xu, C., Li, C.: Selective compensation of power quality problems with a three-phase four-leg shunt active filter. In: Proceedings of the World Congress on Intelligent Control and Automation, pp. 166–171 (2011). https://doi.org/10.1109/WCICA.2011.5970721
7. Zhao, J., Dai, W., Wang, K.: Shunt active power filter and its application. In: International Conference on Challenges in Environmental Science and Computer Engineering, CESCE 2010, vol. 2, pp. 373–376 (2010). https://doi.org/10.1109/CESCE.2010.208
8. Pregitzer, R., Pinto, J.G., João Sepúlveda, M., Afonso, J.L.: Parallel association of shunt active power filters. In: IEEE International Symposium on Industrial Electronics, pp. 2493–2498 (2007). https://doi.org/10.1109/ISIE.2007.4374999
9. Pinto, J.G., Neves, P., Gonçalves, D., Afonso, J.L.: Field results on developed three-phase four-wire shunt active power filters. In: IECON Proceedings (Industrial Electronics Conference), pp. 480–485 (2009). https://doi.org/10.1109/IECON.2009.5414969
10. Singh, B., Al-Haddad, K., Chandra, A.: A review of active filters for power quality improvement. IEEE Trans. Ind. Electron. **46**(5), 960–971 (1999)
11. Popescu, M., Bitoleanu, A., Suru, V., Patrascu, A.: High performance shunt active power filter. In: 2011 7th International Symposium on Advanced Topics in Electrical Engineering, ATEE 2011 (2011)
12. Chaudhari, K.R., Trivedi, T.A.: Analysis on control strategy of Shunt Active Power Filter for three-phase three-wire system. In: 2014 IEEE PES Transmission & Distribution Conference and Exposition-Latin America, PES T&D-LA 2014 - Conference Proceedings, pp. 1–5, October 2014. https://doi.org/10.1109/TDC-LA.2014.6955179
13. Fabricio, E.L.L., Silva, S.C., Jacobina, C.B., Corrêa, M.B.D.R.: Analysis of main topologies of shunt active power filters applied to four-wire systems. IEEE Trans. Power Electron. **33**(3), 2100–2112 (2018). https://doi.org/10.1109/TPEL.2017.2698439
14. Depenbrock, M.: The FBD-method, a generally applicable tool for analyzing power relations. In: ICHPS 1992 - International Conference on Harmonics in Power Systems, pp. 135–141 (1992). https://doi.org/10.1109/ICHPS.1992.559009
15. Staudt, V.: Fryze-Buchholz-Depenbrock: a time-domain power theory. In: 2008 International School on Nonsinusoidal Currents and Compensation, pp. 1–12 (2008)

16. Karimi-Ghartemani, M., Iravani, M.R.: A new phase-locked loop (PLL) system. In: Proceedings of the 44th IEEE 2001 Midwest Symposium on Circuits and Systems, MWSCAS 2001 (Cat. No. 01CH37257), vol. 1, pp. 421–424 (2001). https://doi.org/10.1109/MWSCAS.2001. 986202
17. Araujo, A., Pinto, J.G., Exposto, B., Couto, C., Afonso, J.L.: Implementation and comparison of different switching techniques for shunt active power filters. In: IECON Proceedings (Industrial Electronics Conference), pp. 1519–1525 (2014). https://doi.org/10.1109/IECON. 2014.7048703

A Three-Phase Multilevel AC-DC Converter Operating as a Shunt Active Power Filter: Validation Considering an Industrial Environment

Bruno Nova, Diogo Vaz, Paulo Passos[✉], and Vítor Monteiro

ALGORITMI Research Centre, University of Minho, Guimarães, Portugal
{bruno.nova,diogo.vaz,paulo.passos}@algoritmi.uminho.pt,
vmonteiro@dei.uminho.pt

Abstract. Power quality problems are an issue that requires, each more, particular attention, among others, to prevent equipment failure and improve efficiency. In this context, this paper presents a three-phase four-wire multilevel AC-DC converter operating as a shunt active power filter aiming to reduce the current harmonic distortion, low power factor, and current unbalances, which are introduced by the non-linear loads. The proposed topology comprises a total of six full bridges, where every two full bridges are arranged in a cascade structure and connected to one of the phases of the power grid. Both the proposed topology, as well as the applied control algorithm, are validated using computer simulations considering the most relevant conditions of operation in an industrial environment. The obtained results validate the proposed three-phase multilevel converter when operating as a shunt active power filter, showing that the power quality problems presented in the currents are compensated and the converter operates with the multilevel characteristic for all the conditions of operation.

Keywords: Three-phase multilevel converter · Shunt active power filter · Power quality · Power electronics

1 Introduction

Driven by the evolution of technology, a great majority of the equipment that people resort to contains an electrical/electronic system, which consequently leads to a gradual increase in the consumption of electrical energy. Being essential for the people's daily lives and industries, the expectations are that by the year 2030, the demand for energy in the world will increase about 21% [1]. Therefore, it is essential to develop equipment that ensures an optimum power quality, by reducing or mitigating power quality problems. At the beginning of the power grids, there were only linear loads, i.e., loads that consume currents with the same waveform as the voltage, which means that the power factor was the main problem. However, with the evolution of electronics, new power electronics systems were developed, where, instead of the usual linear

J. L. Afonso et al. (Eds.): SESC 2021, LNICST 425, pp. 141–153, 2022.
https://doi.org/10.1007/978-3-030-97027-7_9

loads, appear non-linear loads, meaning that the current and voltage do not have the same waveform. The proliferation of non-linear loads, such as computers, televisions, household appliances, variable speed drives, uninterruptible power supplies, fluorescent lamps and LEDs, arc welding systems, led to a decrease in cost, an increase in efficiency, and greater control, but new problems appeared, such as harmonic current distortion [2, 3]. The existence of harmonics in the power grid causes several problems, such as an increase in losses, leading to greater heating in equipment such as conductors, transformers, and motors. The harmonic distortion decreases the power factor and in the presence of capacitor banks for power factor correction can accentuate the harmonic distortion due to resonance phenomena. Harmonics cause interference in communication equipment and erratic operation of protection systems, besides causing a malfunction in electronic equipment [4, 5].

Furthermore, there are other power quality problems, such as momentary interruptions, swells, swags, flickers, notches, transients, current and voltage imbalances, and electromagnetic interference [6]. Industrial facilities are the largest producers of current harmonics since its processes use variable speed drives for motors, electric furnaces, electric welders, and energy-saving devices, such as uninterruptible power supplies (UPS) which all lead to a deterioration of the power quality and consequently to high monetary losses. In an industrial context, in addition to higher energy bills, there are other associated costs such as production interruption, the production of defective products, and increased maintenance costs [7]. In the European industry, power quality problems cost more than 150 billion euros per year [8].

.Power quality problems have been studied, to find solutions to mitigate them. For the compensation of the power factor, initially was developed the capacitor bank, being a cheap device, but that only compensates a fixed value of reactive power [9]. For current harmonics compensation, passive filters were initially used, which were tuned only to filter a single frequency but could create resonance phenomena which can be a huge problem [10]. To compensate simultaneously the power factor and the current harmonics, an active parallel power filter was developed. As presented in [11], this equipment allows a dynamic compensation, and compensates the power factor, current harmonics and compensates the current imbalances in three-phase systems. Besides parallel active filters, there are also series active filters that compensate for voltage problems such as presented in [12]. When it is necessary to compensate power quality problems related to voltage and current, a unified power quality conditioner (UPQC) can be used, which is a junction of a shunt active filter and a series active power filter [13].

Over time, the industry has evolved as new techniques and technologies have been developed and it is currently facing the fourth industrial revolution, called industry 4.0. Industry 4.0, which is characterized by the introduction of information and communication technologies, will contribute to make factories intelligent, becoming autonomous and efficient. The areas of automation, control, information technology, integrates the main technologies applied to the manufacturing process in this industrial revolution [14, 15]. Industry 4.0 is based on the following principles [16]: Acquisition and processing of data in real-time, allowing a fast and effective decision making; Existence of a virtual copy of the plants for remote tracking and monitoring of all processes; Decentralization of production processes. The modules of the intelligent factory work in a decentralized way; Production according to demand, creating flexible and self-adjusting manufacturing environments; Use of service-oriented software architectures.

Cyber-physical systems are the basis of the Industry 4.0, which consists of the combination of a software component with mechanical and electronic parts. Control, monitoring, and data exchange are usually performed over the Internet. These systems include sensors, mechanical components, and actuators [17]. The sensors acquire the data, then the data is sent to network-based services, where it's processed, and then as the data is processed, orders are given to the actuators. With Industry 4.0, there is constant communication between physical, digital, and human systems. Concepts such as artificial intelligence, big data, IoT, process simulation, intelligent sensors, advanced human-machine interfaces, cloud computing, and virtual reality will play a key role in the 4.0 industry [15, 18].

Aligned with this context, this paper proposes a three-phase multilevel AC-DC converter operating as a shunt active power filter, where the performed validation was carried out considering the real behavior, in terms of current consumption, of the presented loads in an industry. The organization of the paper is as follows: Sect. 2 presents the proposed topology and the principle of operation; Sect. 3 presents the control algorithm, explaining the implemented control techniques; Sect. 4 presents the simulation results obtained through the PSIM software; Sect. 5 presents the main conclusions.

2 Three-Phase Multilevel Converter: Adopted Topology

In systems that deal with high levels of power, such as industries that are powered by medium voltage, the use of multilevel inverters is an excellent solution, being equipment increasingly used in power electronics [19]. The use of these converters implies the use of a greater number of power semiconductors, but the semiconductors do not have to support such high voltages ratings. Initially, DC-AC converters were used, which produced two or three levels in the output voltage. With the use of multilevel converters, it is possible to generate more output voltage levels, and the more the levels produced, the better is the quality of the output voltage, having less harmonic distortion. Also, there is a reduction of dv/dt and allows a reduction of the switching frequency, reducing the switching losses [20]. There are several topologies of multilevel inverters, the most used are diode clamped, capacitor clamped, and cascade H-Bridge (CHB). The single-phase H-Bridge cascade H-Bridge multilevel converter is based on the serial connection of two or more full-bridge converters. This topology compared to other multilevel topologies does not require diodes and capacitors. The output voltage is the sum of the voltage produced by each converter. Each converter is called a cell, and each cell can produce three voltage levels. For a converter with n cells, the number of voltage levels produced is $2n + 1$ [20]. In Fig. 1 it is presented the proposed topology of the three-phase multilevel converter. Considering that there are two independent DC-links per converter, two PI controllers are implemented, one for each DC-link. Each of them works either in the positive semi-cycle or in the negative semi-cycle of the grid voltage [21]. This way when the grid voltage is higher than zero, the voltage of the upper bus (v_{dc1}) is controlled, and when the grid voltage is lower than zero, the voltage of the lower bus (v_{dc2}) is controlled. As mentioned above, five voltage levels are produced at the output of each converter. The voltage levels produced at the output of each converter are $+v_{dc}$ (v_{dc1} + v_{dc2}), $+v_{dc}/2$ (v_{dc1}), 0, $-v_{dc}/2$ (v_{dc2}) and $-v_{dc}$ ($-v_{dc1} - v_{dc2}$). This type of converter presents several redundant states to synthesize $+v_{dc}/2$, $-v_{dc}/2$, and 0. Thus, to load each dc-link individually in both the positive and negative semi cycle of the grid voltage, it is necessary to select states that allow the current to circulate on the desired DC-link. The following table presents the voltage levels produced, as well as the semiconductors that are connected to produce a certain voltage level. In Table 1, it is represented the states for a single-phase converter, where the output voltage for each phase is between v_{xy}. Since it is implemented two single-phase converters equal to the single-phase converter, the voltage levels are produced are the same on each converter.

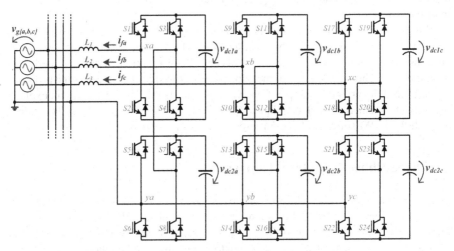

Fig. 1. Proposed three-phase multilevel converter.

Table 1. Selected states of the proposed converter for each phase.

S_1	S_2	S_3	S_4	S_5	S_6	S_7	S_8	Output voltage (v_{xy})
1	0	0	1	1	0	0	1	$+v_{dc}$
0	1	0	1	1	0	0	1	$+v_{dc}/2$
0	1	1	0	1	0	0	1	0
0	1	1	0	1	0	0	1	0
0	1	1	0	0	1	0	1	$-v_{dc}/2$
0	1	1	0	0	1	1	0	$-v_{dc}$

3   Three-Phase Multilevel Converter: Control Algorithm

The power required to regulate the voltage on each DC-link is calculated in the first instance. To calculate this power, two proportional-integral (PI) controllers are used.

Next, the Fryze-Buchholz-Depenbrock power theory (FBD) is applied, to calculate the reference current for the current of each multi-level converter. After the reference current is calculated, current control is applied to calculate the reference voltage that each converter must produce, and this voltage is used for pulse-width modulation (PWM) modulation, to control the switching of power semiconductors. The explanation of power theory, current control, PWM modulation, will be made for one phase, and since the three multilevel converters operate independently for the other phases, the control is the same, being only replicated. To determine the reference of current, the FBD power theory was used. This theory is based on determining the current component that must be supplied by each phase of the power grid, a sinusoidal current in phase with the voltage of the power grid, with the same effective value and 120° apart from the currents of the other phases [22]. The goal is that the power grid provides only the active power, and the harmonics and reactive power are provided by the multilevel converter. The control block diagram applied to each phase of the multilevel is represented in Fig. 2.

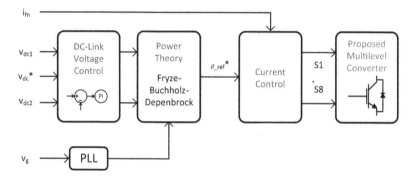

Fig. 2. Block diagram of the proposed control structure for each phase of the converter.

For this purpose, the total power is calculated and the average power, which is the three-phase active power, is calculated. Then the three-phase power is divided by three to determine the power that each phase must provide. This power theory is based on the representation of a load by a conductance in parallel with a current source [22]. The conductance corresponds to the power component of the load that the power grid must provide, i.e., the active power. The current source represents the reactive power and the harmonics that the load consumes. From here, Eq. (1) is used to calculate the reference of current for each phase. Knowing the current in each phase (i_l) and the reference of current of each phase (i_{gref}), a subtraction is made between these two currents to obtain the reference current for each phase of the multilevel converter ($i_{f\_ref}*$), being represented in Eq. (2). Adding Eq. (1) to Eq. (2) gives Eq. (3) where v_g represents the instantaneous value of the voltage in the mains and v_g is the rms value of the grid voltage, where P represents the active power that the grid must provide for each phase and P_{reg} is the power to regulate the DC-link. Each DC bus has an independent PI controller, which allows the DC buses to be loaded separately using the applied PWM modulation level shifting, which is explained in this chapter.

The phase-locked loop (PLL) algorithm is applied for synchronization with the grid voltage. The PLL algorithm produces a sinusoidal signal in phase with the fundamental component of the power grid voltage [23]. This signal produced is used in the calculation of the reference current because it allows the reference current to be sinusoidal, even for a distorted voltage. Equation (4) is used to calculate the reference current, replacing the grid voltage values in Eq. (1). Once the reference current has been calculated, it is used for current control.

$$i_{gref} = \frac{P + P_{reg}}{V_G^2} v_g \tag{1}$$

$$i_{f\_ref} = i_l - i_{gref} \tag{2}$$

$$i_{f\_ref} = i_l - \frac{P + P_{reg}}{V_G^2} v_g \tag{3}$$

$$i_{f\_ref} = i_l - \frac{P + P_{reg}}{V_G^2} v_{pll} \tag{4}$$

After analyzing the converter and its connection to the power grid, the following equations could be described:

$$v_{xy\_ref} = v_g + v_L \tag{5}$$

$$v_{xy\_ref} = v_g + L\frac{di_L}{dt} \tag{6}$$

$$v_{xy\_ref} = v_g[k] + \frac{L}{Ts}\left(i_{f\_ref}[k] - i_{fn}[k]\right) \tag{7}$$

The voltage produced by the converter (v_{xy_ref}), in each phase, is equal to the sum of the grid voltage (v_g) and the voltage in the coupling filter (v_L). By applying the Euler method, it is possible to transform Eq. (6) to the discrete domain, obtaining Eq. (7), where L represents the coupled inductor, Ts represents the sampling period, and i_{fn} it represents the current in the converter. The reference voltage is then compared with a triangular carrier, and the PWM modulation is applied [24, 25]. Three reference currents are calculated, one current for each phase.

The PWM modulation used for the control of semiconductors is based on the level-shifted, which consists of four triangular carrier waves in phase, with the same frequency, with the same amplitude, but with different mean values [26]. The reference signal obtained in Eq. (7), is a sinusoidal signal. After obtaining this sinusoidal reference, it is divided into two modified sinusoidal references. In Fig. 3 (a) and (b), these two modified sinusoidal references are presented. The division of the reference signal in two is due to the fact that the proposed multilevel converter has many redundant states as seen in Sect. 2, and so, to select only the needed ones. Considering only one phase of the proposed topology, the upper full-bridge is modulated by the modified sinusoid sin_1 (Fig. 3 (a)) and the lower full-bridge by the modified sinusoid sin_2 (Fig. 3 (b)).

When the reference signal is greater than 0, the modified sinusoid (sin_1) is used and S1, S2, S3, S4 are switched and S5 and S8 are on and S6 and S7 are off, to get $+vdc$, $+vdc/2$, and 0. When the reference signal is less than 0, the changed sinusoid (sin_2) is used and S5, S6, S7, S8 are switched and S2 and S3 are on and S1 and S4 are off, to obtain $-vdc$, $-vdc/2$ and 0. Figure 4 shows the output voltage of the inverter, where the five voltage levels can be checked. This figure also shows the reference voltage that results from the applied current control. Figure 5, presents the state of each IGBT, where the switching of each IGBT is displayed according to the value of the reference voltage.

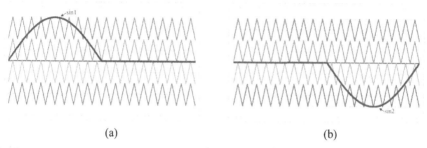

(a)   (b)

Fig. 3. PWM modulation: (a) PWM carriers and the reference signal sin_1; (b) PWM carriers and the reference signal sin_2.

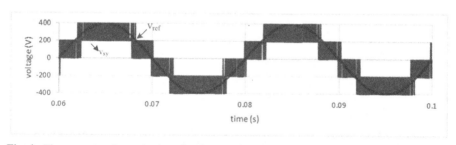

Fig. 4. The output voltage (v_{xy}) and voltage reference (v_{xy_ref}) of the proposed multilevel converter.

4   Three-Phase Multilevel Converter: Computer Validation

This section presents a set of validations resorting to the software simulation tool PSIM. To perform the validation, the DC-links are set at 200 V each to guarantee that the sum of both DC-links presents a higher value than the peak voltage (325 V) of the grid, per phase. The main goal of the computer simulation is to validate the successful operation of the converter as an active power filter, filtering current harmonics.

To validate the operation as shunt active power filter, two different experiments were made. The first experiment consists, in a steady-state, to verify if the active power filter can compensate the harmonic current and guarantee a sinusoidal current waveform on

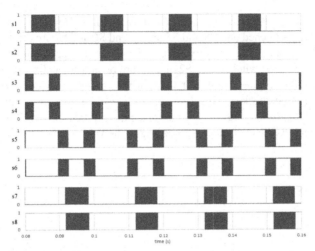

Fig. 5. Pulse-patterns applied to the IGBTs (*S1* to *S8*) of phase *a* of the proposed multilevel converter.

the power grid side. The second experiment consists of starting in a steady state without harmonic loads and then introduce harmonic loads to ensure the dynamic response of the converter. To perform the experiments based on a real industrial environment, three single-phase rectifiers with a RC filter were used in each phase to emulate the loads of the industry, as well as one RL load per phase and one R load per phase. The tests were also carried out considering a distorted voltage (THD%v) of 4% to emulate the real three-phase voltages.

The first experiment is executed with the converter in a steady-state and with the previously described load connected to it. Figure 6 presents the power grid voltages, where it is considered a THD%v value of 4%, as well as the currents consumed by the emulated loads, presenting a THD%i value of about 34%.

The shunt active power filter control algorithm calculates the compensation currents, and as can be seen in Fig. 7, the shunt active power filter produces the compensation currents to obtain a sinusoidal waveform on the power grid side. The compensation currents produced by the shunt active power filter are not going to be symmetrical with the current consumed by the loads since the DC-link needs to be kept balanced, allowing the power grid to only provide the active power needed by the loads.

With this operation, it is possible to verify that the current total harmonic distortion (THD%i) was reduced from around 34% on each phase to 3.78% on phase A, 3.80% on phase B, and 3.90% on phase C. Figure 8 presents the grid-side voltage and current. It's possible to observe that voltage is in phase with the generated current by the multilevel converter and that the power factor is 0.98.

The second experiment aims to validate that the active power filter can compensate for the load's current in a transitory situation. In order to perform this validation, only the non-harmonic loads are connected to the converter, which means that only the dc-link is being controlled. Then the harmonic loads are connected to the converter with the goal to verify if the active power filter can properly calculate the compensation currents and

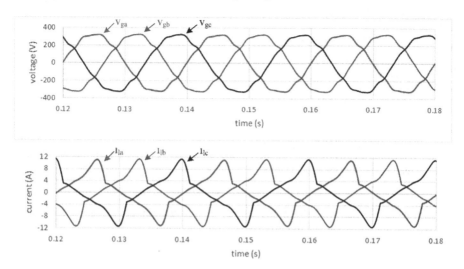

Fig. 6. Results showing the power grid voltages (v_{ga}, v_{gb}, v_{gc}) and the consumed currents (i_{la}, i_{lb}, i_{lc}) by the loads.

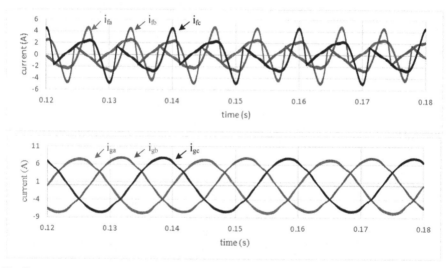

Fig. 7. Validation, in steady-state, of the proposed multilevel AC-DC converter operating as shunt active power filter: Compensation currents (i_{fa}, i_{fb}, i_{fc}); Power grid currents (i_{ga}, i_{gb}, i_{gc}).

reduce the harmonic distortion of the currents. Figure 9 presents the currents measured on the loads, grid, and filter. It is possible to observe the moment when the harmonic loads are connected (0,1 s) as well as the moment where the filter starts to produce the compensation currents (0,1 s) to keep the grid waveform sinusoidal and with low harmonic content. Figure 10 presents the voltage output waveform of each one of the converters that compose this three-phase system. It is possible to observe at 0,1 s the

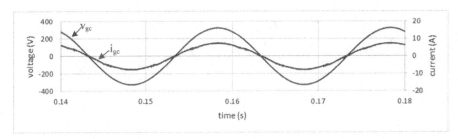

Fig. 8. Validation, in steady-state, of the multilevel AC-DC converter showing in detail, as example for phase c, the power grid current (i_{gc}) and the power grid voltage (v_{gc}).

moment when the harmonic loads are connected because the dc-link sinks for a short moment and then recovers as the filter starts compensating.

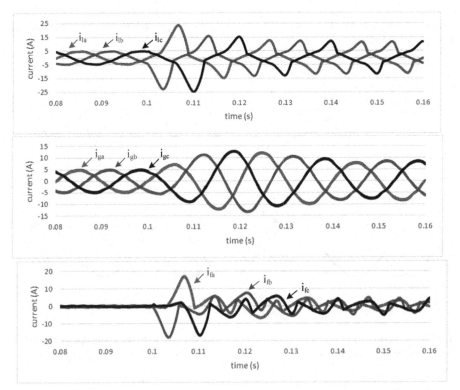

Fig. 9. Validation, in transient-state, of the multilevel AC-DC converter, showing: The currents consumed by the loads (i_{la}, i_{lb}, i_{lc}); The power grid side currents (i_{ga}, i_{gb}, i_{gc}); The compensation currents (i_{fa}, i_{fb}, i_{fc}) of the multilevel AC-DC converter.

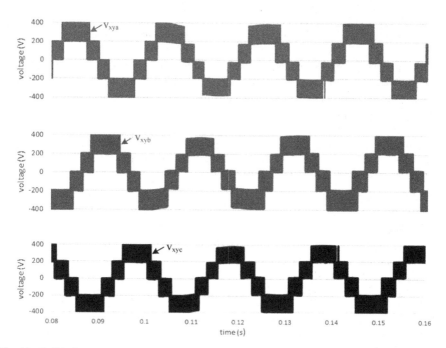

Fig. 10. Validation, in steady-state, of the multilevel AC-DC converter regarding the produced voltages (v_{xya}, v_{xyb}, v_{xyc}), showing in detail the five voltage levels in each phase.

5   Conclusions

Nowadays, in an industrial context, a large amount of the presented loads is characterized by a non-linear behaviour, meaning that the consumed currents present harmonic distortion, leading to deteriorate power quality. Additional, low power factor and unbalances are also critical power quality problems that are presented in industries. As a contribution to mitigate such problems, this paper proposes a three-phase multilevel AC-DC converter, with five different levels, operating as shunt active power filter considering an industrial environment. Due to the fact that this converter can operate with five voltage levels, it allows to reduce, even more, the THD value of the power grid currents when compared to traditional topologies with fewer voltage levels. In this paper, for the adopted multilevel AC-DC converter, the dedicated digital control algorithm is presented, as well as the PWM specific to this converter, allowing to control the DC-links voltages depending on whether the half-cycle of the power grid voltage (i.e., during the positive or negative half-cycle), which improves their voltage balance since they are independent in terms of control. The adoted multilevel AC-DC converter was validated in two different situations: in a steady-state situation and in a transient-state situation. By analysing the obtained results, it is possible to observe that the THD%i value of each phase was reduced from 34% to approximately 4%, while the THD%v of the voltages has a value of around 4%. Even though the THD%i is still 4%, the obtain power factor was almost unitary. The presented results show the correct performance of the adopted multilevel AC-DC converter. Compared to traditional topologies that produce fewer voltage levels, although it applies more semiconductors, the semiconductors are not exposed to such a high dv/dt, which is beneficial since it allows the application of semiconductors with a lower voltage rating. Additionally, since the adopted multilevel AC-DC converter also permits the connection of renewable energy sources on each independent DC-link, represents another important advantage.

Acknowledgment. This work has been supported by FCT – Fundação para a Ciência e Tecnologia within the R&D Units Project Scope: UIDB/00319/2020. This work has been supported by the FCT Project newERA4GRIDs PTDC/EEI-EEE/30283/2017.

References

1. Ferroukhi, R., et al.: Renewable energy benefits: measuring the economics. IRENA Int. Renew. Energy Agency 92 (2016)
2. Akagi, H.: New trends in active filters for improving power quality. In: Proc. IEEE Int. Conf. Power Electron. Drives Energy Syst. Ind. Growth, PEDES, vol. 1, pp. 417–425 (1996)
3. Motta, L., Faundes, N.: Active / passive harmonic filters: Applications, challenges & trends. In: 2016 17th International Conference on Harmonics and Quality of Power (ICHQP), vol. 2016, no. 1, pp. 657–662 (2016)
4. Godbole, P.: Effect of harmonics on active power flow and apparent power in the power system. IOSR J. Electron. Commun. Eng. 39–43 (2013)
5. Subjak, J.S., McQuilkin, J.S.: Harmonics-causes, effects, measurements, and analysis: an update. IEEE Trans. Ind. Appl. **26**(6), 1034–1042 (1990)
6. Afonso, Martins, Couto: Qualidade de energia eléctrica. In: Robótica Automação, Control. Instrumentação, vol. 9, pp. 219–231 (2003)
7. Patrão, C., Delgado, J., De Almeida, A.T., Fonseca, P.: Power quality costs estimation in portuguese industry. In: Proceeding Int. Conf. Electr. Power Qual. Util. EPQU, pp. 337–342 (2011)
8. Targosz, R., Chapman, D.: Cost of Poor Power Quality, pp. 1–13 (2012)
9. Dai, H., Wang, Y., Li, X., Ming, Z., Deng, H.: Characteristic analysis of reactive power compensation device at HVDC converter station. In: 2012 Asia-Pacific Power and Energy Engineering Conference, pp. 1–5 (2012)
10. Marques, H.S., Anunciada, V., Borges, B.V.: Power grid current harmonics mitigation drawn on low voltage rated switching devices with effortless control. Int. J. Electr. Power Energy Syst. **32**(1), 87–99 (2010)
11. Pinto, J.G., Neves, P., Goncalves, D., Afonso, J.L.: Field results on developed three-phase four-wire Shunt Active Power Filters. In: 2009 35th Annual Conference of IEEE Industrial Electronics, pp. 480–485 (2009)
12. Pinto, J.G., Carneiro, H., Exposto, B., Couto, C., Afonso, J.L.: Transformerless series active power filter to compensate voltage disturbances. In: Proceedings of the 2011 14th European Conference on Power Electronics and Applications, EPE 2011, no. Epe, pp. 1–6 (2011)
13. Virmani, R., Gaur, P., Santosi, H., Mittal, A.P., Singh, B.: Performance comparison of UPQC and Active Power Filters for a non-linear load. In: 2010 Joint International Conference on Power Electronics, Drives and Energy Systems & 2010 Power India, pp. 1–8. (2010)

14. Shrouf, F., Ordieres, J., Miragliotta, G.: Smart factories in Industry 4.0: A review of the concept and of energy management approached in production based on the Internet of Things paradigm. In: 2014 IEEE International Conference on Industrial Engineering and Engineering Management, vol. 2015, pp. 697–701 (2014)
15. Da Xu, L., Xu, E.L., Li, L.: Industry 4.0: State of the art and future trends. Int. J. Prod. Res. **56**(8), 2941–2962 (2018)
16. Habib, M.K., Chimsom, C.: Industry 4.0: Sustainability and design principles. In: Proceedings of the 2019 20th International Conference on Research and Education in Mechatronics, REM 2019, vol. 5, pp. 1–8 (2019)
17. Jiang, J.R.: An improved Cyber-Physical Systems architecture for Industry 4.0 smart factories. In: Proc. 2017 IEEE Int. Conf. Appl. Syst. Innov. Appl. Syst. Innov. Mod. Technol. ICASI 2017, pp. 918–920 (2017)
18. Chen, B., Wan, J., Shu, L., Li, P., Mukherjee, M., Yin, B.: Smart factory of industry 4.0: key technologies, application case, and challenges. IEEE Access **6**, 6505–6519 (2017)
19. Gaikwad, A., Arbune, P.A.: Study of cascaded H-Bridge multilevel inverter. In: Int. Conf. Autom. Control Dyn. Optim. Tech. ICACDOT 2016, pp. 179–182 (2017)
20. Mittal, N., Singh, B., Singh, S., Dixit, R., Kumar, D.: Multilevel inverters: A literature survey on topologies and control strategies. In: 2012 2nd International Conference on Power, Control and Embedded Systems, pp. 1–11 (2012)
21. Monteiro, V., Sousa, T.J.C., Sepulveda, M.J., Couto, C., Martins, J.S., Afonso, J.L.: A Novel Multilevel Converter for On-Grid Interface of Renewable Energy Sources in Smart Grids. In: 2019 International Conference on Smart Energy Systems and Technologies (SEST), pp. 1–6 (2019)
22. Staudt, V.: Fryze - Buchholz - Depenbrock: A time-domain power theory. In: 2008 International School on Nonsinusoidal Currents and Compensation, pp. 1–12 (2008)
23. Karimi-Ghartemani, M., Iravani, M.R.: A new phase-locked loop (PLL) system. In: Proceedings of the 44th IEEE 2001 Midwest Symposium on Circuits and Systems. MWSCAS 2001 (Cat. No.01CH37257), vol. 1, pp. 421–424 (2001)
24. Kazmierkowski, M.P., Malesani, L.: Current control techniques for three-phase voltage-source pwm converters: a survey. IEEE Trans. Ind. Electron. **45**(5), 691–703 (1998)
25. Araujo, A., Pinto, J.G., Exposto, B., Couto, C., Afonso, J.L.: Implementation and comparison of different switching techniques for shunt active power filters. In: IECON 2014 - 40th Annual Conference of the IEEE Industrial Electronics Society, pp. 1519–1525 (2014)
26. Aspalli, M.S., Wamanrao, A.: Sinusoidal pulse width modulation (SPWM) with variable carrier synchronization for multilevel inverter controllers. In: 2009 Int. Conf. Control Autom. Commun. Energy Conserv. INCACEC 2009, pp. 1–6 (2009)

Electric Mobility; Power Electronics

Traction and Charging Systems for an Electric Motorcycle

Jorge Carvalho, Tiago J. C. Sousa, and Delfim Pedrosa^(✉)

Centro ALGORITMI, University of Minho, Campus de Azurém, Guimarães, Portugal
dpedrosa@dei.uminho.pt

Abstract. Low energy consumption vehicles such as Electric Motorcycles (EMs) are a very viable solution to reduce energy consumption in the transportation sector. Due to their low power and weight, EMs have high energy efficiency and are optimized for urban transit. In this context, it becomes necessary to develop systems prototypes for any type of Electric Vehicles (EVs). Therefore, the focus of this paper is the implementation of traction and charging systems for an EM. The traction system is composed by a DC motor and a power converter that operates the motor. The power converter control allows the motor to operate in different modes. Besides, the traction system's input is a hand accelerator/brake that can control the motor speed/torque. The charging system acts as an interface between the power grid and the motorcycle system. With this, the first stage of the charger is AC-DC rectification that, besides regulating the DC-link voltage, should also act as a Power Factor Corrector (PFC) and consume a sinusoidal current from the power grid. The charger should also ensure the battery's safety and offer the possibility of regulating the charging rate. This paper details the development of traction and charging systems from the presentation of topologies to the computational simulations, and respective experimental tests and validation.

Keywords: Battery charging · Electric motorcycles · Brushed DC motor · Regenerative braking · Torque control

1 Introduction

Internal Combustion Engine (ICE) vehicles, which use fossil fuels as a source of energy, represent most of the existing worldwide on-road vehicles today [1]. The shortage of these non-renewable resources, as well as the environmental impact they bring, are considered as some of the most critical worldwide issues [2].

Electric traction systems also have much higher energy and performance efficiency than their conventional counterparts. On top of that, electrified vehicles offer performance advantages such as higher responsiveness, i.e., faster acceleration [1]. With this, electrification of transportation is a paradigm shift, and it is one of the most promising solutions to achieve the global goal of reduced and cleaner energy consumption [1, 2].

In regard to Electric Vehicles (EVs) market there are two tendencies. For one, there are models designed for commuting purposes with low battery weight and short-range.

© ICST Institute for Computer Sciences, Social Informatics and Telecommunications Engineering 2022
Published by Springer Nature Switzerland AG 2022. All Rights Reserved
J. L. Afonso et al. (Eds.): SESC 2021, LNICST 425, pp. 157–172, 2022.
https://doi.org/10.1007/978-3-030-97027-7_10

These are lightweight/low-power vehicles and are optimized for low consumption and urban traffic. On the other hand, there are long-range EVs with high-capacity batteries. However, this section of the market has a major disadvantage regarding range compared to ICE vehicles. Other EV disadvantages when contrasted with ICE vehicles are a higher initial cost and time to charge [3].

Considering the limitations and advantages of EVs, a good solution is the use of low-power EVs such as Electric Motorcycles (EMs). EMs have the advantage of having low energy consumption and are optimized for urban driving since they are compact and easy to park [4]. Considering all the advantages of low-power vehicles, EMs prove to be an economic and environment-friendly solution for work commutes in an urban context [4].

To operate an electric motor is necessary the respective controller [5, 6]. In the market, there is a wide range of motor controllers, varying in terms of power, supply voltage, and functionalities. These motor controllers act as an interface for the user to control speed, rotation direction, regulating torque, starting, stopping the motor and it offers protection against overloads and electric faults. The controllers produced for motor applications employ power electronic converters allied with control methods [5, 6]. With this, the EV requires the integration of a motor controller such as described.

For electric motors, by resorting to power electronics it is possible to recover energy during braking. This processing is called regenerative braking [5, 6]. Regenerative braking allows the mechanical energy from the motor's rotation to be converted into electrical energy that is returned to the battery. This process occurs when the brake is applied, the vehicle slows down and the motor works as a generator and thus recharging the battery [7].

The success of EV technology depends on the availability of EV charging stations. To meet this demand, it is necessary to have a solid power grid infrastructure of charging stations. Unidirectional charging is a logical first step because it limits hardware requirements and simplifies interconnection issues [8]. Aside from the interface between the EV system and the power grid, there must be provided charging control for the battery, e.g., keeping track of the charging and discharging rate [8].

EV charging systems can be classified as on-board and off-board [8]. Off-board chargers are the usual charging stations seen in public spaces and are directly connected to the EV batteries. Off-board chargers have their respective power converters placed between the power grid and the EVs. This charging solution is considered a DC charger [8]. On-board chargers, as the name suggests, are integrated in the EV and their topology is based on AC-DC and DC-DC converters [8–10].

This paper proposes and details the implementation of an electric traction system that activates a brushed DC (BDC) motor, as well as an on-board battery charger system for an EM. Both traction and charger systems are connected to a battery and operate independently. The traction system is operated by means of a user input such has a hand accelerator. The battery charging system acts as an interface between the power grid and the battery, providing PFC and charging current regulation The structure of this paper is composed of a brief introduction, covering the EVs state-of-the-art, in Sect. 2 is presented each systems topologies, followed in Sect. 3 by the respective computational simulations, thereafter, in Sect. 4 is shown the hardware implemented, and lastly the experimental tests and validation of two systems.

2   Traction and Charging Systems

Based on the contextualization presented above, it is presented a two-converter topology for the EM traction and charging systems, as shown in Fig. 1.

The topology is composed by the motor and charger, where both have an interface with the battery. Considering that both motor and charger do not operate at the same time, the topologies are developed independently.

The charger acts as the interface between the power grid and the battery and is composed by two stages: the first stage is the AC-DC converter for DC voltage regulation and power factor correction; the second stage is charger converter, for battery current control. On the other hand, the motor converter is connected directly to the battery and controls the DC motor.

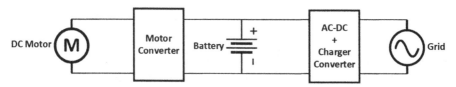

Fig. 1. Presented topology for the implementation of a traction and charging systems using two converters.

2.1   Charger System Topology

For the first stage, the simplest AC-DC converter topology is unidirectional using single-phase diode rectifiers. Usually, the topology used is a Diode Full-Bridge (DFB) that rectifies the grid voltage and producing at the output (DC-link) a constant DC voltage with a certain ripple. The ripple is minimized by the DC-link capacitor, where the ripple is lower with a higher capacitance. On top of those components referred it is also present an inductor after or before the DFB to reduce the power grid current ripple [11]. However, the DFB rectifier has disadvantages such has high effects on the power grid, particularly by absorbing a current with high Total Harmonic Distortion (THD), and an unregulated output voltage that is directly dependent on the power grid voltage level [11].

To achieve a sinusoidal power grid current with THD < 5% (required for the distribution grid), it is opted to implement a Power Factor Corrector (PFC) boost converter, as shown in Fig. 2 [12]. With this, the converter requires two closed-loop controls: one to obtain the reference current for a specific DC-link voltage and the other to regulate the power grid current.

To regulate and control the charging rate and state of the batteries it is required a proper control algorithm. There are diverse charging methods that improve charging safety and regulation, such as the Constant-Current Constant-Voltage (CC–CV) charging method [13]. However, the essential parts of battery chargers are controlling the charging current while regulating the battery conditions, such as State of Charge (SoC) and temperature [14].

Regarding the type of battery used, the most common for EV applications are lithium-ion (Li-ion) batteries [10]. Li-ion batteries are well suited for transportation applications, due to their high energy/power density ratio, slow self-discharge, and high life cycle [15].

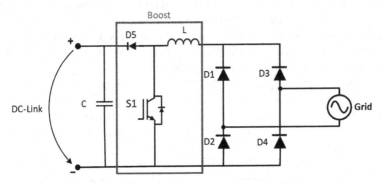

Fig. 2. Electric schematic of the PFC boost rectifier (DFB rectifier + DC-DC boost).

To implement a battery charger, it is required a power converter, and considering that the EV system operates in DC, the options are DC-DC converters. With this, it is implemented a DC-DC buck converter connected to the DC-link resulting in the schematic presented in Fig. 3.

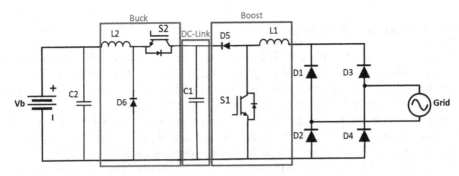

Fig. 3. Electric schematic of the overall charger topology for grid-battery interface.

2.2 Traction System Topology

The motor used in the context of this paper was a BDC motor, despite AC and DC brushless motors also being viable for traction systems applications.

To operate the BDC motor it is opted for a full-bridge or H-Bridge which allows bidirectional current flow, supplies a controllable voltage to a load, and it is constituted by four semiconductors in an H-shape. In Fig. 4 is shown the H-bridge topology, with the equivalent model of a DC motor being supplied by the battery (V_b). The operation of an H-bridge is based on which semiconductors are active, determining a specific operation mode [7, 16]. Considering this, it is possible to reverse the voltage applied to the load and control the current direction, consequently inverting the motor's rotation. Translating to the context of an EV, the H-bridge controls the operation modes, representing acceleration and braking in both directions (forward and reverse), making up to a total of four functioning modes [16].

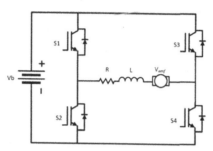

Fig. 4. H-bridge electric schematic applied to the equivalent model of a DC motor, supplied by a battery (V_b).

By observing Fig. 4 it is concluded that each combination of two operating IGBTs define a specific mode. However, both semiconductors of the same leg (S1 and S2 or S3 and S4) cannot be active at the same time, otherwise causing a short circuit. On the other hand, if the two top or two bottom semiconductors are active, the motor coasts and it is idle. Therefore, the remaining four combinations are the most relevant, which define the motor operation. In Table 1 are presented the conditions of each IGBT regarding the four operation modes [16]. The semiconductors can have three states, either fully closed (ON), fully open (OFF) or activated by a PWM wave at the respective gate.

Regenerative braking occurs when it is applied a torque in opposition to the current rotation and the current flows from the motor to the batteries.

Table 1. Motor operation modes and the corresponding combinations of IGBT states.

	S1	S2	S3	S3
1-Forward Motoring	PWM	OFF	OFF	ON
2-Forward Regeneration	OFF	PWM	OFF	ON
3-Reverse Motoring	OFF	ON	PWM	OFF
4-Reverse Regeneration	OFF	OFF	OFF	PWM

For each mode, the motor voltage (V_m) is given by the following equations:

$$V_m = V_b\alpha_1$$

$$(1)$$

$$V_m = V_b(1 - \alpha_2) \tag{2}$$

$$V_m = -V_b\alpha_3 \tag{3}$$

$$V_m = -V_b(1 - \alpha_4), \tag{4}$$

where $\alpha_{1,2,3,4}$ correspond to the PWM duty-cycle applied to the respective semiconductor (1-Forward Motoring, 2-Forward Regeneration, 3-Reverse Motoring, 4-Reverse Regeneration).

On top of that, the back-EMF (V_{emf}), which is the speed-induced voltage of the motor, is given by equation:

$$V_{emf} = km\,v, \tag{5}$$

where km is a motor constant and v the motor rotation speed (rpm).

3 Simulations of the Traction and Charging Systems

A simulation tool allows testing the performance of control systems, as well as manipulate their parameters to obtain the desired behavior. Therefore, it is convenient that the used simulation model is very close to the actual model, and to consider non-ideal aspects of the system components. Besides, problems resulting from design errors can be identified and corrected, thus avoiding damage to electronic components.

All presented simulations were performed using PowerSim Inc's PSIM v9.0.3 simulation software, which is especially suitable for power electronics applications.

3.1 Traction Operation

To simulate the traction system, it is required to simulate the equivalent model of the BDC motor used. With this, in Table 2 are presented the most relevant characteristics of the Motenergy ME1003 BDC motor.

Regarding the traction control, it is used a torque control, since it is more intuitive for a user to operate the motorcycle, similarly to a regular vehicle. With this, the motorcycle speed is controlled indirectly by the torque given by the user input (Fig. 5).

The controller allows an accurate torque control proportional to the current applied on the motor. This control is identical to that of the vehicle with a hand accelerator, where it is given an acceleration reference by means of demanding current [7, 16]. It is important to note that the motor torque is directly proportional to the respective current. The control of the BDC motor is based upon the identification of the respective operation mode. For that, it is required to measure the back-EMF and the motor current (i_m) [17]. After defining the conditions for each mode, it is applied a PI current control that generates a control output u [18].

This value is based on the error between the reference current (i_{ref}), given by the user, and the motor current [16]. With this, for each mode, it is obtained:

Table 2. Technical data of the BDC motor simulated.

Characteristics	Values
Electric Power	15 kW
Armature Resistance	0.012 Ω
Armature Inductance	0.93 mH
Rated Voltage	72 V
Rated Current	200 A
Rated Speed	3000 rpm
Voltage Constant	0.0207 V/rpm
Torque Constant	0.197 Nm/A

Mode 1:

If $i_m \geq 0$ and $V_{emf} \geq 0$, then $\alpha_1 = \frac{1}{V_b}(u + V_{emf})$

Mode 2:

If $i_m < 0$ and $V_{emf} \geq 0$, then $\alpha_2 = 1 - \frac{1}{V_b}(u + V_{emf})$

Mode 3:

If $i_m < 0$ and $V_{emf} < 0$, then $\alpha_3 = -\frac{1}{V_b}(u + V_{emf})$

Mode 4:

If $i_m \geq 0$ and $V_{emf} < 0$, then $\alpha_4 = 1 + \frac{1}{V_b}(u + V_{emf})$

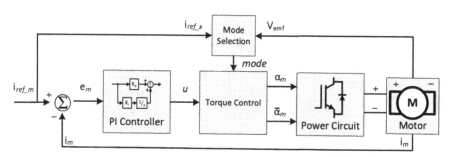

Fig. 5. Block diagram of the traction system torque control.

After implementing the simulation design, it is proceeded to the respective validation. To validate the correct operation of the torque control, the traction system is tested supplied with a 72 V fixed power supply and a 20 Nm mechanical load. On the other hand, to simulate the user input various reference currents are given throughout the simulation, displaying the different modes of operation (Fig. 6 (c)). That being said, in Fig. 6 (a) and Fig. 6 (b) the evolution of mechanical and electrical characteristics are presented, respectively. Observing Fig. 6 (a), from 0 s and 1 s it is possible to confirm that the acceleration/deceleration is proportional to the absolute current value. For the first 0.5 s the motor accelerates with a current of 130 A reaching 1500 rpm, then it is applied the braking, switching to regeneration mode, until speed direction is inverted, causing the motor to accelerate in the opposite direction.

From 0.88 s to 1 s and 1 s to 1.12 s the speed evolution is greater because in those instances the load is applying force in the same direction as the motor, helping decelerate/accelerate as observed in Fig. 6 (b). Transitioning to a practical situation, it is like braking on an uphill or accelerating in a downhill, where in these cases the mechanical load applies torque in the same direction of the motor, increasing acceleration. With this, it is possible to validate the traction system by comparing the intervals of each mode with the evolution of torque and speed, respectively.

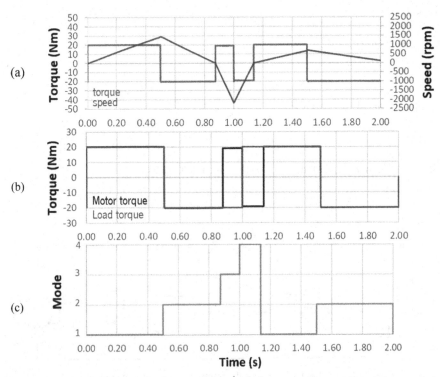

Fig. 6. Motor simulation results with a fixed 72 V power supply: (a) Mechanical characteristics of the motor, speed, and torque; (b) Relation between the torque developed by the motor (motor torque) and the attached load; (c) Motor operation modes from 1 to 4.

To further validate the regenerative braking, it is used the equivalent model of a battery. The battery model is a 2nd order Thevenin circuit. Figure 7 shows the waveforms of the motor current, back-EMF (Fig. 7 (a)) and the battery voltage (Fig. 7 (b)) that can be correlated with the battery SoC.

By observing Fig. 7 (a) it can be validated that during motoring mode the battery is discharged and during braking mode the battery recharges. It is also possible to conclude that, for a greater current, the battery voltage varies faster, as predicted.

3.2 Charging Operation

The requirements set for the AC-DC converter are 3 kW rated power and a DC-link voltage of 400 V. Considering the converter has an input voltage of 230 V (RMS), the rated absorbed grid current (i_g) is 13.05 A (RMS).

The AC-DC converter implemented in simulation is the passive PFC boost topology with a PI current control technique. In this control strategy, the DC-link voltage (V_{dc}) is measured and compared to the reference value ($V_{dc.ref}$), resulting in an error signal ($V_{dc.error}$), that it is subjected to a PI controller. The output of the PI controller is a reference current (i_{ref}), used for the PFC current control. For the proper operation of the AC-DC converter it is necessary to synchronize the system with the power grid voltage. Therefore, it is used a Phase-Locked-Loop (PLL) algorithm, which generates a sinusoidal signal that is an input for the PFC current control.

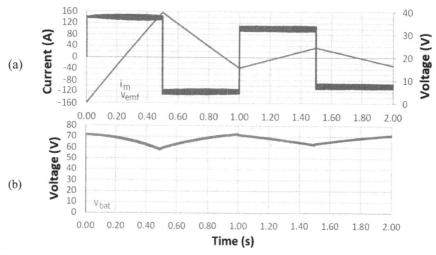

Fig. 7. Motor simulation results with a 72 V battery: (a) Represents the input reference current and the back-EMF voltage produced by the motor; (b) Corresponds to battery voltage evolution throughout the simulation.

Figure 8 presents the simulation results for the AC-DC converter. In this regard, Fig. 8 (a) shows the DC-link voltage active regulation stabilized at 400 V with 20 V of ripple. Figure 8 (b) shows a sinusoidal power grid current with low harmonic content (THD$_f$ of 0.65%) and the current i_{ref} calculated by the DC-link control. With this, it is possible to validate both the DC-link regulation and the PFC current control.

To activate the battery charging control, it is necessary to stabilize the DC-link voltage. Therefore, the buck converter is activated when the input voltage is higher than 390 V. The simulation results of the buck converter are shown in Fig. 9, where are present the reference charging current (i_{ref}) and the battery current (i_{bat}), as well as the battery voltage (v_{bat}).

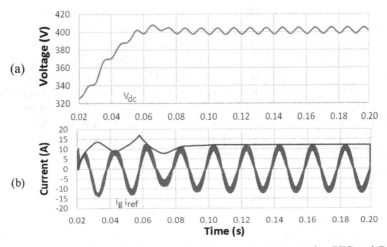

Fig. 8. Simulation waveforms of the AC-DC converter and the respective PFC and DC-link regulation functions.

Figure 9 (a) shows the reference input current and the battery charging current. At the start of the charging process, it is specified a reference current of 20 A, then, at a later stage, this value is lowered to 10 A. Figure 9 (b) shows the battery voltage evolution during the charging process. It is also observable that, during the period of higher current, the battery charges faster concerning the later stage, reaching 80 V. With this, it is possible to confirm the correct functioning of the PI current control.

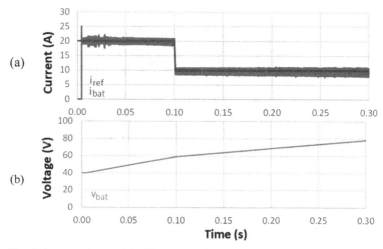

Fig. 9. Simulation waveforms of the buck converter for charging current control: (a) Reference, and battery charging currents. (b) Battery voltage that is correlated with the respective charge.

4   Experimental Tests and Results

The experimental tests conducted are necessary for the development of specific hardware. Therefore, two Printed Circuit Boards (PCBs) were developed. One is a control PCB (Fig. 10 (a)), where signal conditioning of the sensors outputs is performed to be processed by the Analog to Digital (ADC) module of the DSP. The control PCB also has error processing, to detect and act on voltage or current anomalies by turning off the converter's operation, and the driver circuits for the two semiconductors of the charger converters. The other implemented PCB was the charger converter power circuit (Fig. 10 (b)), where are located the semiconductors, DC-link capacitors, voltage and current sensors and the connection to the power grid.

In Fig. 11 is shown the motor traction system, including the control system, where each part is described.

4.1   Traction Operation

For the conducted tests it is used a constant DC power supply of 31 V instead of a battery, therefore the validation of the regenerative braking is conditioned. However, due to the high capacitance on the DC-link input, making up to 10 mF capacitance, it is possible during mode 2 to return energy to these capacitors. This phenomenon is monitored by observing the motor's current direction, which is negative, or rather, from the motor to the capacitor bank. The reference current range used on the tests shown is from -5 A to 15 A, which without a mechanical load the acceleration is already very significant. On top of that tests with a 2 Nm mechanical load were conducted, where the only noticeable differences it is a higher current threshold for the motor to generate enough torque to rotate.

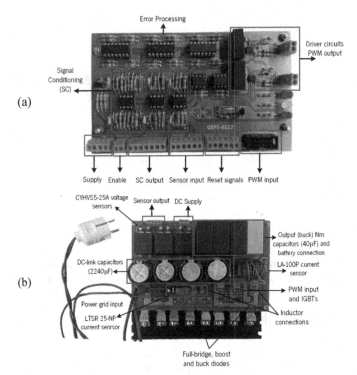

Error Processing

Driver circuits
PWM output

Signal
Conditioning
(SC)

(a)

Supply Enable SC output Sensor input Reset signals PWM input

CYHVS5-25A voltage Sensor output DC Supply
sensors

(b)

DC-link capacitors
(2240μF)

Output (buck) film
capacitors (40μF) and
battery connection

LA-100P current
sensor

PWM input
and IGBTs

Power grid input

LTSR 25-NP
current senrsor

Inductor
connections

Full-bridge, boost
and buck diodes

Fig. 10. Developed PCBs: (a) Control board; (b) Charger power board.

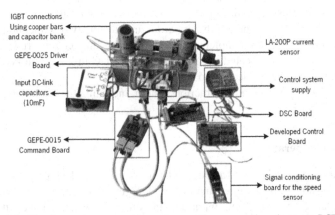

IGBT connections
Using cooper bars
and capacitor bank

LA-200P current
sensor

GEPE-0025 Driver
Board

Input DC-link
capacitors
(10mF)

Control system
supply

DSC Board

Developed Control
Board

GEPE-0015
Command Board

Signal conditioning
board for the speed
sensor

Fig. 11. Traction system assembly and respective connections between PCBs.

Considering the test description above, the motor results are presented in Fig. 12, showing the back-EMF voltage (V_{emf}), the operation mode, the motor current (i_m) and the respective reference (i_{ref}). By observing the waveforms of Fig. 12 it is possible to compare the motor current value with the reference and conclude that the control is functioning properly, and it has a good reaction time. On top of that can also be established the relation between current/torque and the speed evolution.

4.2 Charging Operation

To test the current control, it was set a power grid voltage of 24 V RMS and a DC-link reference voltage of 40 V (10% of the nominal value). To evaluate the PFC behavior, it was measured the reference current (i_{ref}) and the DC-link voltage (V_{dc}), as well as both power grid voltage and current (V_g and i_g). By measuring these quantities, it is expected to obtain results similar to the waveforms obtained in the simulation. For the experimental tests, a 26 Ω resistive load was used on the output. In Fig. 13 (a) is shown the waveform of the power grid current without the PFC current control. In Fig. 13 (b) the DC-link regulation and PFC current controls are activated, and it is possible to verify that the DC-link voltage value is what was expected (40 V with a ripple of 2 V (5%)). On top of that, it is validated the current control considering that the absorbed current has a THD$_f$ of 5.26%.

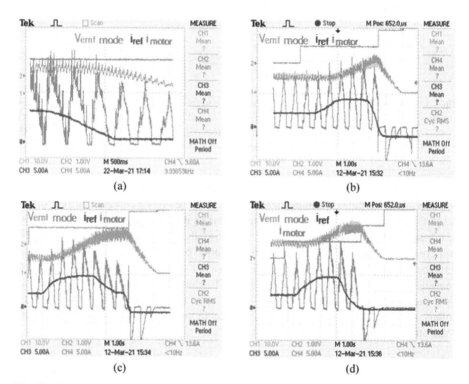

Fig. 12. Waveform results of motor operation showing the waveforms/curves of the back-EMF voltage (CH1: 10 V/div), mode (CH2: modes 0 to 4 (0 no control active) as per established before (1 mode/div)), reference current (CH3: 5 A/div), and motor current (CH4: 5 A/div): (a) Deceleration test while in mode 1; (b) Transition from open loop to control to mode 1 and (c) Acceleration test followed by regenerative braking; (d) Test of modes 1, 2, 3. Time scale of 1 s/div.

To evaluate the PFC behavior, it was measured the reference current (i_{ref}) and the DC-link voltage (V_{dc}), as well as both power grid voltage and current (V_g and i_g). By measuring these quantities, it is expected to obtain results similar to the waveforms obtained in the simulation. For the experimental tests, a 26 Ω resistive load was used on the output. In Fig. 13 (a) is shown the waveform of the power grid current without the PFC current control. In Fig. 13 (b) the DC-link regulation and PFC current controls are activated, and it is possible to verify that the DC-link voltage value is what was expected (40 V with a ripple of 2 V (5%)). On top of that, it is validated the current control considering that the absorbed current has a THD$_f$ of 5.26%.

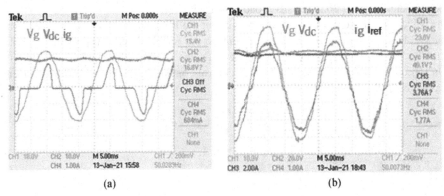

(a)   (b)

Fig. 13. PFC waveform results: (a) Synthesized current without the current control (CH4: 1 A/div), pre-charge DC-link voltage (CH2: 10 V/div) and power grid voltage (CH1: 10 V/div). Time scale of 5 ms/div; (b) Absorbed power grid current (CH4: 1 A/div), reference current, (CH3: 2 A/div), DC-link voltage (CH2: 20 V/div) and grid voltage (CH1: 10 V/div).

The next step to validate the charging system was the buck converter. With this, considering the stipulated values for the PFC tests, a reference charging current of 1 A is set. On the other hand, during the conducted tests it was used a resistive load instead of a battery, which it is not optimal for validating the charging control. However, it is still possible to confirm the correct implementation of the PI control by setting a fixed reference current. Therefore, it was used a resistive load of 13 Ω, and activated the PFC converter as presented above. Figure 14 shows the charger control in steady-state, where can be seen a constant load current of 1 A. On top of that, it is verified that the DC-link voltage remains stable during charging, and that both PFC and charger controls do not destabilize each other.

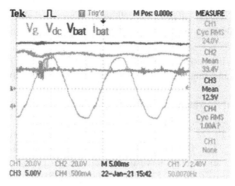

Fig. 14. Buck converter waveform results showing power grid voltage (CH1: 20 V/div), DC-link voltage (CH2: 20 V/div), battery (load) voltage (CH3: 5 V/div) and battery current (CH4: 500 mA/div). Time scale of 5 ms/div.

5   Conclusions

This paper has presented the implementation of traction and battery charging systems for an Electric Motorcycle (EM). Both systems were developed independently and are connected to a battery bank. The traction system is composed by a Brushed DC motor (BDC) and an H-bridge converter that allows four motor operation modes and is supplied by the battery bank. The modes are motoring and regenerative braking, both forward and reverse directions. The control for the traction system is a current/torque control which has a user interface by means of a hand accelerator/brake. The mode transition is performed automatically based on the user's input. The charging system is composed by two stages, where firstly is utilized a PFC boost for AC-DC purposes, to regulate the DC-link voltage while consuming a sinusoidal power grid current. The second stage is composed by a buck DC-DC converter that applies a charging current control for the battery. For the charging system, it is established a 3 kW rated power, with 400 V on the DC-link and a 13 A (RMS) power grid current. The computer simulations and the experimental tests presented allowed the validation of the developed topologies, as well as the hardware implementation.

Acknowledgments. This work has been supported by FCT – Fundação para a Ciência e Tecnologia within the Project Scope: UIDB/00319/2020. This work has been supported by the FCT Project DAIPESEV PTDC/EEI-EEE/30382/2017. Mr. Tiago J. C. Sousa is supported by the doctoral scholarship SFRH/BD/134353/2017 granted by the Portuguese FCT agency.

References

1. Liberto, C., Valenti, G., Orchi, S., Lelli, M., Nigro, M., Ferrara, M.: The impact of electric mobility scenarios in large urban areas: the Rome case study. IEEE Trans. Intell. Transp. Syst. **19**(11), 3540–3549 (2018). https://doi.org/10.1109/TITS.2018.2832004
2. Adib, A., et al.: E-mobility – advancements and challenges. IEEE Access **7**, 165226–165240 (2019). https://doi.org/10.1109/ACCESS.2019.2953020031

3. De Santiago, J., et al.: Electrical motor drivelines in commercial all-electric vehicles: a review. IEEE Trans. Veh. Technol. **61**(2), 475–484 (2012). https://doi.org/10.1109/TVT.2011.217 7873

4. Farzaneh, A., Farjah, E.: a novel smart energy management system in pure electric motorcycle using COA. IEEE Trans. Intell. Veh. **4**(4), 600–608 (2019). https://doi.org/10.1109/TIV.2019. 2938100

5. Boopathi, C.S., Saha, S., Singh, A., Sinha, S.: Regenerative braking in electric vehicles. Int. J. Recent Technol. Eng. **8**(2 Special Issue 11), 3338–3346 (2019). https://doi.org/10.35940/ ijrte.B1562.0982S1119

6. Hsu, Y.C., Kao, S.C., Ho, C.Y., Jhou, P.H., Lu, M.Z., Liaw, C.M.: On an electric scooter with G2V/V2H/V2G and energy harvesting functions. IEEE Trans. Power Electron. **33**(8), 6910–6925 (2018). https://doi.org/10.1109/TPEL.2017.2758642

7. Hasanah, R.N., Andrean, V., Suyono, H., Soeprapto: An effective method of regenerative braking for electric vehicles. Int. J. Adv. Sci. Eng. Inf. Technol. **7**(5), 1943–1949 (2017). https://doi.org/10.18517/ijaseit.7.5.1405

8. Yilmaz, M., Krein, P.T.: Review of battery charger topologies, charging power levels, and infrastructure for plug-in electric and hybrid vehicles. IEEE Trans. Power Electron. **28**(5), 2151–2169 (2013). https://doi.org/10.1109/TPEL.2012.2212917

9. Charger, Q.I.O., Na, T., Zhang, Q., Tang, J., Wang, J.: Active Power Filter for Single-Phase **3**(3), 197–201 (2018)

10. Saber, C., Labrousse, D., Revol, B., Gascher, A.: Challenges facing PFC of a single-phase on-board charger for electric vehicles based on a current source active rectifier input stage. IEEE Trans. Power Electron. **31**(9), 6192–6202 (2016). https://doi.org/10.1109/TPEL.2015. 2500958

11. Kolar, J.W., Friedli, T.: The essence of three-phase PFC rectifier systems part i. IEEE Trans. Power Electron. **28**(1), 176–198 (2013). https://doi.org/10.1109/TPEL.2012.2197867

12. Li, G., Huang, H., Song, S., Liu, B.: A nonlinear control scheme based on input–output linearized method achieving PFC and robust constant voltage output for boost converters. Energy Rep. **7**, 5386–5393 (2021). https://doi.org/10.1016/j.egyr.2021.08.169

13. Liu, H., et al.: An analytical model for the CC-CV charge of Li-ion batteries with application to degradation analysis. J. Energy Storage **29**, 101342 (2020). https://doi.org/10.1016/j.est. 2020.101342

14. Sarrafan, K., Muttaqi, K.M., Sutanto, D.: Real-time estimation of model parameters and state-of-charge of li-ion batteries in electric vehicles using a new mixed estimation model. IEEE Trans. Ind. Appl. **56**(5), 5417–5428 (2020). https://doi.org/10.1109/TIA.2020.3002977

15. Miniguano, H., Barrado, A., Lazaro, A., Zumel, P., Fernandez, C.: General parameter identification procedure and comparative study of Li-Ion battery models. IEEE Trans. Veh. Technol. **69**(1), 235–245 (2020). https://doi.org/10.1109/TVT.2019.2952970

16. Wu, F.K., Yeh, T.J., Huang, C.F.: Motor control and torque coordination of an electric vehicle actuated by two in-wheel motors. Mechatronics **23**(1), 46–60 (2013). https://doi.org/10.1016/ j.mechatronics.2012.10.008

17. Zhang, Q., Wen, B., He, Y.: Rotational speed monitoring of brushed DC motor via current signal. Meas.: J. Int. Meas. Confed. **184**, 109890 (2021). https://doi.org/10.1016/j.measur ement.2021.109890

18. Vidlak, M., Makys, P., Stano, M.: Comparison between model based and non-model based sensorless methods of brushed DC motor. Transp. Res. Proc. **55**(2019), 911–918 (2021). https://doi.org/10.1016/j.trpro.2021.07.059

Electric Vehicle Battery Charger with Vehicle-to-Vehicle (V2V) Operation Mode

Carlos F. V. Martins[✉], Tiago J. C. Sousa, and Delfim Pedrosa

ALGORITMI Research Centre, University of Minho, Guimarães, Portugal
a70902@alunos.uminho.pt

Abstract. This paper presents a validation based on simulation result of an electric vehicle (EV) battery charger for power transfer between two EVs (vehicle-to-vehicle (V2V) operation) using only one converter per EV. The traditional topology needs a connection between the EVs and the power grid, consisting in a combination of two operation modes (V2G and G2V). In addition, the power transfer is made using a total of four power converters, two dc-dc and two dc-ac power converters, which represents more energy losses. In contrast, the presented topology discards a connection with a power grid and the charging operation can be done anywhere through the connection between two EVs. Furthermore, the proposed topology only needs two dc-dc power converters, one per EV, allowing the power transfer between EVs becoming more efficient and useful.

Keywords: Electric Vehicles (EVs) · Battery charging · Vehicle-to-Vehicle (V2V) · Power transfer

1 Introduction

Nowadays, there is an urgent need for a growing concern for environmental sustainability and measures to be adopted for a better future for the Earth. Electric mobility, a growing concept associated with means of transportation, presents itself as an asset in order to reduce greenhouse gas emissions produced by internal combustion engine vehicles (ICEVs) into the atmosphere. However, for electric mobility to actively contribute to the mitigation of this problem, the main means that support it also need to be in constant evolution. One of the main problems it faces is the reduced number of functional charging stations that exist [1–3].

Electric vehicles (EVs) are nothing new among us, having been in existence for over 150 years, but only in the last few years they have presented themselves as a viable alternative to ICEVs in order to reduce emissions of greenhouse gases produced into the atmosphere and the fossil fuels exploration. Through the past years, the ICEV represents about 10% of the total greenhouse emissions every year, and, for that reason, it is a big concern to society to try to reduce that in every way as possible [4]. With the growing acceptance of EVs by society, electric mobility has undergoing an impressive growth

J. L. Afonso et al. (Eds.): SESC 2021, LNICST 425, pp. 173–185, 2022.
https://doi.org/10.1007/978-3-030-97027-7_11

and represents a key agent that helps to mitigate the ICEVs problems for the environment [5, 6].

For an EV to operate, an energy storage element is needed. The battery is the most used energy storage element in EVs, being classified as a secondary battery as it is rechargeable [7]. When used in an EV, its charging process is carried out through the connection to the power grid and its discharge process through the supply of energy for the EV to move, as well as to supply energy to another EV, home or power grid [8].

EV battery chargers can be classified as on-board or off-board, and also as conductive or wireless. Besides the traditional grid-to-vehicle (G2V) operation mode, in the literature can be found other operation modes such as vehicle-to-grid (V2G), vehicle-to-home (V2H) and vehicle-for-grid (V4G). These operation modes have in common the connection between an EV and a power grid, restricting the places to where EVs can be connected [9–14].

A power transfer between two EVs is a strong option to address the presented problems, namely the operation mode presented as vehicle-to-vehicle (V2V). In the literature can be found two concepts associated to V2V, one related to the communication between two vehicles (EV or ICEV) and another to the power transfer between two batteries of different EVs. The V2V operation mode can be used by connecting the EVs to the power grid or directly between them, as seen in Fig. 1. In the first case, the power transfer is carried out using four conversion stages (two stages for each EV), which is based in the combination of V2G and G2V operation modes, with one EV operating as an energy provider and the other as an energy receiver. For this reason, the power transfer efficiency is significantly decreased. In the second case, the power transfer can be performed using four or two conversion stages, being naturally more efficient if only two conversion stages are used. V2V is a recent operation mode and new developments and approaches are expected in the next years to increase the use of EVs and make them more efficient [15–19].

Considering the V2V operation mode and the different topologies proposed for it in the literature, this paper is focused on the power transfer between two EVs using only two conversion stages without external power converters, ensuring a greater efficiency and working only with dc power. The paper is structured as follows: Sect. 2 presents the adopted V2V topology for power transfer, Sect. 3 presents a simulation for the presented topology, and Sect. 4 summarizes the conclusions of the developed work.

2   Adopted V2V Configuration

This section presents the adopted V2V topology for power transfer, using only dc power and discarding the connection to the power grid by using a direct approach between two EVs. Throughout this section will be described how two EVs (EV#1 and EV#2) can transfer power between them only using the on-board dc-dc power converters. It is important to refer that the power converters present in each EV battery charging system are bidirectional to support the presented V2V topology.

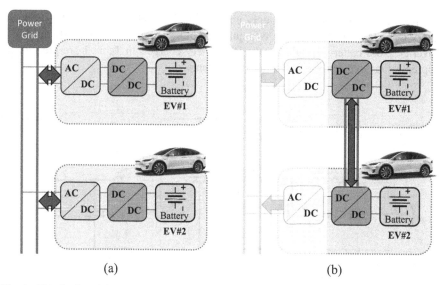

Fig. 1. Topologies of power transfer between two electric vehicles: (a) Conventional indirect V2V power transfer based on the combination of V2G and G2V modes; (b) Direct V2V power transfer using only the on-board dc-dc converters.

2.1 On-Board Dc-Dc Converters

As presented in Fig. 1, each EV battery charger contains a front-end ac-dc converter and a back-end dc-dc converter. Considering two EVs, with only one bidirectional dc-dc power converter in each EV, it is possible to perform charging and discharging processes of the batteries with controlled current, voltage or both, being possible to take this approach as the batteries operate in dc. When the two EVs are connected by the dc-link of battery chargers dc-dc converters, a power exchange between them can be performed, as shown in Fig. 1. Both EVs are connected by the dc-links between the nodes that are common to the front-end and back-end power converters of each battery charger. With two dc-dc converters connected, a bidirectional bridge is accomplished, and both can operate with fully control of charging and discharging current and voltage, being possible for an EV to charge the other under different operating conditions with a high-rate power transfer.

The choice of the bidirectional dc-dc converter for the topology to be implemented relies on the non-isolated buck-boost converter, which changes its operating mode depending on the semiconductor that is being switched. As can be seen in Fig. 2, the connection between the two non-isolated buck-boost converters through the dc-link of each one gives rise to a non-isolated bidirectional split-pi buck-boost dc-dc converter [20, 21].

3 Computational Simulation

This section presents the simulation of the presented V2V power transfer topology, considering the connection between two EVs only use the on-board bidirectional dc-dc power converter present in the battery charger. Each adopted model of the on-board battery charger is composed by a two-quadrant bidirectional buck-boost dc-dc power converter and a battery, simulating the EV battery charger. In Table 1 are present the adopted values to the power converter components.

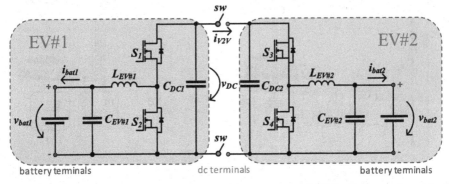

Fig. 2. Connection of the dc-dc converters used in the presented V2V power transfer method between two EVs.

To keep the simulation as real as possible for a power transfer between the batteries of EVs and to the charging and discharging processes, the battery model adopted in this paper is a Thevenin battery model, present in Fig. 3.

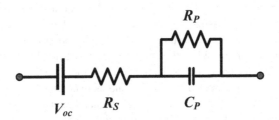

Fig. 3. Adopted Thevenin battery model.

As mentioned in [16], this battery model considers the dynamic operation of the batteries during the charging and discharging processes of an EV, which is enough to validate the presented V2V power transfer. The used parameters for the charging and the discharging process are present in Table 2. The chosen software to perform all the simulations is PSIM v9.1 from PowerSim.

3.1 V2V Operation Mode Conditions

Since V2V can guarantee bidirectional power flow between two EVs, four modes of operation for power transfer will be addressed to simulate all the battery conditions. However, to prove the operation of the adopted battery charger, different operating

Table 1. Component values used in simulation.

Variable	Value
L_{EV}	600 μH
C_{EV}	10 nF
C_{DC}	480.1 μH

Table 2. Battery simulation parameters.

Variable	Value
V_{oc}	200 V
R_s	80 mΩ
R_p	100 kΩ
C_P *(charging)*	0.2 F
C_P *(discharging)*	0.1 F

parameters will be defined to be assigned to each mode. Table 3 shows the four chosen operating modes and the different parameters defined for their operation, considering the EV user's needs and the battery conditions. In the Table 3, variables V_{bat1} and V_{bat2} represent the battery voltages of EV#1 and EV#2, respectively. The sign of the current i_{V2V} represents the power flow direction, indicating which EV is charging and discharging.

Table 3. Defined operation modes for V2V power transfer according to the batteries voltage.

Mode	V2V power transfer	Condition
I	$i_{V2V} > 0$	$V_{bat1} > V_{bat2}$
II		$V_{bat1} < V_{bat2}$
III	$i_{V2V} < 0$	$V_{bat2} > V_{bat1}$
IV		$V_{bat2} < V_{bat1}$

Being defined a maximum operating power of 3 kW for simulating the V2V power transfer, the nominal operating voltage and current values need to be defined. These values are scaled according to the desired requirements and for the operation of the V2V charging system under nominal conditions. In Table 4 are presented the voltage values and the charging and discharging current values for each battery.

For a correct functioning of the implemented power converter, it is necessary to have a dc-link voltage higher than the battery voltage so that a controlled power transfer can exist. The reference voltage set for the dc-link was 400 V and needs to be controlled to remain constant. To ensure that the dc-link voltage and current remains at the defined reference value, a PI control technique using PWM modulation was used. To control the charging and discharging processes applied to each of the EV batteries, a method was adopted for each one. For the charging process, the constant current-voltage charging method was adopted and for the discharging process, which controls the dc-link, the constant power method was used. The constant power discharge method allows controlling the voltage and current of the dc-link simultaneously, resulting in a superior performance to the constant voltage method.

Table 4. Defined nominal operating values for the system.

Variable	Minimum	Maximum
v_{bat1}	150 V	300 V
v_{bat2}	150 V	300 V
i_{charge}	0 A	10 A
$i_{discharge}$	0 A	16 A

Figure 4 shows the result of the PI control technique applied to the discharging process, responsible for controlling the voltage and current in the dc-link. In Fig. 4(a) it is possible to verify that the dc-link voltage is controlled to 400 V, and it only suffers two voltage disturbances during the charging process. The first is related to the start of the charging process, started after the dc-link reaches 400 V, and the second when the charging is finished. Figure 4(b) portrays the current present in the connection between the two EVs during the power transfer. In the same way as in voltage, two disturbances are visible in its value, represent the beginning and the end of the power transfer.

Once the operating modes of the system have been defined and the nominal operating values and the control applied to its operating modes have been validated, the results obtained in the computational simulations for each of the assigned modes are then presented.

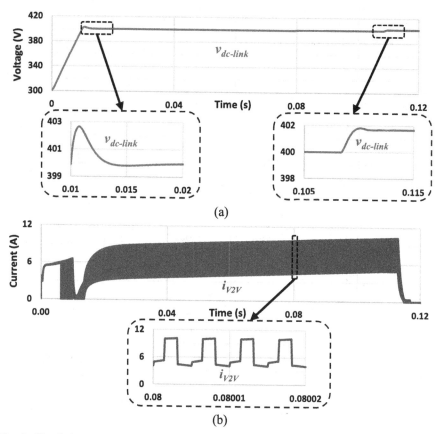

Fig. 4. Simulation result of the dc-link voltage control implemented for V2V power transfer between two EVs: (a) Dc-link voltage ($v_{dc\text{-}link}$); (b) Dc-link current (i_{V2V}).

Mode I

To perform the simulation for V2V operation in Mode I, the nominal operating values defined previously need to be in consideration. Figure 5 shows the charging process applied to EV#2 and the discharging process applied to EV#1, existing energy transfer from EV#1 to EV#2 in both mode I and mode II, according to the operating conditions defined in Table 3. In Fig. 5(a) it is possible to see the beginning of V_{bat2} charging process at 0.01 s, with a value of 200 V and constant current, and finished when it reaches 300 V at 0.113 s. During 0.108 s and 0.113 s, the charging process went from constant current to constant voltage, being terminated when the current reaches about 0 A. On the other hand, as shown in Fig. 5(b), V_{bat1} starts the discharging process with a value of 300 V and finishes with 290 V, validating the power transfer between both batteries.

Considering the voltage values of both batteries and that the charging method adopted is constant current, with a charging current of 10 A being defined, it is possible to verify that the discharging current will increase as the battery voltage drops while that the charging current remains constant throughout the entire process. The current i_{bat2}

(i_{charge}) has a current ripple peak-to-peak value of 500 mA and i_{bat1} ($i_{discharge}$) has a slightly higher current ripple peak-to-peak value of 700 mA.

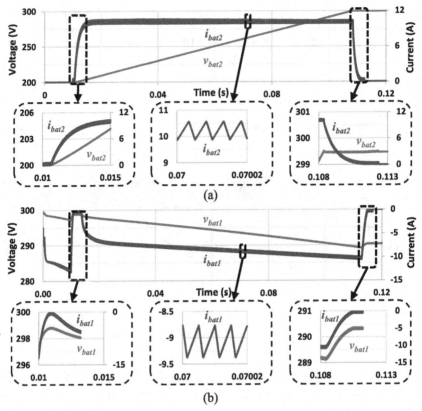

Fig. 5. Simulation results for V2V power transfer in mode I: (a) Charging process applied to EV#1; (b) Discharging process applied to EV#2.

Mode II

Respecting the same operating condition for energy transfer as in mode I, Fig. 6 shows the case for V2V power transfer in mode II. In Fig. 6(a), V_{bat2} starts the charging process at 0.015 s with a mean value of 240 V and finishes when it reaches 300 V at 0.076 s. As it can be seen in Fig. 5, the same process happens during 0.075 s and 0.08 s as in mode I. In mode II, V_{bat1} has lower voltage than V_{bat2}, and starts the discharging process with 200 V and finishes with 190 V. Comparing the mean value of charge and discharge currents obtained with mode I, it is possible to verify they have the same charge current (10 A), previously defined, but the discharge current has increased. In Fig. 6(a) it is possible to see the discharging process and to verify that the discharge current (i_{bat1}) reaches a value of 15 A, because the battery voltage in the process of discharging (V_{bat1}) is lower than in mode I, according to the operation condition present in Table 3, naturally increasing the current respecting the theory of the input power being equal to the output power. Comparing the current ripple with mode I, it is possible to verify that it is equal, although the discharge current (i_{bat1}) values are higher.

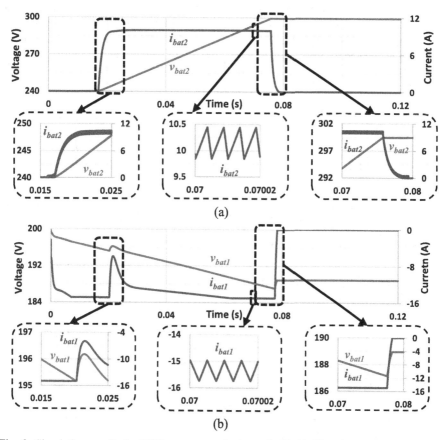

Fig. 6. Simulation results for V2V power transfer in mode II: (a) Charging process applied to EV#1; (b) Discharging process applied to EV#2.

Mode III

According to the condition previously defined for mode III and mode IV, the power transfer in these two modes will be performed from EV#2 to EV#1. The charging process is then applied to EV#1, while to EV#2 is applied the discharging process.

Figure 7 shows the result obtained during the simulation of V2V power transfer in mode III. In this mode, as the voltage applied to each battery is equal to mode I in their respective charging and discharging processes, the results obtained for one of the processes will be equal to mode I. Similarly, to the previous mode I, the current i_{bat1} has the same average values and a peak-to-peak ripple with value of 500 mA, while i_{bat2} has a value of 700 mA. As already mentioned, through a detailed analysis of the charging (Fig. 7(a)) and discharging (Fig. 7(b)) processes, the results obtained in mode III are the same as in mode I, proving the bidirectionality in power transfer and the topology adopted.

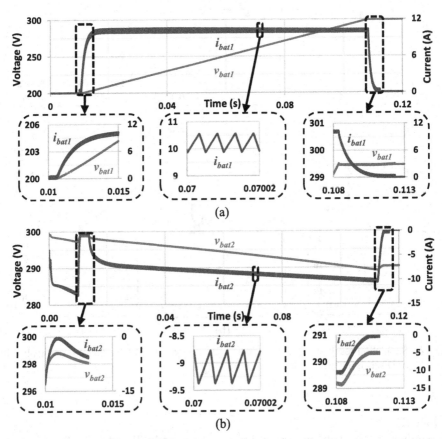

Fig. 7. Simulation results for V2V power transfer in mode III: (a) Discharging process applied to EV#2; (b) Charging process applied to EV#1.

Mode IV

Finally, the results obtained in operation mode IV are be analyzed, proving the functioning of all defined modes. By analyzing Fig. 8, it is possible to verify that the results obtained are equal to mode II, as expected. Figure 8(a) portrays the charging process and Fig. 8(b) the discharging process, verifying the power transfer from EV#2 to EV#1. It is also possible to verify that the obtained results present the same behavior as mode II although the direction of power transfer is different, which would be expected since the voltages defined for each battery are the same.

Once the computational simulations are presented for all four operation modes, it is possible to claim that the V2V topology, using only the dc-dc converters present in the charging system of an EV, allows power transfer between EVs with different battery voltages independently of the power flow direction.

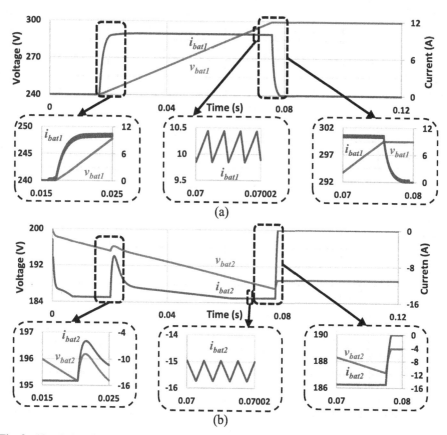

Fig. 8. Simulation results of the adopted topologies for V2V power transfer mode IV: (a) Discharging process applied to EV#2; (b) Charging process applied to EV#1.

4   Conclusions

This paper presents a validation based on simulation result of an EV battery charger for vehicle–to–vehicle (V2V) power transfer between two EVs without using additional power converters. The presented V2V operation is easy to implement, using only the dc-dc converters present in the on–board battery chargers of the EVs, and numerous advantages are associated with its use. Without the necessity to connect to a power grid, the EVs perform the power transfer through the direct connection of the dc–link of the on-board dc-dc converters. It should be noted that the direct connection via the dc-link is not available in nowadays EVs.

The implemented V2V configuration was validated through computational simulations. To prove the flexibility, safety and efficiency of the system, several operating modes were attributed to the adopted configuration. The defined operating modes were also intended to prove the bidirectional power transfer under different operating conditions, validating its operation with different voltage values assigned to the batteries. With the adopted procedures, the performed computational simulations and obtained results, the adopted V2V topology is then considered valid.

However, additional metrics will be used in further investigation in order to improve the power, safety and efficiency. Metrics with the adoption of new power converter topologies for on–board battery chargers, such as interleaved topologies, and advanced methods for controlling the current can be implemented.

Acknowledgments. This work has been supported by FCT – Fundação para a Ciência e Tecnologia within the Project Scope: UIDB/00319/2020. This work has been supported by the FCT Project DAIPESEV PTDC/EEI-EEE/30382/2017. Mr. Tiago J. C. Sousa is supported by the doctoral scholarship SFRH/BD/134353/2017 granted by the Portuguese FCT agency.

References

1. Abdelkafi, N., Makhotin, S., Posselt, T.: Business model innovations for electric mobility — what can be learned from existing business model patterns? Int. J. Innov. Manag. **17**(01), 1340003 (2013). https://doi.org/10.1142/S1363919613400033
2. 21st Session of the Conference of the Parties to the United Nations Framework Convention on Climate Change. https://www.c2es.org/content/cop-21-paris/, Last Accessed 12 Aug 2021
3. Finger, M., Audouin, M.: The Governance of Smart Transportation Systems: Towards New Organizational Structures for the Development of Shared, Automated, Electric and Integrated Mobility. Springer (2018)
4. CO_2 and Greenhouse Gas Emissions. https://ourworldindata.org/co2-and-other-greenhouse-gas-emissions. Last Accessed 12 Aug 2021
5. Global EV Outlook 2020 – Entering the decade of electric drive?. https://www.iea.org/reports/global-ev-outlook-2020, Last Accessed 13 Aug 2021
6. Global EV Outlook 2019 Scaling up the transition to electric mobility. https://www.iea.org/reports/global-ev-outlook-2019. Last Accessed 14 Aug 2021
7. Nikolian, A., De Hoog, J., Fleurbay, K., Timmermans, J., Van De Bossche, P., Van Mierlo, J.: Classification of electric modelling and characterization methods of lithium-ion batteries for vehicle applications. Eur. Electr. Veh. Congr. 1–15 (2014)
8. Ngo, T., Lee, K., Won, J., Nam, K.: Study of single-phase bidirectional battery charger for high power application. Proc. ICEMS. 958–962 (2012)
9. Monteiro, V., Pinto, J.G., Afonso, J.L.: Operation modes for the electric vehicle in smart grids and smart homes: present and proposed modes. IEEE Trans. Veh. Technol. **65**(3), 1007–1020 (2016)

10. Xu, N.Z., Chung, C.Y., Member, S., Reliability evaluation of distribution systems including vehicle-to-home and vehicle-to-grid. IEEE Trans. Power Syst. 1–10 (2015)
11. Monteiro, V., Exposto, B., Ferreira, J.C., Afonso, J.L.: Improved vehicle-to-home (iV2H) operation mode: experimental analysis of the electric vehicle as off-line UPS. IEEE Trans. Smart Grid **8**(6), 2702–2711 (2017)
12. Jung, S., Choi, S.: A high efficiency Bi-directional EV charger with seamless mode transfer for V2G and V2H application. IEEE Trans. Veh. Technol. 1–5 (2016)
13. Guo, X., Li, J., Wang, X.: Impact of grid and load disturbances on electric vehicle battery in G2V/V2G and V2H mode. IEEE Energy Convers. Congr. Expo. 5406–5410 (2015)
14. Pinto, J.G., Monteiro, V., Goncalves, H., Exposto, B., Pedrosa, D., Couto, C., et al.: Bidirectional battery charger with grid-to-vehicle vehicle-to-grid and vehicle-to-home technologies. Proc. IECON. 10–13 (2013)
15. Sousa, T.J.C., Monteiro, V., Fernandes, J.C.A., Couto, C., Meléndez, A.A.N., Afonso, J.L.: New perspectives for vehicle-to-vehicle (V2V) power transfer. In: IECON 2018 – 44th Annual Conference of the IEEE Industrial Electronics Society, pp. 5183–5188 (2018)
16. Sousa, T., Machado, L., Pedrosa, D., Martins, C., Monteiro, V., Afonso, J.L.: Comparative analysis of vehicle-to-vehicle (V2V) power transfer configurations without additional power converters. In: 2020 IEEE International Conference on Compatibility, pp. 1–6 (2020)
17. Sakr, N., Sadarnac, D., Gascher, A.: A review of on-board integrated chargers for electric vehicles. In: 16th European Conference on Power Electronics and Applications, pp. 1–10 (2014)
18. Vempalli, S.K., Deepa, K., Prabhakar, G.: A novel V2V charging method addressing the last mile connectivity. IEEE International Conference on Power Electronics Drives and Energy Systems (PEDES), pp. 1–6 (2018)
19. Bulut, E., Kisacikoglu, M.C.: Mitigating range anxiety via vehicle-to-vehicle social charging system. IEEE 85th Vehicular Technology Conference (VTC Spring), pp. 1–5 (2017)
20. Viana, C., Keshani, M., Lehn, P.W.: Interleaved buck-boost integrted DC fast charger with bidirectional fault blocking capability. In: 20th Workshop on Control and Modeling for Power Electronics (COMPEL), pp. 1–7 (2019)
21. Alzahrani, A., Shamsi, P., Ferdowsi, M.: Single and Interleaved Split-Pi DC-DC Converter. In: IEEE 6th International Conference on Renewable Energy Research and Applications (ICRERA), pp. 995–1000 (2017)

Renewable Energy

A Short Term Wind Speed Forecasting Model Using Artificial Neural Network and Adaptive Neuro-Fuzzy Inference System Models

Yahia Amoura[1(✉)], Ana I. Pereira[1,2], and José Lima[1,3]

[1] Research Centre in Digitalization and Intelligent Robotics (CeDRI),
Instituto Politécnico de Bragança, Bragança, Portugal
{yahia,apereira,jllima}@ipb.pt
[2] ALGORITMI Center, University of Minho, Braga, Portugal
[3] INESC TEC - INESC Technology and Science, Porto, Portugal

Abstract. Future power systems encourage the use of renewable energy resources, among them wind power is of great interest, but its power output is intermittent in nature which can affect the stability of the power system and increase the risk of blackouts. Therefore, a forecasting model of the wind speed is essential for the optimal operation of a power supply with an important share of wind energy conversion systems. In this paper, two wind speed forecasting models based on multiple meteorological measurements of wind speed and temperature are proposed and compared according to their mean squared error (MSE) value. The first model concerns the artificial intelligence based on neural network (ANN) where several network configurations are proposed to achieve the most suitable structure of the problem, while the other model concerned the Adaptive Neuro-Fuzzy Inference System (ANFIS). To enhance the results accuracy, the invalid input samples are filtered. According to the computational results of the two models, the ANFIS has delivered more accurate outputs characterized by a reduced mean squared error value compared to the ANN-based model.

Keywords: Artificial Neural Network · Adaptive Neuro-Fuzzy Inference System · Wind speed · Temperature · Mean Square Error

1 Introduction

The deployment of renewable energy sources (RES) such as wind power generation systems has gained significant attention in many countries following the objective established by the European Union (EU) to confront climate change in the framework for action on climate and energy for the period of 2021–2030 [1]. Wind is an abundant and non-polluting source, considered as one of the most requested approaches in generation to ensure a sustainable energy supply and

© ICST Institute for Computer Sciences, Social Informatics and Telecommunications Engineering 2022
Published by Springer Nature Switzerland AG 2022. All Rights Reserved
J. L. Afonso et al. (Eds.): SESC 2021, LNICST 425, pp. 189–204, 2022.
https://doi.org/10.1007/978-3-030-97027-7_12

a key element of micro-grids for the implementation of a smart grid infrastructure [2]. Therefore, wind power generation forecasting is essential for the optimal operation of a power system with a high level penetration of wind energy conversion systems but the latter encounters several challenges due to the intermittent effect of the wind [3].

The uncertainties associated with wind power may endanger system reliability and power quality, as a consequence a grid integration challenges, such as balance management and reserve capacity [4].

Because of weather pressure difference, air density, topography and other factors, wind speed is considered one of the hardest meteorological parameters to predict. As a result, the power delivered by the wind turbine will be quite difficult to predict [5]. Therefore, the prediction model will mostly be non-linear and should respect the accuracy rules as much as possible. Consequently, remarkable progress has been achieved in the improvement of wind speed and/or power prediction methods. In the literature, multiple prediction methods have been proposed and performed, each employing a different technology and giving good results with a different forecasting horizon. The recent studies in the context of wind prediction have focused on short-term wind predictions, ranging from a few minutes to a few days, in view to the relevance of these data for power systems that require a day ahead scheduling operations, as the case of the power flows circulating in micro-grids systems. Nevertheless, it is usually very difficult to make a long-term prediction because strategies designed for long-term prediction horizons are less effective in the short term [6].

In the latest years, with the increasing computation speed of computers, researchers have proposed a number of power prediction models for wind speeds based on complex statistics and artificial intelligence techniques [7]. The AI-based models that rely on a large number of historical data for constructing an input/output mapping function are widely adopted, the new methods are also based on the adaptive neuro-fuzzy inference system (ANFIS), fuzzy logic methods, support vector machine (SVM), neuro-fuzzy network and evolutionary optimization algorithms [8]. For instance, in [9], Saeed et al. have devloped an ANN model based on Multiple Layer Perceptron (MLP) architecture with three layers (input, hidden, and output) on the basis of the input data concerning previous recorded wind speed, air pressure, air humidity and air temperature obtained by local meteorological station. In [10], the authors proposed a new two-step hybrid approach based on the association of Artificial Neural Network (ANN), Genetic Algorithm (GA), and Hilbert-Huang transforms (HHT), for day-to-day wind energy forecasting, the concept is focused on two steps: the first one employs Numerical Weather Prediction (NWP) to forecast the wind speed at the wind farm site. The second step maps actual wind speed versus power characteristics recorded by SCADA (system control and data acquisition) system. Then, the future day wind velocity predicted from the first step is incorporated into the following step to predict the prospective day's wind power. Other methods based on ANN have been developed on [11,12]. Yang et al. [13], developed an ANFIS method for intercepting the incomplete and incorrect wind data. The performance trials are proved by twelve sets of real wind data collected from North China wind farms, respectively interpolated and evaluated. The computational results demonstrated the performance of the ANFIS method. The authors in [14] had shown an SVM-based strategy for wind energy prediction, indeed, the computational analysis is performed by using real measurement of wind velocity, the results prove that the proposed SVM method is more effective than the persistence model. Jursa and Rohrig have published a novel approach to short-term forecasting based on evolutionary optimization methods for neural network automated specification and nearest neighbor search. The computational results proved that the wind speed forecasting error can be reduced using the proposed automated specification method. Moreover, there are other hybrid methods, as suggested by [16], where the authors had proposed a hybrid approach, based on the combination of ANN with wavelet transform, for short-term wind power forecasting in Portugal.

According to the growing use of wind power in the electricity system, the accurate prediction of wind speed becomes increasingly important, as indicated above, many researchers have done developments on wind power prediction. In this work, the wind speed is predicted accurately using multiple local meteorological measurements for each five minutes concerning the previously recorded wind speed and temperature measured at laboratory level of Polytechnic Institute of Bragança, Portugal. The input data set is composed of 103104 samples. The contribution of this paper represents a comparative study in term of accuracy between two wind speed forecasting models, one based on the artificial neural network intelligence (ANN), in which several configurations are proposed by changing the: training, testing and validation samples, while the other is based on Adaptive Neuro-Fuzzy Inference System (ANFIS) model. The two approaches are compared regarding to their Mean Squared Error (MSE) value. Furthermore, in order to achieve an increase accuracy stage for the two models, it is proposed to introduce a filtering system on the initial data set devoted to eliminating the out-of-valid samples, then, the filtered list of data set will be used as a new input for the learning process of the two models.

The remaining parts of the paper are organized as follows: Sect. 2 illustrates the study data used in the prediction models regarding wind and temperature samples, in Sect. 3 the forecasting models including the Artificial Intelligence of Neural Network (ANN) and the Adaptive Neuro-Fuzzy Inference System (ANFIS) are explained. The computational results of the two forecasting models are presented, compared and discussed in Sect. 4. Finally, Sect. 5 concludes the study and proposes guidelines for future works.

2   Study Data

In this study, a real meteorological measurements were collected using a data monitoring system composed of an *anemometer* placed at 10 m from the ground to record the wind speed values and a *K-type thermocouple* to measure the temperature data. The monitoring system can record the sensors' measurements with an interval of five minutes. The data are measured by the meteorological station of the laboratory of the Polytechnic Institute of Bragança in Portugal (latitude: 41° 47′52, 5876° ″ N - longitude: 6° 45′55, 692° ″ W) as shown in Fig. 1, for the length of time from January 1, 2019 to December 31, 2019.

Fig. 1. Satellite view of the study area.

The input samples represent a set of measurements quantified at 103104 values recorded each five minutes for both wind speed and temperature data. Figure 2a and 2b show the wind speed and temperature data respectively measured each five minutes and their average value for each hour.

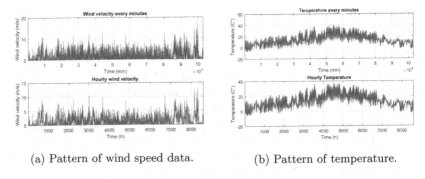

(a) Pattern of wind speed data.   (b) Pattern of temperature.

Fig. 2. Study data in 5 min' interval in Polytechnic Institute of Bragança.

3   Artificial Intelligence Proposed Models

Wind speed prediction is a widely discussed topic, several models have already been proposed in the literature as defined in Sect. 1. In this paper to develop a wind speed prediction system with two Artificial Intelligence (AI) techniques, an ANFIS and ANN based-models are used. The wind speed is predicted accurately using multiple local meteorological measurements. The proposed models uses the previously recorded wind speed V_i and temperature T_i together to predict the future value of wind speed V_{i+1}, where i is the discrete sampling taken for a step of 5 min and 60 min. The principle of the two *AI* models are explained in the following.

3.1 Artificial Neural Network

The structure of the ANN based on a feed-forward network is composed of three layers: an input layer, an output layer, and a hidden layer as illustrated in Fig. 3.

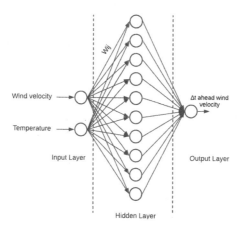

Fig. 3. Structure of the ANN model.

The neural network is initially trained while employing the initial weights. Following the back-propagation principle, for the error correction, the inputs including wind speed V_i and temperature T_i are weighted together by W_{ij} via the Levenberg-Marquardt algorithm that is chosen for its fast convergence, hence, the neural network weights are updated to achieve a more consistent level of prediction following the Eq. (1) [17]:

$$W_{ij} = W_{(i-1)j} + \eta \times \left[V_i^d - V_i^p\right] \times X \tag{1}$$

where W_{new} and W_{old} are respectively the new and the currently updated weights. η is the network learning rate equal to 1%. V_i^d and V_i^p are the desired and predicted outputs respectively. X is the current input at which the network made false predictions.

The activation function $f(s)$ used for the output layer neuron is taken in a sigmoid as following [17]:

$$f(S) = \frac{1}{1 - e^{-S}} \tag{2}$$

where S represents the sum of the products between the inputs data V_i and T_i respectively with their corresponding weights W_{ij} written as:

$$S = V_i(t) \times W_{i1} + T_i(t) \times W_{i2} + b \tag{3}$$

where b is the bias.

Then, the output of the activation function will represent the predicted output V_i^p, However, The performances of the prediction model are measured using the mean square error (MSE) value as [18]:

$$MSE = \frac{1}{n} \sum_{i=1}^{n} (V_i^d - V_i^p)^2 \tag{4}$$

where n is the number of periods.

Therefore, The feed-forward network with a back-propagation principle assures the adjusting of weights which is determined at the offline training as described in Fig. 4.

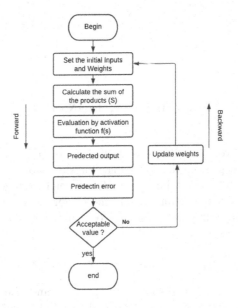

Fig. 4. Back-propagation learning process.

In this work, there are 103104 pairs of input samples, to achieve an accurate model, it is proposed to train the neural network with the most persistent values by eliminating the invalid samples, to do this, the latter are excluded from the data set through a data filter. The filter returns a logical array whose elements are true when an outlier or invalid value is detected in the corresponding element of the data set. An outlier is defined as a value that deviates by more than three median absolute deviations (MAD) from the median [19]. The adopted learning process is described in the flowchart of Fig. 5.

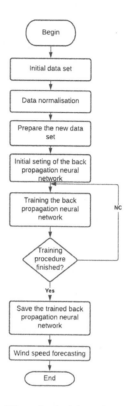

Fig. 5. The adopted learning process.

3.2   Adaptive Neuro-Fuzzy Inference System

The second AI model adopted in this study is the ANFIS framed by combining two intelligent models: the fuzzy inference system (FIS) and the neural network (NN). It has the potential to capture the benefits of both in a single framework. Moreover, the adopted inference system is based on the Sugeno fuzzy model corresponding to a set of fuzzy if-then rules that have the learning capability to approximate non-linear functions [20].

The proposed model includes five layers [21], comprised of two types of nodes: fixed and adaptable as illustrated in Fig. 6.

The first layer commonly called fuzzification, takes the input values including the previously recorded data of temperature $T_i(t)$ and wind velocity $V_i(t)$ to determine the membership function belong to them. The membership degrees of each function are computed by using the premise parameter set, namely

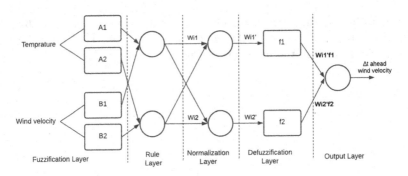

Fig. 6. Structure of the ANFIS model.

$\{A, B, C\}$. In order to firing the fuzzy rules, the rule layer is responsible for generating the firing strengths for the rules, as indicated before, the ANFIS is based on sugeno fuzzy model responsible for generating two principal rules [22]:

– *Rule 01:* if $T_i(t)$ is A1 and $V_i(t)$ is B1 then, $f_1 = P_1 T_i(t) + Q_1 V_i(t) + r_1$

– *Rule 02:* if $T_i(t)$ is A2 and $V_i(t)$ is B2 then, $f_1 = P_2 T_i(t) + Q_2 V_i(t) + r_2$

Where, $\{A_1, A_2, B_1, B_2\}$ are the fuzzy membership functions and $\{P_1, P_2, Q_1, Q_2, r_1, r_2\}$ are the linear parameters of consequent part of the rule. As result, the output of each node is the product of all incoming signals. The third layer is intended for normalizing the computed firing strengths by dividing each value for the total firing strength as follow:

$$W'_{i1} = \frac{W_{i1}}{W_{i1} + W_{i2}} \tag{5}$$

$$W'_{i2} = \frac{W_{i2}}{W_{i1} + W_{i2}} \tag{6}$$

The fourth layer takes as input the normalized values and the consequence parameter set $\{P_\alpha, Q_\alpha, r_\alpha\}$ with $\alpha = \{1, 2\}$ as demonstrated above, in this inference system, the output of each rule is a linear combination of the input variables added by a constant term, the output returned by this layer follows the defuzzification process as [23]:

$$O_4^1 = W'_{i1} \times f_1 = W'_{i1} \times (P_1 T_i(t) + Q_1 V_i(t) + r_1) \tag{7}$$

$$O_4^2 = W'_{i2} \times f_2 = W'_{i2} \times (P_2 T_i(t) + Q_2 V_i(t) + r_2) \tag{8}$$

Those values are then passed to the last layer to return the final output which is the weighted average of the output for each rule denoted by the sum of the two equations (7) and (8). Figure 7 represent the schematic diagram of fuzzy based inference system.

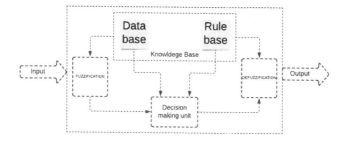

Fig. 7. The schematic diagram of fuzzy based inference system.

4   Results and Discussions

4.1   ANN Model

The multi-layer neural network proposed is being trained with the predefined function "nntool" in *MatLab*. The feed-forward network based on a back-propagation algorithm ensures the adjustment of the weights which is identified in the offline training following the mechanism explained above in Fig. 4.

In order to investigate multiple local meteorological data type effect, two data sets are provided, the first one consists of using as inputs: the samples of wind speed and temperature taken in a time interval of 5 min between each measurement and the second one consists in taking them in 60 min interval, therefore the predicted values will track the character of the inputs values.

Furthermore, to evaluate the performance of the ANN wind speed prediction model. It is proposed to test it with several configurations by changing the number of training, validation, and testing samples as indicated in Tables 1 and 2 of the MSE values. Five successive tests have been executed for each configuration, the results are evaluated by the best, worst and average values of the resulting mean square error.

The neural network model involves randomly dividing the available measured set of samples into three parts, a training set, a testing set, and a validation set or hold-out set. The model is fitted on the training set. Then a test dataset independent of the training dataset follows the same distribution behavior as the training dataset, this later is used only to assess the performance. The fitted model is used to predict the future wind velocity for the observations in the validation set according to the input sample types. Finally, the resulting validation set error rate is assessed using Mean Square Error (MSE) since the problem concerns a quantitative response.

According to the computation results of Tables 1 and 2, it is noticeable that the error value for an interval measurement of ($\Delta t = 60$ min) are less significant than the one of ($\Delta t = 5$ min). The results can be justified by the large number of data sets involved in the training of the second model.

Table 1. MSE results for different learning configurations of the ANN model considering 5 min interval time data.

Configuration	$\Delta t = 5$ min		
	MSE cases		
	Best	Worst	Average
Training = 70%, Testing = 15% Validation = 15%	0.51	0.52	0.51
Training = 80%, Testing = 10% Validation = 10%	0.49	0.52	0.50
Training = 85%, Testing = 5% Validation = 10%	0.49	0.51	0.49
Training = 50%, Testing =25% Validation = 25%	0.52	0.58	0.54
Training = 85%, Testing = 10 % Validation = 5%	0.52	0.62	0.54
Training = 90%, Testing = 5% Validation = 5%	**0.46**	**0.53**	**0.50**
Training = 40%, Testing = 35% Validation = 25%	0.50	0.51	0.50
Training = 40%, Testing = 25% Validation = 35%	0.50	0.51	0.50

Table 2. MSE results for different learning configurations of the ANN model considering 60 min interval time data.

Configuration	$\Delta t = 60$ min		
	MSE cases		
	Best	Worst	Average
Training = 70%, Testing = 15% Validation = 15%	0.55	0.69	0.61
Training = 80%, Testing = 10% Validation = 10%	0.58	0.67	0.61
Training = 85%, Testing = 5% Validation = 10%	0.58	0.65	0.57
Training = 50%, Testing = 25% Validation = 25%	0.56	0.62	0.60
Training = 85%, Testing = 10 % Validation = 5%	0.54	0.70	0.62
Training = 90%, Testing = 5% Validation = 5%	**0.59**	**0.64**	**0.60**
Training = 40%, Testing = 35% Validation = 25%	0.60	0.65	0.61
Training = 40%, Testing = 25% Validation = 35%	0.63	0.68	0.65

Figure 8 shows the mean square error results for five successive tests considering different training configurations of the ANN based-model.

The results provided more pertinent MSE values in terms of precision by selecting a training configuration composed of samples (Training = 90%, Testing = 5% Validation = 5%) adaptable to the five successive tests considering both types of input data as shown in Fig. 9.

In addition to adjusting the weights by the back-propagation algorithm for precision improvement, it is proposed to further reduce the mean square error value by filtering out the most non-conforming training input values deleting the outliers values, as illustrated above in Fig. 5.

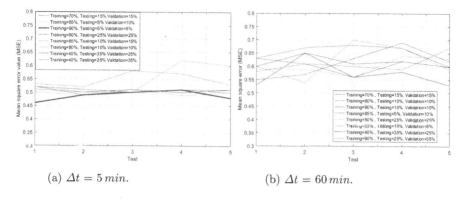

(a) $\Delta t = 5\,min.$ (b) $\Delta t = 60\,min.$

Fig. 8. MSE values for each configuration after five successive tests.

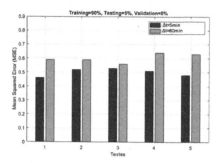

Fig. 9. MSE results for five successive tests considering the combination: Training = 90%, Testing = 5% Validation = 5%.

Figures 10 and 11 represent the filtered data results for measurement interval of 5 min and 60 min respectively.

By adopting this approach, according to Figs. 12, 13 and Tables 3 and 4, the mean square error results experienced an interesting improvement either for 5 min or 60 min interval time measurement. This comes back to the nature of the input data. Likewise, the elimination of invalid pairs (wind speed - temperature) allowed model training with more persistent data.

To evaluate the first part of the results based on the artificial neural network model, the best wind speed forecasting model would be to establish a network configuration considering the input learning samples for a measurement interval of $\Delta t = 5$ min divided by 90% for training, 10% for testing, and 10% for validation as well as considering the exclusion of invalid or outliers values.

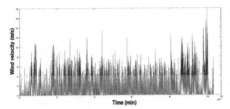 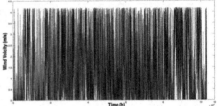

(a) The pattern of wind speed data in 5 min' interval with outlier values.   (b) The pattern of temperature data in 5 min' interval without outlier values.

Fig. 10. Data filtration for 5 min' interval time.

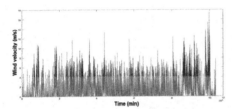 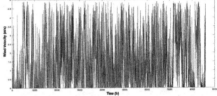

(a) The pattern of wind speed data in 60 min' interval with outlier values.   (b) The pattern of temperature data in 60 min' interval without outlier values.

Fig. 11. Data filtration for 60 min' interval time.

4.2   ANFIS Model

As another forecasting approach, an ANFIS model based on both ANN and Fuzzy Inference Systems (FIS) Sugeno-based was designed to forecast the wind speed in horizon of one day with a time-step of five minutes. The variants of the algorithm used in the study are two input membership functions tuned using the training data including the two processing parameters, namely the wind speed and the temperature that was generated from the set of filtered data deleting the outliers values.

The filtered dataset used as ANFIS inputs in the training, testing, and validation phases are taken with the same sampling configuration as the best one achieved on the ANN model, in like manner, the experiments samples were divided into three groups: for training: 90%, testing = 5%, and validation = 5% of ANFIS.

The mean squared error value is used to compare predicted and actual values of wind speed for model validation and further conclude its effectiveness. The reduced number of input membership functions brings a simple ANFIS network structure. for that, the results had shown an interesting convergence to the target. According to the Fig. 14 describing the variation of the value of the MSE according to the epochs reflecting the number of times that the learning algorithm was working through the entire dataset knowing that in each epoch the samples in the dataset has the opportunity to update the internal model

Table 3. MSE values with and without outlier data for 5 min interval considering the samples combination: Training = 90%, Testing = 5% Validation = 5%.

MSE	Cases		
	With outlier	Without outlier	Deviation
Best	0.46	0.20	56.52%
Worst	0.53	0.28	47.16%
Average	0.50	0.24	52%

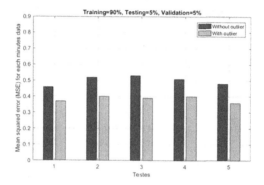

Fig. 12. MSE values for five successive tests considering with and without outlier data for 5 min interval time.

parameters. Furthermore, the fuzzy system is assigned to the epoch for which the least learning error is reached. If two epochs are equal in terms of learning error, the fuzzy system of the preceding epoch is returned. The learning algorithm had run through 1000 epoch until the MSE from the model has been sufficiently minimized to 0.11. The results of the ANFIS model have shown the effectiveness of the latter comparing with the ANN model as shown in Table 5, With well-chosen set samples of ANN configurations, and fully compliant data, the ANFIS has resulted in an 90% accurate forecasting model.

Table 4. MSE values with and without outlier data for 60 min interval considering the samples combination: Training = 90%, Testing = 5% Validation = 5%.

MSE	Cases		
	With outlier	Without outlier	Deviation
Best	0.59	0.42	28.8%
Worst	0.64	0.56	12.5%
Average	0.60	0.47	21.66%

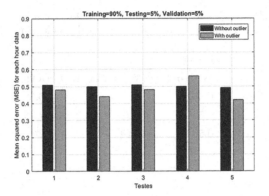

Fig. 13. MSE values for five successive tests considering with and without outlier data for 60 min interval time.

Table 5. Comparison of MSE between ANN and ANFIS models.

Model	Adaptive Neuro Fuzzy Inference System	Artificial Neural Network
Mean Square Error	0.11	0.24

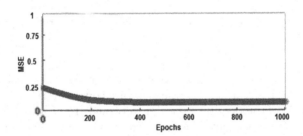

Fig. 14. Learning error curve of the adaptive neuro-fuzzy inference system.

5   Conclusions and Future Work

The wind speed prediction is very important for the electricity trades, strategic scheduling, commitment decision and wind farm investigations for all perspectives. In this paper, the previously recorded wind speed and temperature were used to forecast the future wind speed values in the horizon of one day with a time-step of five minutes and sixty minutes respectively. For this purpose two artificial intelligence models have been proposed, the first one was the artificial intelligence of the neural network (ANN) based on the back-propagation algorithm and the second one concerned Adaptive Neuro-Fuzzy Inference System (ANFIS) sugeno-based. To improve the accuracy of computational results for both models, the input set of training data was filtered to achieve a set without outlier values. Several configurations were proposed for the model learning, after five successive tests for each one, the best configuration was to opt for a sampling of 90% training, 5% testing and 5% validation. Comparing the the Mean Square Error (MSE) values resulting from the two models, the ANFIS has outperformed the ANN model in term of accuracy. As continuation of this work it is envisaged to combine different learning mechanisms with optimization methods to obtain accurate results effective in short and especially long term prediction.

References

1. Buck, M., Graf, A., Graichen, P.: The big picture. Ten priorities for the next European Commission to meet the EU's 2030 targets and accelerate towards 2050. European Energy Transition (2019). https://www.agora-energiewende.de
2. Tascikaraoglu, A., Uzunoglu, M.: A review of combined approaches for prediction of short-term wind speed and power. Renew. Sustain. Energy Rev. **34**, 243–254 (2014). https://doi.org/10.1016/j.rser.2014.03.033
3. Naik, J., Satapathy, P., Dash, P.K.: Short-term wind speed and wind power prediction using hybrid empirical mode decomposition and kernel ridge regression. Appl. Soft Comput. **70**, 1167–1188 (2018). https://doi.org/10.1016/j.asoc.2017.12.010
4. Georgilakis, P.S.: Technical challenges associated with the integration of wind power into power systems. Renew. Sustain. Energy Rev. **12**(3), 852–863 (2008). https://doi.org/10.1016/j.rser.2006.10.007
5. Sohoni, V., Gupta, S.C., Nema, R.K.: A critical review on wind turbine power curve modelling techniques and their applications in wind based energy systems. J. Energy **2016**, 1–18 (2016). https://doi.org/10.1155/2016/8519785
6. Lei, M., Shiyan, L., Chuanwen, J., Hongling, L., Yan, Z.: A review on the forecasting of wind speed and generated power. Renew. Sustain. Energy Rev. **13**(4), 915–920 (2009). https://doi.org/10.1016/j.rser.2008.02.002
7. Soman, S.S., Zareipour, H., Malik, O., Mandal, P.: A review of wind power and wind speed forecasting methods with different time horizons. In: North American Power Symposium (2010). https://doi.org/10.1109/naps.2010.5619586
8. Chang, W.Y.: A Literature review of wind forecasting methods. J. Power Energy Eng. **2**, 61–168 (2014). ee.2014.24023. https://doi.org/10.4236/jp
9. Samadianfard, S., et al.: Wind speed prediction using a hybrid model of the multilayer perceptron and whale optimization algorithm. J. Energy Rep. **6**, 1147–1159 (2020). https://doi.org/10.1016/j.egyr.2020.05.001
10. Zheng, D., Shi, M., Wang, Y., Eseye, A., Zhang, J.: Day-ahead wind power forecasting using a two-stage hybrid modeling approach based on SCADA and meteorological information, and evaluating the impact of input-data dependency on forecasting accuracy. Energies **10**(12), 1988 (2017). https://doi.org/10.3390/en10121988
11. Wu, Y.K., Lee, C.Y., Tsai, S.H., Yu, S.N.: Actual experience on the short-term wind power forecasting at Penghu-From an Island perspective. In: Proceedings of the 2010 International Conference on Power System Technology, pp. 1–8 (2010). https://doi.org/10.1109/powercon.2010.5666619
12. Chang, W.Y.: Application of back propagation neural network for wind power generation forecasting. Int. J. Digit. Cont. Technol. Its Appl. 502–509 (2013). https://doi.org/10.4156/jdcta.vol7.issue4.61
13. Yang, Z.L., Liu, Y.K., Li, C.R.: Interpolation of missing wind data based on ANFIS. Renew. Energy **36**, 993–998 (2011). https://doi.org/10.1016/j.renene.2010.08.033

14. Zeng, J.W., Qiao. W.: support vector machine-based short-term wind power forecasting. In: Proceedings of the IEEE/PES Power Systems Conference and Exposition, Phoenix, pp. 1–8 (2011). https://doi.org/10.1109/psce.2011.5772573
15. Jursa, R., Rohrig, K.: Short-term wind power forecasting using evolutionary algorithms for the automated specification of artificial intelligence models. Int. J. Forecast. **24**, 694–709 (2008). https://doi.org/10.1016/j.ijforecast.2008.08.007
16. Catalão, J.P.S., Pousinho, H.M.I., Mendes, V.M.F.: Short-term wind power forecasting in Portugal by neural networks and wavelet transform. Renew. Energy **36**, 1245–1251 (2011). https://doi.org/10.1016/j.renene.2010.09.016
17. Hecht-Nielsen. R.: Theory of the backpropagation neural network. In: Neural Networks for Perception, pp. 65–93. Academic Press, Boston (1992). https://doi.org/10.1109/ijcnn.1989.118638
18. Dongale, T.D., Patil, K.P., Vanjare, S.R., Chavan, A.R., Gaikwad, P.K., Kamat, R.K.: Modelling of nanostructured memristor device characteristics using artificial neural network (ANN). J. Comput. Sci. **11**, 82–90 (2015). https://doi.org/10.1016/j.jocs.2015.10.007
19. Ronald, P.K.: Outliers in process modeling and identification. IEEE Trans. Control Syst. Technol. **10**, 55–63 (2002). https://doi.org/10.1109/87.974338
20. Gholami, A., et al.: A methodological approach of predicting threshold channel bank profile by multi-objective evolutionary optimization of ANFIS. Eng. Geol. **239**, 298–309 (2018). https://doi.org/10.1016/j.enggeo.2018.03.030
21. Abdulshahed, A.M., Longstaff, A.P., Fletcher, S.: The application of ANFIS prediction models for thermal error compensation on CNC machine tools. Appl. Soft Comput. **27**, 158–168 (2015). https://doi.org/10.1016/j.asoc.2014.11.012
22. Sushmita, M., Hayashi, Y.: Neuro-fuzzy rule generation: survey in soft computing framework. IEEE Trans. Neural Netw. **11**, 748–768 (2000). https://doi.org/10.1109/72.846746
23. Vahidnia, M.H., Alesheikh, A.A., Alimohammadi, A., Hosseinali, F.: A GIS-based neuro-fuzzy procedure for integrating knowledge and data in landslide susceptibility mapping. Comput. Geosci. **36**, 1101–1114 (2017). https://doi.org/10.1016/j.cageo.2017.04.004

Maximization of Solar Power Extraction from Photovoltaic Modules Using Energy Harvesting Solutions for Smart Cities

José A. Salgado[1](✉), Vitor Monteiro[1], J. G. Pinto[1], Ruben E. Figueiredo[1],
Joao L. Afonso[1], and Jose A. Afonso[2]

[1] ALGORITMI Research Centre, University of Minho, Guimarães, Portugal
jose.salgado@algoritmi.uminho.pt
[2] CMEMS-UMinho Center, University of Minho, Guimarães, Portugal

Abstract. Smart cities integrate a wide and diverse set of small electronic devices that use Internet communication capabilities with very different purposes and features. A challenge that arises is how to feed these small devices. Among the various possibilities, energy harvesting presents itself as the most economical and sustainable. This paper describes the design and simulation of an electronic circuit dedicated to maximizing the solar power extraction from photovoltaic (PV) modules. For this purpose, an integrated circuit (IC) dedicated to energy harvesting is used, namely the LTC3129. This IC is a DC-DC converter that uses the maximum power point control (MPPC) technique, which aims to keep its input voltage close to a defined reference value. The designed circuit is used with three photovoltaic modules, each one of a different PV technology: monocrystalline silicon, polycrystalline silicon and amorphous silicon. These PV modules are installed in a weather station to correlate the power produced with the meteorological conditions, in order to assess which solar photovoltaic technology is best for a given location. The equivalent circuit of a solar cell is used in simulation to represent a photovoltaic module. The values of the components of the equivalent circuit are adjusted so they have the same characteristics of the modules installed in the weather station. With each module, a power resistor of the same value is used as load, for comparison purposes. For the case of the monocrystalline silicon technology, the use of the LTC3129 converter increases the power extraction by 47.6% compared to when this converter is not used between the PV module and the load.

Keywords: Photovoltaic modules · DC-DC converter · Maximum power point control · LTSpice software · LTC3129 DC-DC converter

1 Introduction

With the current growth of the world population, the global energy demand has been also increasing, which has been depleting the available fossil fuel resources [1]. Adding to the limitations of available resources, these types of energy are associated with global

© ICST Institute for Computer Sciences, Social Informatics and Telecommunications Engineering 2022
Published by Springer Nature Switzerland AG 2022. All Rights Reserved
J. L. Afonso et al. (Eds.): SESC 2021, LNICST 425, pp. 205–215, 2022.
https://doi.org/10.1007/978-3-030-97027-7_13

warming and depletion of the ozone layer. For this reason, renewable energy sources have been attracting the attention from scientists and governments as an alternative to fossil resources [2].

There is a diverse range of renewable energy sources, such as solar energy, geothermal energy, hydropower and wind power. Among these sources, solar energy is one of the most popular, due to the economic and environmental benefits of its conversion into electricity [2]. The most common method to convert solar energy into electricity is by the use of photovoltaic (PV) panels. The PV market is growing at a rate of 35–40% a year, being one of the fastest growing technologies [3].

Photovoltaics can be made from different materials. Depending on the material used, the characteristics of the PV cell, module or panel will be different. The most popular and used material is the silicon, which has a high availability in the Earth's crust. Variations of silicon are used to develop PV technologies, with crystalline silicon being the most prevalent. There are different sub-types of crystalline silicon, with the most popular being monocrystalline and polycrystalline silicon. Non-crystalline silicon is also a material adopted to make PV, especially with thin film technologies, with amorphous silicon being the most developed technology [4]. Of the three technologies mentioned, monocrystalline silicon PV modules are the most efficient, but also more expensive. Polycrystalline silicon PV modules are slightly less efficient [5], but less expensive than the monocrystalline silicon photovoltaics, with its efficiency/cost ratio making it the most type used of them all. Amorphous silicon PV modules have the advantage of being flexible and are very popular in small applications [4].

The most basic component of a PV is the solar cell. A single solar cell has its own electrical characteristics, which is not very useful for electrical energy. An association of solar cells, in series, parallel or both, forms a solar module, which can already be useful in small-scale applications, whereas, an association of multiple solar modules form a solar panel.

To decide the best solar panel technology for a specific geographical location, it is very important to have information about the weather conditions. Some factors that have impact the solar energy production, like the temperature and solar irradiance, can have different effects for different technologies of PV [6, 7], changing the power produced by solar panels or modules and, consequently, the MPP (Maximum Power Point). To solve this problem, the MPPT (Maximum Power Point Tracking) technique [8] is normally used. A MPPT algorithm will always search for the MPP and thus, maximize the power extraction from solar panels or modules.

For smaller power levels obtained from external energy sources, as is the case of photovoltaic modules, it is introduced the process called energy harvesting. This process is normally used to power wireless devices, such as wearable electronics or wireless sensor networks [9]. Besides solar, it is also used with energy sources like thermoelectric or piezoelectric [9]. Dedicated integrated circuits to energy harvesting that increase the efficiency of power extraction from these sources are normally used.

Concerning related work, in [10] the modelling and simulation of a photovoltaic energy harvesting circuit was developed. The converter LTC3105 was used with the equivalent circuit of a solar cell. The used converter is very similar to the converter used in this paper, but dedicated to smaller power sources. The objective of the paper was to find the optimal output power of the system used. In [11] a maximum efficiency extracting technique for endoscopic capsules using Wireless Power Transfer (WPT) was presented. The converter LTC3129-1 was used in order to boost the power conversion efficiency of the WPT receiver. The use of the converter outperformed an LDO (Low-Dropout) by boosting the power range of the endoscopic capsules.

The solution proposed in this paper was developed in the context of a PV module evaluation system that integrates a weather station and a client machine (smartphone or computer), as shown in Fig. 1. The weather station measures various meteorological variables, namely: wind speed, wind direction, solar irradiance, and temperature. This weather station prototype also integrates three PV modules of different technologies: monocrystalline silicon, polycrystalline silicon and amorphous silicon, which are three of the most common photovoltaics technologies. All the gathered data is pre-processed by a microcontroller and stored locally in an SD card before it is transferred to the client machine for analysis. The data collected by the weather station can be periodically transferred to a cloud server over the Internet, from where it can be accessed using the client machine, or be directly transferred to the client machine when the user approaches the weather station through the establishment of a wireless network connection between the weather station and the client machine. The weather station is powered by a LiPo battery and it is recharged by an extra PV module when the weather conditions allow. Based on the analysis of the data gathered by this system, it will be possible to correlate the power produced by each PV module with the particular meteorological conditions measured by the weather station, in order to evaluate which PV technology is best suited for a given location.

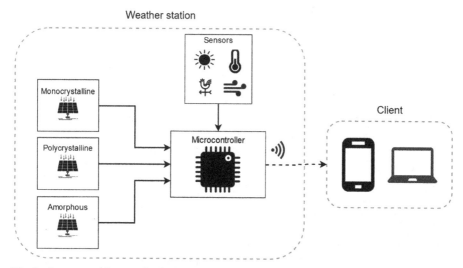

Fig. 1. System architecture in the context of a PV module evaluation system that integrates a weather station and a client machine (smartphone or computer).

The work described in this paper focuses on the design and validation of a circuit to maximize the power extraction from the PV modules installed in the weather station. This solution is based on the use of the LTC3129 [12] DC-DC converter, which implements the MPPC (Maximum Power Point Control) technique. To validate the designed solution, this work uses simulations developed with the LTSpice software [13]. LTspice is a SPICE-based analog electronic circuit simulator computer software, produced by the semiconductor manufacturer Analog Devices.

2 Designed Circuit for Maximization of Solar Power Extraction

This section describes the design of the circuit used to maximize the solar power extraction from the PV modules and explains the decisions behind the choices of the components. Table 1 shows the main characteristics of the three PV modules integrated in the weather station. For comparison purposes, the modules ideally would need to have the same area. However, such was not possible, since the acquired amorphous silicon module has a significantly larger area than the other ones. Therefore, to solve this problem, after measuring the power produced by each module, the average power per 1000 mm^2 is calculated to establish the comparison.

Table 1. Characteristics of the photovoltaic modules integrated in the weather station.

	Monocrystalline	Polycrystalline	Amorphous
Maximum power	1 W	1 W	0.6 W
Short circuit current	250 mA	250 mA	300 mA
Operating current	200 mA	200 mA	200 mA
Short circuit voltage	6 V	6 V	4.15 V
Operating voltage	5 V	5 V	3 V
Area	5100 mm^2	5580 mm^2	6696 mm^2

To maximize the power extraction by low power PV modules, integrated circuits with MPPT capabilities or variations of this technique are normally used. In one of these variations, called MPPC, the converter will try to have its input voltage equal to the set reference value. This technique takes advantage on the fact that the MPP voltage, unlike the current, does not vary much with variations in the weather conditions. Table 2 presents some converters dedicated to energy harvesting that can be used with low power PV modules, such as the ones installed in the weather station.

Taking into consideration the characteristics of the PV modules acquired, the LTC3129 [12] converter was chosen due to the voltage ranges of these modules. It allows an input voltage from 2.42 V to 15 V, which is suited for the PV modules voltage range, and a maximum output current of 200 mA. Depending on the operation mode adopted, the converter can achieve a quiescent current of just 1.3 μA. This converter has integrated MPPC capabilities, in which the reference voltage can be programmed.

Figure 2 presents the circuit with the LTC3129 converter used with each PV module. The datasheet [12] of the converter was followed in order to choose the components

Table 2. DC-DC converters dedicated to energy harvesting available in the market.

IC	Topology	Technique	Input voltage range (V)	Output voltage range (V)	Maximum power (mW)
LTC3105	Boost	MPPC	0.225–5	1.6–5.25	–
LTC3129	Buck/Boost	MPPC	2.42–15	1.5–15.75	–
LTC3331	Buck/Boost	–	3–19	3.45–4.2	–
BQ25570	Boost	MPPT	0.1–5.1	2–5.1	510
SPV1040	Boost	MPPT	0.3–5.5	2–5.2	3000

needed for the implementation of the converter. It is recommended to use an input capacitor higher than 22 μF when using the MPPC capabilities of the converter, so we used a capacitor of 47 μF.

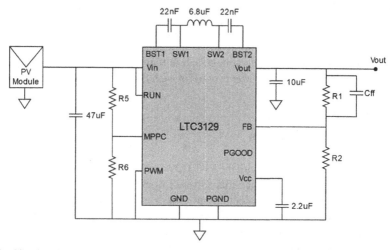

Fig. 2. Circuit using the LTC3129 converter for each photovoltaic module to maximize power extraction.

To achieve the goal of maintaining the input voltage equal to the programmed reference value, it is necessary to connect an external inductor to the converter. The current in the inductor is adjusted by the IC (Integrated Circuit) in order to maintain a minimum voltage at the input, when using high impedance sources, such as the case of PV modules. The reference voltage (V_{MPPC}) can be set with a voltage divider in the MPPC pin, according to Eq. (1) [12].

$$Vmppc = 1.175\left(1 + \frac{R5}{R6}\right) \tag{1}$$

The output voltage (V_{OUT}) can be determined with (2) [12] by using two resistors, one between the Vout pin and the FB pin, and another between the FB pin and ground.

The value of the output voltage can be set from 1.4 V to 15.75 V.

$$V_{OUT} = 1.175\left(1 + \frac{R1}{R2}\right) \tag{2}$$

To reduce the output ripple and increase the transient response, it is recommended the use of a feed-forward capacitor (C_{FF}) in parallel with R1 (in the order of MΩ). The value of this capacitor can be calculated with Eq. (3) [12].

$$C_{FF}(pF) = \frac{66}{R1} \tag{3}$$

At the output of the converter, a power resistor (R_L) of known value was added. The power (P) is then calculated with the voltage (V_{OUT}) measured at the output, using Eq. (4). This voltage is measured by the weather station using the microcontroller ADC (Analog-To-Digital Converter), and a voltage divider is dimensioned taking into account the maximum voltage allowed by the ADC (3.3 V).

$$P = \frac{Vout^2}{R_L} \tag{4}$$

The value of MPPC reference voltage and output voltage are set according to each module's characteristics. A converter is used for each PV module installed in the weather station.

3   Results and Discussion

To validate the designed circuit with the LTC3129 converter, simulations were developed using the LTSpice software. Since this software does not have a component for solar cell, module or panel, the equivalent circuit of a solar cell was used in the simulation. This circuit is composed by a current source, a diode, a series resistor and a shunt resistor [14]. The values of these components determine the characteristics of the PV modules. These values were adjusted to represent the characteristics of the PV modules used (Table 1). Since the monocrystalline and polycrystalline modules exhibit very similar characteristics, the same equivalent circuit was used. Figure 3 shows the equivalent circuits for the amorphous module and monocrystalline/polycrystalline modules.

The power-voltage relationship (P/V) graph was obtained for both equivalent circuits by doing a DC voltage sweep from 0 V to the open circuit voltage of the modules. Figure 4 shows the P/V graph for the monocrystalline and polycrystalline modules, whereas Fig. 5 shows the P/V graph for the amorphous module.

A 50 Ω load was added to the output of the equivalent circuit of the monocrystalline and polycrystalline module, in order to obtain the values of the output power without the converter, for comparison purposes. The graphs for both power and voltage of the circuit output were plotted, as shown in Fig. 6. It can be noticed that the output voltage (5.58 V, in red) is far from the voltage in the point of maximum power (5.00 V), and the output power (blue) is only 624 mW, also far from the MPP (1 W).

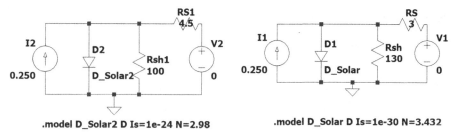

Fig. 3. Equivalent circuits and their components values for the photovoltaic modules: Amorphous module (left) and monocrystalline/polycrystalline modules (right).

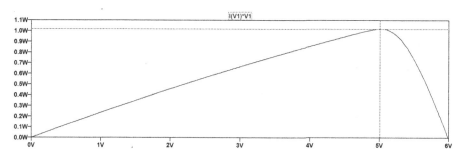

Fig. 4. Power vs. voltage graph for the monocrystalline/polycrystalline module (MPP with 5.00 V and 1.02 W).

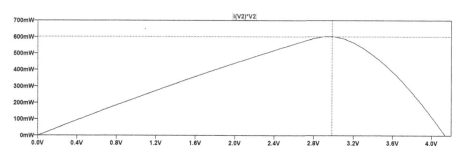

Fig. 5. Power vs. voltage graph for the amorphous module (MPP with 2.98 V and 603 mW).

For validation purposes in the simulation it was only used a single converter, in this case with the equivalent circuit of the monocrystalline and polycrystalline PV module. In practice, in the weather station, a converter would be used for each of the PV modules installed. The converter was added between the equivalent circuit of the PV module and the load, using the MPPC functionality. Figure 7 presents the circuit designed according to Fig. 2 in Sect. 2 of this paper.

The MPPC voltage (V_{MPPC}) was set to different values to test its impact in the power produced by the module. The value of the load was maintained at 50 Ω. In this case, it is assumed that the module is in ideal weather conditions (will produce maximum power). The results can be seen in Table 3.

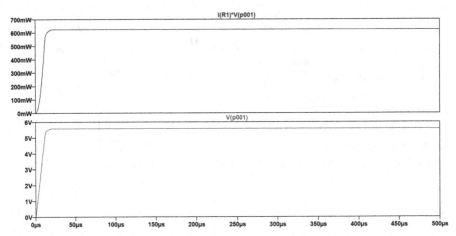

Fig. 6. Output power (624 mW) and voltage (5.58 V) in the equivalent circuit of the monocrystalline/polycrystalline module. (Color figure online)

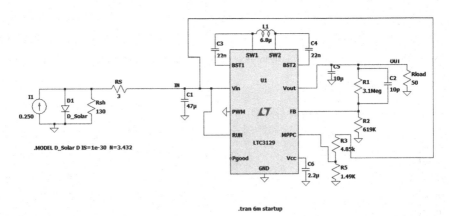

Fig. 7. LTC3129 converter between the model of the monocrystalline/polycrystalline module and the load.

Table 3. Obtained results by varying the MPPC reference voltage.

V_{IN} (V)	V_{MPPC} (V)	V_{OUT} (V)	Load (Ω)	Output power (mW)
3.94	4.0	6.09	50	741
4.45	4.5	6.47	50	837
4.77	4.8	6.68	50	892
5.00	5.0	6.79	50	921
5.42	5.5	6.15	50	759

The maximum output power is obtained when the value of V_{MPPC} is 5 V, which is the voltage of the maximum power point of the monocrystalline and polycrystalline PV modules. As expected, the converter will always try to maintain Vin close to the set value of V_{MPPC}. The output power is relatively higher than when the converter was not used between the module and the load (Fig. 6), with a 47.6% increase in the output power ($V_{MPPC} = 5$ V). Figure 8 presents the power graph in the converter output and the values of V_{IN} and V_{OUT}, for the best case in Table 3 ($V_{MPPC} = 5$ V).

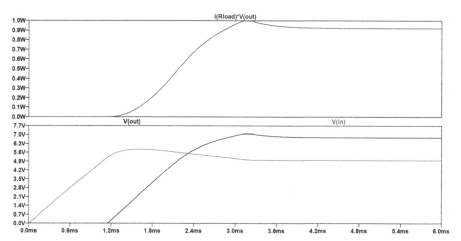

Fig. 8. Values of the output power in the converter and the values of V_{IN} and V_{OUT} ($V_{MPPC} = 5$ V, $R_{LOAD} = 50$ Ω).

The results obtained previously were for a case in which the weather conditions are ideal, with the photovoltaic module producing the maximum power possible. To simulate the module in a situation where the weather conditions are not ideal (such that the voltage and current values are lower, and consequently, the value of the maximum power point also decreases), it was necessary to change some values of the equivalent circuit. For this purpose, the value of the current source was reduced from 250 mA to 200 mA and the ideality factor of the diode (N) was changed from 3.432 to 3.1. This resulted in an MPP of 4.50 V, instead of the previous value of 5.00 V. For the first graph in Fig. 9, the value of the reference voltage was maintained at 5.00 V, whereas for the second graph the reference voltage was changed to 4.50 V.

These results highlight a technical limitation of the MPPC technique when comparing to the MPPT technique. A MPPC reference voltage needs to be set when designing the circuit, but this voltage will not always be optimal. Although the voltage value of the MPP will not vary too much with changing weather conditions, unlike the current, there will still be situations in which the voltage at the MPP can move slightly from the programmed MPPC reference voltage. When designing a circuit using the MPPC technique, some study needs to be done in order to estimate the best value for the MPPC reference voltage. The best value will primarily depend on the photovoltaic module characteristics, but also on the average weather conditions of the location where the module is going to be installed.

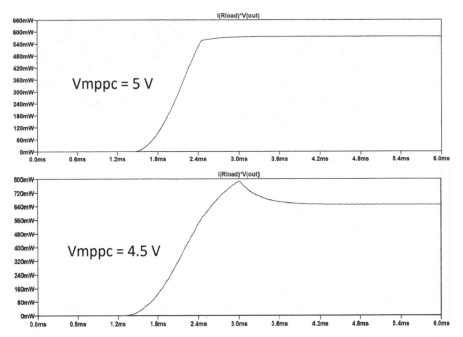

Fig. 9. Graphs of the output power of the converter when the PV module is not in ideal conditions (575 mW @ V_{MPPC} = 5 V; 651 mW @ V_{MPPC} = 4.5 V).

4 Conclusions

This paper presents the design and simulation of a circuit that maximizes the power extraction from PV modules. For this purpose, it uses the LTC3129 DC-DC converter, which implements the MPPC technique. Simulations were developed using the LTSpice software. To represent the PV modules in the simulation, their equivalent circuits were used, and the values of the components were changed to represent the acquired PV modules characteristics. The DC-DC converter was inserted between the PV module equivalent circuit and the load, and the MPPC technique was tested. As expected, the DC-DC converter always tried to maintain the input voltage close to the defined reference value, and so the MPPC technique was validated. When the reference voltage was set to the MPP voltage of the monocrystalline/polycrystalline module, there was an increase of 47.6% in the output power in the load when using the converter, compared to when the converter was not used, and thus, the maximization of power extraction from the PV modules was confirmed.

Acknowledgment. This work was supported by FCT national funds, under the national support to R&D units grant, through the reference project UIDB/04436/2020 and UIDP/04436/2020.

References

1. Panwar, N.L., Kaushik, S.C.: Surendra Kothari, Role of renewable energy sources in environmental protection: a review. Renew. Sustain. Energy Rev. **15**, 1513–1524 (2011)
2. Raza, M.Q., Nadarajah, M., Ekanayake, C.: On recent advances in PV output power forecast. Sol. Energy **136**, 125–144 (2016)
3. Pazheri, F.R., Othman, M.F., Malik, N.H.: A review on global renewable electricity scenario. Renew. Sustain. Energy Rev. **31**, 835–845 (2014)
4. Askari, M.B., Mirzaei, A.V.M., Mirhabibi, M.: Types of solar cells and applicatioons. Am. J. Opt. Photonics **3**, 94–113 (2015)
5. Nayak, P.K., Mahesh, S., Snaith, H.J., Cahen, D.: Photovoltaic solar cell technologies: analysing the state of the art. Nat. Rev. Mater. **4**(4), 269–285 (2019)
6. Guo, B., Javed, W., Figgis, B.W., Mirza, T.: Effect of dust and weather conditions on photovoltaic performance in Doha, Qatar. First Workshop on Smart Grid and Renewable Energy (SGRE) 2015
7. Perraki, V., Kounavis, P.: Effect of temperature and radiation on the parameters of photovoltaic modules. J. Renew. Sustain. Energy. **013102** (2016)
8. Subudhi, B., Pradhan, R.: A comparative study on maximum power point tracking techniques for photovoltaic power systems. IEEE Tran. Sustain. Energy **4**(1), 89–98 (2013). https://doi.org/10.1109/TSTE.2012.2202294
9. Ruan, T., Chew, Z.J., Zhu, M.: Energy-aware approaches for energy harvesting powered wireless sensor nodes. IEEE Sens. J. **17**, 2165–2173 (2017)
10. Adiloa, A.S., Husi, G.: Modelling and simulating photovoltaic energy harvesting circuit: an analysis based on trial and error approximation for optimal output power of a harvester. In: International Conference on Engineering, Technology and Innovation (ICE/ITMC) (2017)
11. Zhang, H., Zhong, Z., Wu, W.: Extracting maximum efficiency of wireless power transfer in endoscopic capsule applications. In: International Applied Computational Electromagnetics Society Symposium (ACES) (2017)
12. Linear Technology: LTC3129: 15V, 200mA Synchronous Buck-Boost DC/DC Converter with 1.3 μA Quiescent Current, pp. 1–30 (2013)
13. Analog Devices: LTSpice | Design Center | Analog Devices. [Online]. Available at: https://www.analog.com/en/design-center/design-tools-and-calculators/ltspice-simulator.html
14. Cubas, J., Pindado, S., De Manuel, C.: «Explicit expressions for solar panel equivalent circuit parameters based on analytical formulation and the lambert W-function», Energies. **7**(7), 4098–4115 (2014)

Author Index

Printed in the United States
by Baker & Taylor Publisher Services